More praise for *Reviving Ophelia*

"With sympathy and focus she cites case histories to illustrate the struggles required of adolescent girls to maintain a sense of themselves. . . . Pipher offers concrete suggestions for ways by which girls can build and maintain a strong sense of self."

—*Publishers Weekly*

"This book is the first to explore carefully the many aspects of adolescence. It does so without blaming, vilifying, or shouting 'Victim here.' Instead Dr. Pipher uses clear, jargonless language and fascinating stories to challenge readers to look at what our culture does to teenage girls. Parents, teachers, and therapists alike will profit from Dr. Pipher's knowledge."

—Dr. Mary Kenning
Juvenile Justice System
Minneapolis

"Adolescent girls have always fallen through the cracks, but now they are tumbling into a chasm. Dr. Pipher goes deep inside their world and comes back with a clearheaded and compassionate report. We owe it to ourselves and our daughters to read this book."

—Carol Spindel

REVIVING OPHELIA

■

SAVING THE SELVES OF ADOLESCENT GIRLS

MARY PIPHER, Ph.D.

Ballantine Books • New York

All clients are composite characters drawn from my life experience and clinical work. Names and details have been changed to protect confidentiality.

This edition published by arrangement with G. P. Putnam's Sons.

Library of Congress Catalog Card Number: 94-94639

ISBN: 0-345-39282-5

Cover design by Ruth Ross
Cover photo © Edgeworth Productions/The Stock Market

Manufactured in the United States of America

First Ballantine Books Edition: March 1995

10 9 8 7 6 5 4 3 2

Acknowledgments

Thank you to my family—Jim, Zeke and Sara and all the Brays, Pages and Piphers.

I appreciate my writers' groups—Nebraska Wesleyan Writers' Group and Prairie Trout. I thank these writers for their help with this project: Pam Barger, Claudia Bepko, Carol Bly, Emilie Buchwald, Paul Gruchow, Twyla Hansen, Carolyn Johnsen, Jo-Anne Krestan, Margaret Nemoede, Marjorie Saiser, Leon Satterfield, Carol Spindel and Elizabeth Weber. I thank my writing teachers: Kent Haruf, Bill Kloefkorn and my first teacher, Charles Stubblefield.

The following people helped me with the book: Nancy Bare, Randy Barger, Beatty Brasch, Ellen Brt, Laura Freeman, Sherri Hanigan, Anna Harms, Sally Jones, Karen Kelly, Brooke and Cathy Kindler, Mary Kenning, Dixie Lubin, Jane Masheter, Frank McPherson, Natalie Porter, Carrie Rodgerson, Jan and Amy Stenberg, Susan Whitmore and Jan Zegers. And I thank all my clients, whom I cannot name, for the many lessons they have taught me.

I thank my friend and editor, Jane Isay, and her assistant, Rona Cohen. I thank my literary agent, Susan Lee Cohen, and my booking agent, Jane Pasanen, at the Chelsea Forum.

To the memory of Frank and Avis Bray

Contents

When I wrote *Hunger Pains: The American Women's Tragic Quest for Thinness* in the 1980s, I was attempting to understand the epidemic of eating disorders that had hit women in our community. I asked myself, Why is this happening to so many women now? I found many answers in an analysis of the culture and its message to women about weight and beauty.

Reviving Ophelia is my attempt to understand my experiences in therapy with adolescent girls. Many girls come into therapy with serious, even life-threatening problems, such as anorexia or the desire to physically hurt or kill themselves. Others have problems less dangerous but still more puzzling, such as school refusal, underachievement, moodiness or constant discord with their parents. Many are the victims of sexual violence.

As I talked to these girls, I became aware of how little I really understood about the world of adolescent girls today. It didn't work to use my own adolescent experience from the early 1960s to make generalizations. Girls were living in a whole new world.

As a therapist, I often felt bewildered and frustrated. These feelings led to questions: Why are so many girls in therapy in the 1990s? Why are there more self-mutilators? What is the meaning of lip, nose and eyebrow piercings? How do I help thirteen-year-olds deal with herpes or genital warts? Why are drugs and alcohol so common in the stories of seventh-graders? Why do so many girls hate their parents?

Meanwhile my own daughter was in adolescence. She and her friends were riding a roller coaster. Sometimes they were happy and interested in their world; other times they just seemed wrecked. They were hard on their families and each other. Particularly junior high seemed like a crucible. Many confident, well-adjusted girls were transformed into sad and angry failures.

Many of my friends had daughters in adolescence. When we talked we were confused, angry and unsure how to proceed. Many of us felt tormented by our daughters, who seemed upset with us for the smallest things. We had raised our daughters to be assertive and confident, and they seemed to be insecure and concerned with their femininity. One dilemma came up again and again: How could we encourage our daughters to be independent and autonomous and still keep them safe? How could we inspire them to take on the world when it was a world that included kidnappers and date rapists? Even in our small city with its mostly middle-class population, girls often experienced trauma. How could we help girls heal from that trauma? And what could we do to prevent it?

This last year I have struggled to make sense of this. Why are girls having more trouble now than my friends and I had when we were adolescents? Many of us hated our adolescent years, yet for the most part we weren't suicidal and we didn't develop eating disorders, cut ourselves or run away from home.

At first blush, it seems things should be better now. After all, we have the women's movement. Hasn't that helped? The answer, as I think about it, is yes and no. Many of my friends, middle-aged and middle-class women like myself, are entitled in ways few women have been since the beginning of time. Many of us are doing things our mothers never dreamed of doing.

But girls today are much more oppressed. They are coming of age in a more dangerous, sexualized and media-saturated culture. They face incredible pressures to be beautiful and sophisticated, which in junior high means using chemicals and being sexual. As they navigate a more dangerous world, girls are less protected.

As I looked at the culture that girls enter as they come of age, I was struck by what a girl-poisoning culture it was. The more I looked around, the more I listened to today's music, watched television and movies and looked at sexist advertising, the more convinced I became that we are on the wrong path with our daughters. America today limits girls' development, truncates their wholeness and leaves many of them traumatized.

This book is an attempt to share my thinking with parents, educators, health and mental-health professionals, policymakers and anyone else who works for and with girls. It's also for girls. In the sixties Betty Friedan wrote of "the problem with no name." She pointed out that many women were miserable but couldn't articulate the source of that misery. Adolescent girls today also face a problem with no name. They know that something is very wrong, but they tend to look for the source within themselves or their families rather than in broader cultural problems. I want to help them see their lives in the context of larger cultural forces.

I believe that most Americans share the concerns I have for our daughters. Hillary Rodham Clinton, Tipper Gore, Janet Reno, Marian Wright Edelman and many others are sounding the alarm. I hope this book offers a description of a particular point in girls' lives. With puberty girls crash into junk culture. One way to think about all the pain and pathology of adolescence is to say that the culture is just too hard for most girls to understand and master at this point in their development. They become overwhelmed and symptomatic.

What can we do to help them? We can strengthen girls so that they will be ready. We can encourage emotional toughness and self-protection. We can support and guide them. But most important, we can change our culture. We can work together to build a culture that is less complicated and more nurturing, less violent and sexualized and more growth-producing. Our daughters deserve a society in which all their gifts can be developed and appreciated. I hope this book fosters a debate on how we can build that society for them.

REVIVING OPHELIA

Chapter 1

SAPLINGS IN
THE STORM

■

When my cousin Polly was a girl, she was energy in motion. She danced, did cartwheels and splits, played football, basketball and baseball with the neighborhood boys, wrestled with my brothers, biked, climbed trees and rode horses. She was as lithe and as resilient as a willow branch and as unrestrained as a lion cub. Polly talked as much as she moved. She yelled out orders and advice, shrieked for joy when she won a bet or heard a good joke, laughed with her mouth wide open, argued with kids and grown-ups and insulted her foes in the language of a construction worker.

We formed the Marauders, a secret club that met over her garage. Polly was the Tom Sawyer of the club. She planned the initiations, led the spying expeditions and hikes to haunted houses. She showed us the rituals to become blood "brothers" and taught us card tricks and how to smoke.

Then Polly had her first period and started junior high. She tried to keep up her old ways, but she was called a tomboy and chided for not acting more ladylike. She was excluded by her boy pals and by the girls, who were moving into makeup and romances.

This left Polly confused and shaky. She had temper tantrums and withdrew from both the boys' and girls' groups. Later she quieted down and reentered as Becky Thatcher. She wore stylish clothes and watched from the sidelines as the boys acted and spoke. Once again she was accepted and popular. She glided smoothly through our small society. No one spoke of the changes or mourned the loss of our town's most dynamic citizen. I was the only one who felt that a tragedy had transpired.

Girls in what Freud called the latency period, roughly age six or seven through puberty, are anything but latent. I think of my daughter Sara during those years—performing chemistry experiments and magic tricks, playing her violin, starring in her own plays, rescuing wild animals and biking all over town. I think of her friend Tamara, who wrote a 300-page novel the summer of her sixth-grade year. I remember myself, reading every children's book in the library of my town. One week I planned to be a great doctor like Albert Schweitzer. The next week I wanted to write like Louisa May Alcott or dance in Paris like Isadora Duncan. I have never since had as much confidence or ambition.

Most preadolescent girls are marvelous company because they are interested in everything—sports, nature, people, music and books. Almost all the heroines of girls' literature come from this age group—Anne of Green Gables, Heidi, Pippi Longstocking and Caddie Wood-lawn. Girls this age bake pies, solve mysteries and go on quests. They can take care of themselves and are not yet burdened with caring for others. They have a brief respite from the female role and can be tomboys, a word that conveys courage, competency and irreverence.

They can be androgynous, having the ability to act adaptively in any situation regardless of gender role constraints. An androgynous person can comfort a baby or change a tire, cook a meal or chair a meeting. Research has shown that, since they are free to act without worrying if their behavior is feminine or masculine, androgynous adults are the most well adjusted.

Girls between seven and eleven rarely come to therapy. They don't need it. I can count on my fingers the girls this age whom I have seen: Coreen, who was physically abused; Anna, whose parents were divorcing; and Brenda, whose father killed himself. These girls were courageous and resilient. Brenda said, "If my father didn't want to stick around, that's his loss." Coreen and Anna were angry, not at themselves, but rather at the grown-ups, who they felt were making mistakes. It's amazing how little help these girls needed from me to heal and move on.

A horticulturist told me a revealing story. She led a tour of junior-high girls who were attending a math and science fair on her campus. She showed them side oats grama, bluestem, Indian grass and trees—

redbud, maple, walnut and willow. The younger girls interrupted each other with their questions and tumbled forward to see, touch and smell everything. The older girls, the ninth-graders, were different. They hung back. They didn't touch plants or shout out questions. They stood primly to the side, looking bored and even a little disgusted by the enthusiasm of their younger classmates. My friend asked herself, What's happened to these girls? What's gone wrong? She told me, "I wanted to shake them, to say, 'Wake up, come back. Is anybody home at your house?' "

Recently I sat sunning on a bench outside my favorite ice-cream store. A mother and her teenage daughter stopped in front of me and waited for the light to change. I heard the mother say, "You have got to stop blackmailing your father and me. Every time you don't get what you want, you tell us that you want to run away from home or kill yourself. What's happened to you? You used to be able to handle not getting your way."

The daughter stared straight ahead, barely acknowledging her mother's words. The light changed. I licked my ice-cream cone. Another mother approached the same light with her preadolescent daughter in tow. They were holding hands. The daughter said to her mother, "This is fun. Let's do this all afternoon."

Something dramatic happens to girls in early adolescence. Just as planes and ships disappear mysteriously into the Bermuda Triangle, so do the selves of girls go down in droves. They crash and burn in a social and developmental Bermuda Triangle. In early adolescence, studies show that girls' IQ scores drop and their math and science scores plummet. They lose their resiliency and optimism and become less curious and inclined to take risks. They lose their assertive, energetic and "tomboyish" personalities and become more deferential, self-critical and depressed. They report great unhappiness with their own bodies.

Psychology documents but does not explain the crashes. Girls who rushed to drink in experiences in enormous gulps sit quietly in the corner. Writers such as Sylvia Plath, Margaret Atwood and Olive Schreiner have described the wreckage. Diderot, in writing to his young friend Sophie Volland, described his observations harshly: "You all die at 15."

Fairy tales capture the essence of this phenomenon. Young women eat poisoned apples or prick their fingers with poisoned needles and fall asleep for a hundred years. They wander away from home, encounter great dangers, are rescued by princes and are transformed into passive and docile creatures.

The story of Ophelia, from Shakespeare's *Hamlet,* shows the destructive forces that affect young women. As a girl, Ophelia is happy and free, but with adolescence she loses herself. When she falls in love with Hamlet, she lives only for his approval. She has no inner direction; rather she struggles to meet the demands of Hamlet and her father. Her value is determined utterly by their approval. Ophelia is torn apart by her efforts to please. When Hamlet spurns her because she is an obedient daughter, she goes mad with grief. Dressed in elegant clothes that weigh her down, she drowns in a stream filled with flowers.

Girls know they are losing themselves. One girl said, "Everything good in me died in junior high." Wholeness is shattered by the chaos of adolescence. Girls become fragmented, their selves split into mysterious contradictions. They are sensitive and tenderhearted, mean and competitive, superficial and idealistic. They are confident in the morning and overwhelmed with anxiety by nightfall. They rush through their days with wild energy and then collapse into lethargy. They try on new roles every week—this week the good student, next week the delinquent and the next, the artist. And they expect their families to keep up with these changes.

My clients in early adolescence are elusive and slow to trust adults. They are easily offended by a glance, a clearing of the throat, a silence, a lack of sufficient enthusiasm or a sentence that doesn't meet their immediate needs. Their voices have gone underground—their speech is more tentative and less articulate. Their moods swing widely. One week they love their world and their families, the next they are critical of everyone. Much of their behavior is unreadable. Their problems are complicated and metaphorical—eating disorders, school phobias and self-inflicted injuries. I need to ask again and again in a dozen different ways, "What are you trying to tell me?"

Michelle, for example, was a beautiful, intelligent seventeen-year-old. Her mother brought her in after she became pregnant for the third time in three years. I tried to talk about why this was happening. She smiled a Mona Lisa smile to all my questions. "No, I don't care all that much for sex." "No, I didn't plan this. It just happened." When Michelle left a session, I felt like I'd been talking in the wrong language to someone far away.

Holly was another mystery. She was shy, soft-spoken and slow-moving, pretty under all her makeup and teased red hair. She was a Prince fan and wore only purple. Her father brought her in after a suicide attempt. She wouldn't study, do chores, join any school activities or find a job. Holly answered questions in patient, polite monosyllables. She really talked only when the topic was Prince. For several weeks we talked about him. She played me his tapes. Prince somehow spoke for her and to her.

Gail burned and cut herself when she was unhappy. Dressed in black, thin as a straw, she sat silently before me, her hair a mess, her ears, lips and nose all pierced with rings. She spoke about Bosnia and the hole in the ozone layer and asked me if I liked rave music. When I asked about her life, she fingered her earrings and sat silently.

My clients are not different from girls who are not seen in therapy. I teach at a small liberal arts college and the young women in my classes have essentially the same experiences as my therapy clients. One student worried about her best friend who'd been sexually assaulted. Another student missed class after being beaten by her boyfriend. Another asked what she should do about crank calls from a man threatening to rape her. When stressed, another student stabbed her hand with paper clips until she drew blood. Many students have wanted advice on eating disorders.

After I speak at high schools, girls approach me to say that they have been raped, or they want to run away from home, or that they have a friend who is anorexic or alcoholic. At first all this trauma surprised me. Now I expect it.

Psychology has a long history of ignoring girls this age. Until recently adolescent girls haven't been studied by academics, and they have long baffled therapists. Because they are secretive with adults and full of contradictions, they are difficult to study. So much is happening internally that's not communicated on the surface.

Simone de Beauvoir believed adolescence is when girls realize that men have the power and that their only power comes from consenting to become submissive adored objects. They do not suffer from the penis envy Freud postulated, but from power envy.

She described the Bermuda Triangle this way: Girls who were the subjects of their own lives become the objects of others' lives. "Young girls slowly bury their childhood, put away their independent and imperious selves and submissively enter adult existence." Adolescent girls experience a conflict between their autonomous selves and their need to be feminine, between their status as human beings and their vocation as females. De Beauvoir says, "Girls stop being and start seeming."

Girls become "female impersonators" who fit their whole selves into small, crowded spaces. Vibrant, confident girls become shy, doubting young women. Girls stop thinking, "Who am I? What do I want?" and start thinking, "What must I do to please others?"

This gap between girls' true selves and cultural prescriptions for what is properly female creates enormous problems. To paraphrase a Stevie Smith poem about swimming in the sea, "they are not waving, they are drowning." And just when they most need help, they are unable to take their parents' hands.

Olive Schreiner wrote of her experiences as a young girl in *The Story of an African Farm.* "The world tells us what we are to be and shapes us by the ends it sets before us. To men it says, work. To us, it says, seem. The less a woman has in her head the lighter she is for carrying." She described the finishing school that she attended in this way: "It was a machine for condensing the soul into the smallest possible area. I have seen some souls so compressed that they would have filled a small thimble."

Margaret Mead believed that the ideal culture is one in which there is a place for every human gift. By her standards, our Western culture is far from ideal for women. So many gifts are unused and unappreciated. So many voices are stilled. Stendhal wrote: "All geniuses born women are lost to the public good."

Alice Miller wrote of the pressures on some young children to deny their true selves and assume false selves to please their parents. *Reviving Ophelia* suggests that adolescent girls experience a similar pressure to split into true and false selves, but this time the pressure comes not from parents but from the culture. Adolescence is when girls experience social pressure to put aside their authentic selves and to display only a small portion of their gifts.

This pressure disorients and depresses most girls. They sense the pressure to be someone they are not. They fight back, but they are fighting a "problem with no name." One girl put it this way: "I'm a perfectly good carrot that everyone is trying to turn into a rose. As a carrot, I have good color and a nice leafy top. When I'm carved into a rose, I turn brown and wither."

Adolescent girls are saplings in a hurricane. They are young and vulnerable trees that the winds blow with gale strength. Three factors make young women vulnerable to the hurricane. One is their developmental level. Everything is changing—body shape, hormones, skin and hair. Calmness is replaced by anxiety. Their way of thinking is changing. Far below the surface they are struggling with the most basic of human questions: What is my place in the universe, what is my meaning?

Second, American culture has always smacked girls on the head in early adolescence. This is when they move into a broader culture that is rife with girl-hurting "isms," such as sexism, capitalism and lookism, which is the evaluation of a person solely on the basis of appearance.

Third, American girls are expected to distance from parents just at the time when they most need their support. As they struggle with countless new pressures, they must relinquish the protection and closeness they've felt with their families in childhood. They turn to their none-too-constant peers for support.

Parents know only too well that something is happening to their daughters. Calm, considerate daughters grow moody, demanding and distant. Girls who loved to talk are sullen and secretive. Girls who liked to hug now bristle when touched. Mothers complain that they can do nothing right in the eyes of their daughters. Involved fathers bemoan their sudden banishment from their daughters' lives. But few parents realize how universal their experiences are. Their daughters are entering a new land, a dangerous place that parents can scarcely comprehend. Just when they most need a home base, they cut themselves loose without radio communications.

Most parents of adolescent girls have the goal of keeping their daughters safe while they grow up and explore the world. The parents' job is to protect. The daughters' job is to explore. Always these different tasks have created tension in parent-daughter relationships, but now it's even harder. Generally parents are more protective of their daughters than is corporate America. Parents aren't trying to make money off their daughters by selling them designer jeans or cigarettes, they just want them to be well adjusted. They don't see their daughters as sex objects or consumers but as real people with talents and interests. But daughters turn away from their parents as they enter the new land. They befriend their peers, who are their fellow inhabitants of the strange country and who share a common language and set of customs. They often embrace the junk values of mass culture.

This turning away from parents is partly for developmental reasons. Early adolescence is a time of physical and psychological change, self-absorption, preoccupation with peer approval and identity formation. It's a time when girls focus inward on their own fascinating changes.

It's partly for cultural reasons. In America we define adulthood as a moving away from families into broader culture. Adolescence is the time for cutting bonds and breaking free. Adolescents may claim great independence from parents, but they are aware and ashamed of their parents' smallest deviation from the norm. They don't like to be seen with them and find their imperfections upsetting. A mother's haircut or a father's joke can ruin their day. Teenagers are furious at parents who say the wrong things or do not respond with perfect answers. Adolescents claim not to hear their parents, but with their friends they discuss endlessly all parental attitudes. With amazing acuity, they sense nuances, doubt, shades of ambiguity, discrepancy and hypocrisy.

Adolescents still have some of the magical thinking of childhood and believe that parents have the power to keep them safe and happy. They blame their parents for their misery, yet they make a point of not telling their parents how they think and feel; they have secrets, so things can get crazy. For example, girls who are raped may not tell their parents. Instead, they become hostile and rebellious. Parents bring girls in because of their anger and out-of-control behavior. When I hear about this unexplainable anger, I ask about rape. Ironically, girls are often angrier at their parents than at the rapists. They feel their parents should have known about the danger and been more protective; afterward, they should have sensed the pain and helped.

Most parents feel like failures during this time. They feel shut out, impotent and misunderstood. They often attribute the difficulties of this time to their daughters and their own failings. They don't understand that these problems go with the developmental stage, the culture and the times.

Parents experience an enormous sense of loss when their girls enter this new land. They miss the daughters who sang in the kitchen, who read them school papers, who accompanied them on fishing trips and to ball games. They miss the daughters who liked to bake cookies, play Pictionary and be kissed goodnight. In place of their lively, affectionate daughters they have changelings—new girls who are sadder, angrier and more complicated. Everyone is grieving.

Fortunately adolescence is time-limited. By late high school most girls are stronger and the winds are dying down. Some of the worst problems—cliques, a total focus on looks and struggles with parents— are on the wane. But the way girls handle the problems of adolescence can have implications for their adult lives. Without some help, the loss of wholeness, self-confidence and self-direction can last well into adulthood. Many adult clients struggle with the same issues that overwhelmed them as adolescent girls. Thirty-year-old accountants and realtors, forty-year-old homemakers and doctors, and thirty-five-year-old nurses and schoolteachers ask the same questions and struggle with the same problems as their teenage daughters.

Even sadder are the women who are not struggling, who have forgotten that they have selves worth defending. They have repressed the pain of their adolescence, the betrayals of self in order to be pleasing. These women come to therapy with the goal of becoming even more pleasing to others. They come to lose weight, to save their marriages or to rescue their children. When I ask them about their own needs, they are confused by the question.

Most women struggled alone with the trauma of adolescence and have led decades of adult life with their adolescent experiences unexamined. The lessons learned in adolescence are forgotten and their memories of pain are minimized. They come into therapy because their marriage is in trouble, or they hate their job, or their own daughter is giving them fits. Maybe their daughter's pain awakens their own pain. Some are depressed or chemically addicted or have stress-related illnesses—ulcers, colitis, migraines or psoriasis. Many have tried to be perfect women and failed. Even though they followed the rules and did as they were told, the world has not rewarded them. They feel angry and betrayed. They feel miserable and taken for granted, used rather than loved.

Women often know how everyone in their family thinks and feels except themselves. They are great at balancing the needs of their coworkers, husbands, children and friends, but they forget to put themselves into the equation. They struggle with adolescent questions still unresolved: How important are looks and popularity? How do I care for myself and not be selfish? How can I be honest and still be loved? How can I achieve and not threaten others? How can I be sexual and not a sex object? How can I be responsive but not responsible for everyone?

As we talk, the years fall away. We are back in junior high with the cliques, the shame, the embarrassment about bodies, the desire to be accepted and the doubts about ability. So many adult women think they are stupid and ugly. Many feel guilty if they take time for themselves. They do not express anger or ask for help.

We talk about childhood—what the woman was like at ten and at fifteen. We piece together a picture of childhood lost. We review her own particular story, her own time in the hurricane. Memories flood in. Often there are tears, angry outbursts, sadness for what has been lost. So much time has been wasted pretending to be who others wanted. But also, there's a new energy that comes from making connections, from choosing awareness over denial and from the telling of secrets.

We work now, twenty years behind schedule. We reestablish each woman as the subject of her life, not as the object of others' lives. We answer Freud's patronizing question "What do women want?" Each woman wants something different and particular and yet each woman wants the same thing—to be who she truly is, to become who she can become.

Many women regain their preadolescent authenticity with menopause. Because they are no longer beautiful objects occupied primarily with caring for others, they are free once again to become the subjects of their own lives. They become more confident, self-directed and energetic. Margaret Mead noticed this phenomenon in cultures all over the world and called it "pmz," postmenopausal zest. She noted that some cultures revere these older women. Others burn them at the stake.

Before I studied psychology, I studied cultural anthropology. I have always been interested in that place where culture and individual psychology intersect, in why cultures create certain personalities and not others, in how they pull for certain strengths in their members, in how certain talents are utilized while others atrophy from lack of attention. I'm interested in the role cultures play in the development of individual pathology.

For a student of culture and personality, adolescence is fascinating. It's an extraordinary time when individual, developmental and cultural factors combine in ways that shape adulthood. It's a time of marked internal development and massive cultural indoctrination.

I want to try in this book to connect each girl's story with larger cultural issues—to examine the intersection of the personal and the political. It's a murky place; the personal and political are intertwined in all of our lives. Our minds, which are shaped by the society in which we live, can oppress us. And yet our minds can also analyze and work to change the culture.

An analysis of the culture cannot ignore individual differences in women. Some women blossom and grow under the most hostile conditions while others wither after the smallest storms. And yet we are more alike than different in the issues that face us. The important question is, Under what conditions do most young women flower and grow?

Adolescent clients intrigue me as they struggle to sort themselves out. But I wouldn't have written this book had it not been for these last few years when my office has been filled with girls—girls with eating disorders, alcohol problems, posttraumatic stress reactions to sexual or physical assaults, sexually transmitted diseases (STDs), self-inflicted injuries and strange phobias, and girls who have tried to kill themselves or run away. A health department survey showed that 40 percent of all girls in my midwestern city considered suicide last year. The Centers for Disease Control in Atlanta reports that the suicide rate among children age ten to fourteen rose 75 percent between 1979 and 1988. Something dramatic is happening to adolescent girls in America, something unnoticed by those not on the front lines.

At first I was surprised that girls were having more trouble now. After all, we have had a consciousness-raising women's movement since the sixties. Women are working in traditionally male professions and going out for sports. Some fathers help with the housework and child care. It seems that these changes would count for something. And of course they do, but in some ways the progress is confusing. The Equal Rights Amendment was not ratified, feminism is a pejorative term to many people and, while some women have high-powered jobs, most women work hard for low wages and do most of the "second shift" work. The lip service paid to equality makes the reality of discrimination even more confusing.

Many of the pressures girls have always faced are intensified in the 1990s. Many things contribute to this intensification: more divorced families, chemical addictions, casual sex and violence against women. Because of the media, which Clarence Page calls "electronic wallpaper," girls all live in one big town—a sleazy, dangerous tinsel town with lots of liquor stores and few protected spaces. Increasingly women have been sexualized and objectified, their bodies marketed to sell tractors and toothpaste. Soft- and hard-core pornography are everywhere. Sexual and physical assaults on girls are at an all-time high. Now girls are more vulnerable and fearful, more likely to have been traumatized and less free to roam about alone. This combination of old stresses and new is poison for our young women.

Parents have unprecedented stress as well. For the last half-century, parents worried about their sixteen-year-old daughters driving, but now, in a time of drive-by shootings and car-jackings, parents can be panicked. Parents have always worried about their daughters' sexual behavior, but now, in a time of date rapes, herpes and AIDS, they can be sex-phobic. Traditionally parents have wondered what their teens were doing, but now teens are much more likely to be doing things that can get them killed.

This book will tell stories from the front lines. It's about girls because I know about girls. I was one, I see them in therapy, I have a teenage daughter and I teach primarily young women. I am not writing about boys because I have had limited experience with them. I'm not saying that girls and boys are radically different, only that they have different experiences.

I am saying that girls are having more trouble now than they had thirty years ago, when I was a girl, and more trouble than even ten years ago. Something new is happening. Adolescence has always been hard, but it's harder now because of cultural changes in the last decade. The protected place in space and time that we once called childhood has grown shorter. There is an African saying, "It takes a village to raise a child." Most girls no longer have a village.

Parents, teachers, counselors and nurses see that girls are in trouble, but they do not realize how universal and extreme the suffering is. This book is an attempt to share what I have seen and heard. It's a hurricane warning, a message to the culture that something important is happening. This is a National Weather Service bulletin from the storm center.

Chapter 2

THEORETICAL ISSUES— FOR YOUR OWN GOOD

■

CAYENNE (15)

In a home video made when she was ten, Cayenne was wiry and scrappy, all sixty-eight pounds of her focused on the ball as she ran down the soccer field. Her red ponytail bobbed, her face shone with sweat as she ducked in and around the other players, always hustling. When she scored a goal, she held her arms over her head in a moment of self-congratulation. She tossed her parents a proud smile and moved into position for another play.

Her parents loved her willingness to take on the universe. One day she dressed up like a belly dancer, the next like an astronaut. She liked adults and babies, boys and girls, dogs and sparrows. An absolute democrat, Cayenne treated everyone with respect, and she expected the same.

When outraged, she took on the world. She got a black eye from fighting with a boy who said that girls couldn't play soccer. Once she dunked a much older boy who was throwing rocks at a little turtle. She threatened to hit kids who were racist. Because she was good at standing up for herself and concerned with justice, her teachers predicted she'd go to law school.

In elementary school Cayenne didn't fret much about her appearance. She weighed in once a year at the doctor's office and was pleased with gains in her height and weight chart. She wore jeans and T-shirts unless forced to dress up. Her mother had to beg her to go shopping and remind her to brush her hair.

She walked to school every day with her best friend, Chelsea. She and Chelsea biked together, watched television, played on the same ball teams and helped each other with chores. They talked about everything—parents, school, sports and interests. They shared their dreams. Chelsea wanted to be a pilot, and Cayenne wanted to be a doctor. They made up elaborate fantasies in which Chelsea would fly Cayenne into a remote Alaskan village to deliver a baby or amputate the leg of a fisherman.

Cayenne liked school. Her grades were good and she loved projects, especially science projects. Twice she was on the Olympics of the Mind team. She'd known most of the kids in her class since kindergarten. She played ball with them and went to their houses for birthday parties.

Cayenne got along well with her parents. Marla, her older sister, had been the moodier and more disobedient child. As an adolescent, Marla sneaked out of the house to drink with her friends. Cayenne felt sorry for her parents when Marla yelled or made them worry, and she promised she would never act that way.

Of course, Cayenne wasn't perfect. She'd never liked to clean her room and was fidgety in church. She preferred junk food to fruits and vegetables. About twice a year Cayenne would be cranky and sullen for a day, but mostly she was easy-going. Bad days were so rare that they were events, like Groundhog Day. Her parents came to depend on Cayenne as their emotional centerboard, and they jokingly called her "Old Faithful."

At twelve, Cayenne had her first period. As her body grew rapidly, it became awkward and unpredictable. She gained weight, especially in her hips, and she got acne. Cayenne moved from her neighborhood school to a junior high with 2,000 students. She was nervous the first day because she'd heard rumors that seventh-graders' heads were stuffed in the toilets and that boys pulled down the girls' blouses. Fortunately these things didn't happen, but she came home upset that some boys teased her and that the girls wore makeup and expensive clothes. She was criticized for her JCPenney jeans, and even Chelsea begged her to give up soccer practice and spend Saturday at the mall.

Cayenne grew quieter and less energetic. For the first time she needed to be coaxed into doing things with the family. She stopped wanting hugs from her parents and brushed them away when they approached her. She didn't laugh or talk to them.

Her parents expected some of this. When Cayenne became self-conscious about her appearance, it saddened them, but they knew this was "normal." They were more upset when she quit playing soccer and when her grades dropped, even in science, which Cayenne now considered hard and boring.

Meanwhile Chelsea's parents divorced and Chelsea fell in with a wild crowd. She invited Cayenne to join and called her a "Muffy" when she hesitated. Eventually Cayenne became part of the group. Her parents suspected that this crowd might be using alcohol or drugs. They encouraged Cayenne to do more with other girls, but she complained about cliques. They tried to steer her toward sports and school activities, but she felt these things were for nerds.

I met Cayenne the winter of her ninth-grade year. Her family physician had referred her to me after she was diagnosed with herpes. He believed that the family and Cayenne needed help dealing with this infectious disease.

She scrunched between her parents wearing a T-shirt that said "If you don't like loud music, you're too fucking old." Her body posture signaled "My parents can force me to be here but nobody can make me talk." When I offered her a soda, she rolled her eyes and said, "Color me excited."

Her mother said, "Cayenne acts like she's allergic to us. Everything we do is wrong."

Her dad talked about her grades, her friends, her herpes and depression, but most of all he mourned their lost relationship. Cayenne had been so close to them and so much fun. She was no longer "Old Faithful"—her bad days outnumbered her good. He thought that even Marla had been easier. At least she hadn't contracted a sexually transmitted disease. After he shared his concerns, he asked, "Does Cayenne need to be hospitalized, or is she just acting like a fifteen-year-old?"

Good question, I thought to myself. Later I met with Cayenne alone. Her blue eyes were icy under her frizzy red hair. She glared at me, almost daring me to make her talk. I sensed that while her surface behavior was angry and withdrawn, underneath she was hurting. I searched for a way to begin.

Finally Cayenne asked, "Do shrinks analyze dreams?"

"Do you have one?"

Cayenne told me of a recurring dream in which she was asleep in her upstairs bedroom. She heard footsteps on the stairs and knew who was coming. She listened, terrified, as the steps grew louder. An old man leading a goat walked into her room. He had a long, sharp knife. Cayenne lay in her bed unable to move while he began slicing at her toes. He sliced off pieces of her and fed her to the goat. She usually awoke when he reached her knees. She'd be covered with sweat and her heart would be racing wildly. Afterward she was afraid to go back to sleep for fear the man would return.

When she finished I asked her what she thought the dream meant. She said, "It means I'm afraid of being cut up and eaten alive."

Over the next few months Cayenne talked in fragments, almost in code. Sometimes she talked so softly that I couldn't hear her. She wasn't happy in junior high and missed her old school. She missed her sister, Marla, who was away at college. Although she was sure it was they, not she, who had changed, Cayenne missed the closeness she had had with her parents.

Cayenne's demeanor was cautious and her speech elliptical, but she kept coming. She hated her looks. She thought her hair was too bright, her hips and thighs too flabby. She tried to lose weight but couldn't. She dyed her hair, but it turned a weird purple color and dried out. She felt almost every girl was prettier. She said, "Let's face it, I'm a dog."

She didn't feel comfortable around her old friends. We talked about the girls in her class who teased her about her clothes and about the boys who gave her a hard time. Cayenne had problems with most of her friends. Everything was unpredictable. One week she felt reasonably comfortable and accepted, the next she felt like a pariah. She told her friends secrets only to have them spread all over the school. She was included one day in a clique and left out the next. Some days guys called her a slut, other days these same boys would flirt with her.

She felt pressure to use drugs and alcohol. She said, "I was the perfect angel in grade school. I never planned to smoke or drink, but all of a sudden, alcohol was everywhere. Even the president of the Just Say No Club got loaded all the time."

School, which had once been fun, was now a torment. She felt stupid in her math and science classes and bored in everything else. She said to me, "School's just the way the government baby-sits kids my age."

We talked about her parents' rules, which had grown much stricter after the herpes. Her protests were surprisingly weak. She felt ambivalent about her parents—part of her felt guilty about all the fights with them, while another part blamed them for not understanding the pressure she was under and keeping her safe.

I recommended she write down three things every day that she felt proud of. I asked her to write me a letter telling me her good qualities. She wrote that she was proud of mowing the lawn, doing dishes and going to church with her grandmother. As for good qualities, she liked her navel and her feet. When I pressed her for personality characteristics, she liked her courage and directness. At least, she could remember being that way.

One session, dressed in sweats and red-nosed from a bad cold, Cayenne told me that Chelsea was afraid she was pregnant. She had missed a period and showed positive on a home testing kit. We had a general discussion of girls getting pregnant, teenage mothers, abortion and birth control pills. Cayenne was happy to discuss her friend's sexual behavior, but volunteered nothing about her own.

The next session she said that Chelsea was not pregnant and had renounced sex until she was sixteen. She and Chelsea had gone to the movies to celebrate. We talked about *Mermaids,* the movie they had seen, in which a teenage girl has graphic sex with a guy she barely knows. I asked Cayenne what she thought of that. She said, "It tells it like it is."

I'd just seen *Medicine Man,* the story of a male scientist who is in the rain forest searching for a cure for cancer. Sean Connery is visited by a female scientist forty years younger than he, wearing short shorts and a tight, low-cut top. He's shocked to find that a scientist is female and refuses to work with her. She's snooty and terrified of snakes. Then she has an accident, Sean saves her, and she falls weeping into his arms. Reduced to a helpless blob of jelly, the female scientist becomes more feminine and likable. She follows Sean around and he rewards her with smiles and caresses. In the end she gives up her career to help him find the cure for cancer.

I thought it was sexist and told her why. "This movie says it's okay for women to be scientists if they are beautiful, young and seductive. But they must allow themselves to be rescued by a man and give up their careers to serve his needs."

As I wondered aloud if a movie like this could influence a girl's grades in science, I told Cayenne about the MTV I had watched in a hotel room in Chicago. I was shocked by the sexual lyrics and scenes. In the first video, openmouthed and moaning women writhed around the male singer. In the second video, four women with vacant eyes gyrated in low-cut dresses and high black boots. Their breasts and bottoms were photographed more frequently than their faces. When I expressed dismay, she said, "That's nothing; you should see the Guns 'N' Roses videos."

We talked about *Silence of the Lambs*. Much to my dismay, she insisted on describing to me the pictures of skinned women and oozing body parts. I realized as she talked how different we were. Violence and casual sex that upset me didn't bother her. In fact, Cayenne was proud of being able to watch scary and graphic scenes—it proved she wasn't a wimp. Despite our different reactions to media, the talk raised important issues—lookism, sexism, cultural stereotypes of men and women, and the importance of sex and violence in movies.

Finally Cayenne was ready to talk about her own sexual experiences, at first in a tentative way, and later in a more relaxed manner. She made fun of the school films with their embryos and cartoon sperm that looked like tadpoles. She said her parents told her to wait for sex until she was out of high school and involved with someone whom she loved.

I asked, "How does your experience fit with what your parents told you?"

Cayenne looked at me wide-eyed. "My parents don't know anything about sex."

She pushed back her frizzy bangs. "In seventh grade everyone was sex-crazy. Kids kept asking me if I did it, if I wanted to get laid, stuff like that. Guys would grab at me in the halls. I was shocked, but I didn't show it. Later I got used to it."

By the middle of her eighth-grade year, Cayenne wanted to have sex. Her friends said it was fun and they teased her about being a virgin. But she was scared—she wondered if it would hurt, if she would get AIDS or become pregnant or if the boy would lose respect for her. She knew that "boys who have sex are studs, but girls who do it are sluts."

The summer before ninth grade she and Chelsea went to an unsupervised party. A guy she knew from the Olympics of the Mind team was there. Tim had been innocent and clean-cut in sixth grade. Now he was a sophomore with long hair pulled back in a headband and a sarcastic sense of humor.

Tim's friend had invited ten girls and nine guys. He opened his parents' liquor cabinet and poured crème de menthe for the girls and scotch for the guys. Cayenne hated the cough-syrupy taste of liqueur, but because she was nervous, she drank it. Tim came over and sat by

Cayenne. He complimented her shirt and joked about all the geeks at the party. He poured refills. Tim's friend put on a Madonna tape and turned off all the lights.

Cayenne was nervous and excited. Tim put his arm around her and kissed her on the forehead. They whispered for a while, then began to make out. All the other kids were doing the same thing or more. Some moved off into other rooms.

Cayenne told me, "I knew this would be the night. I was scared, but ready. I was surprised by how fast things happened. We had sex in the first hour of the party."

After that night she and Tim called each other for the next month. They talked about school, music and movies—never sex. They lived in different parts of town and couldn't figure out how to meet each other. Twice they made elaborate plans that fell through. After a while both became interested in kids at their own schools and they drifted apart.

I asked her how she felt about Tim now. Cayenne rubbed her forehead. "I wish it had been more romantic."

Cayenne was a typical therapy client. She had had a reasonably happy childhood. With puberty, the changes and challenges in her life overwhelmed her, at least temporarily. Her grades fell, she dropped out of sports and relinquished her dream of being a doctor. As she moved from the relatively protected space of an elementary school into the more complex world of junior high, all her relationships grew turbulent. She had decisions to make about adult issues such as alcohol and sex. While she was figuring things out, she contracted herpes.

When I first worked with girls like Cayenne, I was lost myself. I had been educated by male psychologists in the 1970s. With the exception of Carol Gilligan's work, almost all theory about teenagers had been authored by men such as Lawrence Kohlberg and E. H. Erikson, who had mainly studied boys.

I found girls to be obsessed with complicated and intense relationships. They felt obligated and resentful, loving and angry, close and distant, all at the same time with the same people. Sexuality, romance and intimacy were all jumbled together and needed sorting. Their symptoms seemed connected to their age and their common experiences. Certain themes, such as concern with weight, fear of rejection and the need for perfection, seemed rooted in cultural expectations for women rather than in the "pathology" of each individual girl. Girls struggled with mixed messages: Be beautiful, but beauty is only skin deep. Be sexy, but not sexual. Be honest, but don't hurt anyone's feelings. Be independent, but be nice. Be smart, but not so smart that you threaten boys.

Adolescent girls presented me with all kinds of problems that my education and experience didn't help me solve. When I stubbornly tried traditional methods of psychotherapy, they didn't work. Girls dropped out of therapy, or even worse, they came in obediently, chatted obligingly and accomplished nothing. Because they were my most difficult cases, I thought a great deal about my adolescent clients. I wanted to conceptualize their problems in a way that actually led to positive action, and I tried to connect their surface behaviors with their deeper struggles. I found help from the writings of Alice Miller.

Alice Miller was an expert on the sacrifice of wholeness. In *The Drama of the Gifted Child,* she describes how some of her patients lost their true selves in early childhood. She believed that as young children her patients faced a difficult choice: They could be authentic and honest, or they could be loved. If they chose wholeness, they were abandoned by their parents. If they chose love, they abandoned their true selves.

Her patients' parents, because of their own childhood experiences, regarded parts of their children's personalities as unacceptable. They taught their children that only a small range of thoughts, emotions and behaviors would be tolerated. The children disowned that which wasn't tolerated. If anger was not tolerated, they acted as if they felt no anger. If sexual feelings were not permitted, they acted as if they had no sexual urges.

As children, her patients chose parental approval and experienced a loss of their true selves. They stopped expressing unacceptable feelings and engaging in the unacceptable behaviors, at least in front of adults. They stopped sharing the unsanctioned thoughts. The part of them that was unacceptable went underground and eventually withered from lack of attention. Or that part of them that was unacceptable was projected onto others.

Miller believed that as the true self was disowned, the false self was elevated. If others approved, the false self felt validated and the person was temporarily happy. With the false self in charge, all validation came from outside the person. If the false self failed to gain approval, the person was devastated.

This loss of the true self was so traumatic that her patients repressed it. They had only a vague recollection of what was lost, a sense of emptiness and betrayal. They felt vulnerable and directionless—happy when praised and devastated when ignored or criticized. They were like sailboats without centerboards. Their self-worth changed with whatever way the wind blew.

Miller contrasted adults with false selves to authentic adults who experienced all feelings, including pain, in an honest way. Authentic adults accepted themselves rather than waiting for others to accept them. This state of psychological health she called vibrancy.

Her weapon against mental illness was "the discovery and emotional acceptance of the truth of each individual." She encouraged her patients to accept what happened to them as young children. Only then could they become authentic people.

Miller wrote about this process as if it were an either-or phenomenon. But in fact this process of creating false selves in children follows a continuum that ranges from basic socialization to abuse. It is present in all families: All parents accept and reject some of their children's behaviors and teach children to sacrifice some wholeness to social acceptability. However, even the most authoritarian parents usually don't succeed in totally destroying the true selves of their children.

Miller wrote in a different time and place about a different kind of family from the average family in America in the 1990s. What is timeless and important about Miller's work is her description of the process by which the self splits. With great clarity she describes the splitting into political versus personal selves. She documents the damage that this splitting can do and describes the process by which healing can occur.

I think that a process analogous to Miller's occurs for girls in early adolescence. Whereas Miller sees the parents as responsible for the splitting in early childhood, I see the culture as splitting adolescent girls into true and false selves. The culture is what causes girls to abandon their true selves and take up false selves.

Often parents are fighting hard to save their daughters' true selves. Parents encourage their daughters to stay with their childhood interests and argue with them over issues such as early sexual activity, makeup, diets and dating. They encourage athletics and math and science classes. They dislike the media values and resist cultural definitions of their daughters as consumers or sex objects. They do not want their daughters to sell their souls for popularity. They are fighting to preserve wholeness and authenticity.

But because of girls' developmental stage, parents have limited influence. Cayenne, for example, would barely speak to her parents. As daughters move into the broader culture, they care what their friends, not their parents, think. They model themselves after media stars, not parental ideals.

With puberty, girls face enormous cultural pressure to split into false selves. The pressure comes from schools, magazines, music, television, advertisements and movies. It comes from peers. Girls can be true to themselves and risk abandonment by their peers, or they can reject their true selves and be socially acceptable. Most girls choose to be socially accepted and split into two selves, one that is authentic and one that is culturally scripted. In public they become who they are supposed to be.

Authenticity is an "owning" of all experience, including emotions and thoughts that are not socially acceptable. Because self-esteem is based on the acceptance of all thoughts and feelings as one's own, girls lose confidence as they "disown" themselves. They suffer enormous losses when they stop expressing certain thoughts and feelings.

Cayenne exemplifies the process of disowning the true self. With puberty she went from being a whole, authentic person to a diminished, unhappy version of herself. Her dream of being cut into pieces and fed to a goat reflects quite exactly her loss of wholeness. Many girls report dreams like Cayenne's. They dream of drowning, of being paralyzed and of being stuck in quicksand. A common dream is of being attacked and unable to scream or fight back in any way. The attackers can vary—men, schoolmates, insects or snakes. The important elements of the dream are the attack, the paralysis and the imminent destruction of the self.

With adolescence, Cayenne begins to operate from a false self. When she says "Let's face it, I'm a dog," she is accepting society's right to define her solely on the basis of her appearance. She is even defining herself that way. Earlier, she fought to save a turtle or defend an ideal, now she is used to being "grabbed," and no longer protests when her bodily integrity is threatened.

As she adopts a false self, Cayenne loses her confidence and calmness. She loses her clear, direct speech. She distances from her parents, who encourage her to remain true to her self. Her surface behavior and her deeper feelings are not congruent. She no longer behaves in a way that meets her true needs.

Her decisions are not thoughtful, conscious choices, but rather reactions to peer pressure. She's pressured to use chemicals and to have sex. Cayenne is off course and unfocused. Her long-term goal to be a doctor is abandoned.

Cayenne experienced what all girls experience in early adolescence—rigorous training for the female role. At this time girls are expected to sacrifice the parts of themselves that our culture considers masculine on the altar of social acceptability and to shrink their souls down to a petite size. Claudia Bepko and Jo-Ann Krestan call it "indoctrination into the code of goodness," which they argue is essentially unchanged since the fifties. The rules remain the same: be attractive, be a lady, be unselfish and of service, make relationships work and be competent without complaint.

This is when girls learn to be nice rather than honest. Cayenne told me, "The worst punishment is to be called a bitch. That will shut anyone up." She continued, "Girls are supposed to smile. If I'm having a bad day, teachers and kids tell me to smile. I've never heard them say that to a guy."

Adolescent girls discover that it is impossible to be both feminine and adult. Psychologist I. K. Broverman's now classic study documents this impossibility. Male and female participants in the study checked off adjectives describing the characteristics of healthy men, healthy women and healthy adults. The results showed that while people describe healthy men and healthy adults as having the same qualities, they describe healthy women as having quite different qualities than healthy adults. For example, healthy women were described as passive, dependent and illogical, while healthy adults were active, independent and logical. In fact, it was impossible to score as both a healthy adult and a healthy woman.

The rules for girls are confusing and the deck is stacked against them, but they soon learn that this is the only game in town. One friend remembered that when she was in seventh grade, she wished someone would tell her what the rules were. She said, "It was so hard to play the games correctly without knowing the rules."

While the rules for proper female behavior aren't clearly stated, the punishment for breaking them is harsh. Girls who speak frankly are labeled as bitches. Girls who are not attractive are scorned. The rules are reinforced by the visual images in soft- and hard-core pornography, by song lyrics, by casual remarks, by criticisms, by teasing and by jokes. The rules are enforced by the labeling of a woman like Hillary Rodham Clinton as a "bitch" simply because she's a competent, healthy adult.

Many of the girls I teach at the university can remember some of their choices—the choice to be quiet in class rather than risk being called a brain, the choice to diet rather than eat when they were hungry, the choice to go out with the right crowd rather than the crowd they liked, the choice to be polite rather than honest, or to be pretty rather than have fun. One girl put it this way: "You have to suffer to be beautiful." But generally, girls are inarticulate about the trauma at the time it happens. The issues that adolescent girls struggle with are barely discussed in the culture. Language doesn't fit their experiences. Protest is called delinquency, frustration is called bitchiness, withdrawal is called depression and despair is labeled hormonal. Many battles for the self are won and lost without reports from the front lines.

There are many different experiences that cause girls to relinquish their true selves. In early adolescence girls learn how important appearance is in defining social acceptability. Attractiveness is both a necessary and a sufficient condition for girls' success. This is an old, old problem. Helen of Troy didn't launch a thousand ships because she was a hard worker. Juliet wasn't loved for her math ability.

The *Ladies' Guide to Health,* written in 1888, pointed out that while boys were dressed for winter in wool pants, jackets and sweaters, girls were dressed in silks and laces that fell gracefully from their shoulders and left their arms exposed. The author bemoaned the deaths of girls from diphtheria and pneumonia.

Teen magazines are a good example of the training in lookism that girls receive. Once when my daughter was sick I wanted to buy her some light reading. When I picked up her antibiotics at the drugstore, I leafed through the magazines. The models all looked six feet tall and anorexic. The emphasis was on makeup, fashion and weight. Girls were encouraged to spend money and to diet and work out in order to develop the looks that would attract boys. Apparently attracting boys was the sole purpose of life, because the magazines had no articles on careers, hobbies, politics or academic pursuits. I couldn't find one that wasn't preaching the message "Don't worry about feeling good or being good, worry about looking good."

Girls come of age in a misogynistic culture in which men have most political and economic power. Girls read a history of Western civilization that is essentially a record of men's lives. As Dale Spender says, "Women's accomplishments are relegated to the lost and found." As girls study Western civilization, they become increasingly aware that history is the history of men. History is His Story, the story of *Man*-kind.

I discovered this when I read H. G. Wells' *Outline of History* and Winston Churchill's *History of the Western World*. Both are primarily histories of war and the distribution of property. Women's lives were ignored except as they influenced the course of men's lives. I remember wondering, Where were the women during all these events? My daughter made the same observation about her history text: "It's so boring, just a bunch of kings and generals fighting each other. What were the women doing anyway?"

Girls move into a culture with a Constitution that gave white men, not all Americans, the right to vote, and that has yet to pass an equal rights amendment. They join a culture in which historical documents proclaim the rights of man. As Tillie Olson observed, women's voices have been silenced through the ages, and the silencing continues in the present.

By junior high girls sense their lack of power, but usually they cannot say what they sense. They see that mostly men are congressmen, principals, bankers and corporate executives. They notice that famous writers, musicians and artists are mostly men. But they don't focus on the political—their complaints are personal.

What girls say about gender and power issues depends on how they are asked. When I ask adolescent girls if they are feminists, most say no. To them, feminism is a dirty word, like communism or fascism. But if I ask if they believe men and women should have equal rights, they say yes. When I ask if their schools are sexist, they are likely to say no. But if I ask if they are ever harassed sexually at their school, they say yes and tell me stories. If I ask who writes most of the material they study at school, they know it's men. If I ask who is more likely to be a principal, they say a man. If I ask who has more power, they say men.

I encourage girls to think about these issues and bring me examples of discrimination. One girl noticed that the mountains in Colorado that were named for men had their last names. She brought in a map to point out Mount Adams, Mount Audubon, Babcock Peak, Mount Edwards, Mount Garfield, Hilliard Peak, Mount Sneffels and Mount Richthofen. The few natural features that are named for women are named with only the woman's first name, such as Mount Alice, Mount Emma, Mount Eva, Lake Emmaline, Lake Agnes, Maggie Gulch and Mount Flora.

Girls complain that they do more chores than their brothers. Or that they make less money baby-sitting than their brothers do mowing lawns. Or that parents praise brothers' accomplishments more than theirs. An athlete complained that her track coach spent more time with the boys. Another noted that only the female gymnasts had to weigh in at practices. A softball player complained that sports coverage was better for men's events than for her own. A musician noticed that most rock stars were male.

I was a reader and I remember the trouble I had with misogynistic writers. I loved Tolstoy, but it broke my heart to realize when I read *The Kreutzer Sonata* that he detested women. Later I had the same experience with Schopenhauer, Henry Miller and Norman Mailer. My daughter, Sara, read Aristotle in her philosophy class. One night she read a section aloud to me and said, "This guy doesn't respect women." I wondered what it means to her that one of the wisest men of the ages is misogynistic.

It's important for girls to be exposed to more women writers, but it's equally important to change the way women are portrayed in the media. Not many girls read Tolstoy today, but almost all watch television. On the screen they see women mainly depicted as half-clad and half-witted, often awaiting rescue by quick-thinking, fully clothed men. I ask girls to watch the ways women are portrayed on television. We'll talk about their observations and I'll ask, "What does this teach you about the role of women?"

Cayenne noticed that television almost never features old, heavy or unattractive women. She also noticed that on TV even if a woman is a doctor or a scholar, she looks like a *Playboy* bunny. Another noticed that women are often victims of violence. Lots of plots have to do with women being raped, beaten, chased or terrorized by men. She also noticed that some sex scenes have scary music and some violent scenes have sexy music so that sex and violence are all mixed up.

She noticed that male voices carry more authority in commercials. Men are the doctors and scientists who give product endorsements. She observed that women's bodies sell products that have nothing directly to do with women—tires, tractors, liquor and guns.

Another client hated the Old Milwaukee beer ads that feature the Swedish Bikini Team in which a group of bikini-clad women parachute onto a beach to fulfill the sexual fantasies of a beer-drinking man. She said, "Women are portrayed as expensive toys, as the ultimate recreation." She brought in cologne ads. A Royal Copenhagen ad shows a semi-naked woman kissing a man. The tag line is: "Some of the wildest things happen below deck." A Santa Fe ad has a couple in bed with the woman's body in the foreground and it reads: "It's pretty hot in Santa Fe." She showed me a Courvoisier ad showing a woman in a short tight skirt sitting on a man's lap locked in a passionate embrace. She said, "It looks like he'll get sex if he buys this alcohol."

To my embarrassment, one client brought in a magazine from my own waiting room. It was an alumni magazine that features arts and sciences. In the glossy thirty-five-page magazine, there were forty-five photographs, forty-four of which pictured males. The one female pictured was on the last page in an article on ballet classes. A male teacher posed with a young girl in a tutu.

My psychology students are aware that the field is male-dominated. While 90 percent of the students are women, almost all the theorists and the famous therapists are men. It's hard to find books about psychotherapy written by women or films of women psychotherapists.

Ironically, bright and sensitive girls are most at risk for problems. They are likely to understand the implications of the media around them and be alarmed. They have the mental equipment to pick up our cultural ambivalence about women, and yet they don't have the cognitive, emotional and social skills to handle this information. They are paralyzed by complicated and contradictory data that they cannot interpret. They struggle to resolve the unresolvable and to make sense of the absurd. It's this attempt to make sense of the whole of adolescent experience that overwhelms bright girls.

Less perceptive girls may miss the meaning of sexist ads, music and shows entirely. They tend to deny and oversimplify problems. They don't attempt to integrate aspects of their experience or to "connect the dots" between cultural events and their own lives. Rather than process their experience, they seal in confusion.

Often bright girls look more vulnerable than their peers who have picked up less or who have chosen to deal with all the complexity by blocking it out. Later, bright girls may be more interesting, adaptive and authentic, but in early adolescence they just look shelled.

Girls have four general ways in which they can react to the cultural pressures to abandon the self. They can conform, withdraw, be depressed or get angry. Whether girls feel depression or anger is a matter of attribution—those who blame themselves feel depressed, while those who blame others feel angry. Generally they blame their parents. Of course, most girls react with some combination of the four general ways.

To totally accept the cultural definitions of femininity and conform to the pressures is to kill the self. Girls who do this are the "Muffys" and "Barbie dolls" with hair and smiles in place and a terrible deadness underneath. They are the ones who make me want to shout, "Don't give up, fight back." Often girls who try to conform overshoot the mark. For example, girls with anorexia have tried too hard to be slender, feminine and perfect. They have become thin, shiny packages, outwardly carefully wrapped and inwardly a total muddle.

Girls have long been trained to be feminine at considerable cost to their humanity. They have long been evaluated on the basis of appearance and caught in myriad double binds: achieve, but not too much; be polite, but be yourself; be feminine and adult; be aware of our cultural heritage, but don't comment on the sexism. Another way to describe this femininity training is to call it false self-training. Girls are trained to be less than who they really are. They are trained to be what the culture wants of its young women, not what they themselves want to become.

America today is a girl-destroying place. Everywhere girls are encouraged to sacrifice their true selves. Their parents may fight to protect them, but their parents have limited power. Many girls lose contact with their true selves, and when they do, they become extraordinarily vulnerable to a culture that is all too happy to use them for its purposes.

Alice Miller said, "It is what we cannot see that makes us sick." It's important for girls to explore the impact the culture has on their growth and development. They all benefit from, to use on old-fashioned term, consciousness-raising. Once girls understand the effects of the culture on their lives, they can fight back. They learn that they have conscious choices to make and ultimate responsibility for those choices. Intelligent resistance keeps the true self alive.

Chapter 3

DEVELOPMENTAL ISSUES— "I'M NOT WAVING, I'M DROWNING"

■

CHARLOTTE (15)

Rain drummed on the office windows and rolled down the casings as Rob and Sue, looking weary, talked about their daughter. Charlotte was fifteen, but looked much older in her heavy makeup and tight dress. Her face had a hardness that I hate to see in anyone, especially in someone so young.

Sue thought that Charlotte's problems went back to her divorce, which had occurred when Charlotte was three. Charlotte hadn't missed her father, who was an abusive alcoholic, but she had missed Sue, who immediately began a full-time job at a Quick Stop. Sue looked at her nicotine-stained fingers and said, "After the divorce, I had less of everything—time, money, patience. I think that hurt Charlotte."

As Sue talked, Charlotte sat stiffly, her mouth a tight, thin line.

Rob changed the subject. "Sue and I met at a singles group and dated for ten months. We got married when Charlotte was eight. She was our flower girl. Really a cute kid."

"Charlotte was okay till junior high, but then things started going wrong fast," Sue said. "She developed an attitude. She started smoking and dressing like a slut. She slipped out to drink with older kids."

"She's not the only one in trouble," Rob said. "Three of her friends have babies. Our town has one thousand people and three liquor stores. Kids have nothing to do but get into trouble."

Sue added, "We haven't been great supervisors. Rob commutes to manage a Safeway, and I run the Quick Stop at home."

Charlotte was in about every kind of trouble an adolescent girl could be in. She was flunking ninth grade. She smoked cigarettes, drank whiskey and used pot. She had an older boyfriend. She barely spoke to her parents and had tantrums when they tried to keep her safe. A month ago, when they insisted on a drug and alcohol evaluation, Charlotte ran away from home.

For three weeks Rob and Sue worried that she'd been kidnapped or killed. Sue said, "You don't know what fear is until you have a daughter hitchhiking around the country." Then Charlotte called from Seattle to say she wanted to come home. She sounded frightened and promised to do whatever her parents wanted. They called for a therapy appointment.

I asked Charlotte if she was willing to work with me for a while. She shrugged elaborately, feigning exasperation. But over the next few months Charlotte and I figured a few things out. She really had been okay in elementary school. She had played ball every summer until the town's insurance was canceled and Little League was discontinued. She liked hanging out at the Quick Stop, drinking root beer and reading the magazines. She was happy when Rob became her dad. He took her camping and bought her a new bike. He made her mom laugh.

But adolescence changed everything. First it was the ordinary stuff: fights with girls and teasing by the boys. Her breasts developed early and boys were always rubbing against her, grabbing her from behind and calling her names. She also was heavier than most of her classmates and worried about her weight. She bought some diet pills and lost weight rapidly. Charlotte loved the light, airy feeling she had on those pills. She started smoking cigarettes to help herself lose weight. Charlotte stole her Virginia Slims from the Quick Stop.

Rob and Sue hated her smoking, but they smoked too and couldn't take the high moral ground on this issue. Sue and Rob didn't like her friends, her constant dieting, her music, her falling grades or her mouthiness. Conversations became tense and angry. Charlotte stayed in her room or out of the house as much as she could.

The summer of her eighth-grade year she started "partying," a euphemism for getting loaded with friends. She met kids at a sand pit south of town and drank beer and cheap wine around a bonfire until dawn. She told me, "Getting baked erased my life."

Once Rob showed up looking for her, but she hid behind a cotton-wood tree while her friends lied about her whereabouts. Several times Sue and Rob called the police to help them find her. She was grounded, but she slipped out her window and went anyway. Finally Rob and Sue had what Charlotte described as an "emotional meltdown." They gave up and let her do what she wanted.

That is, they gave up until she began dating Mel. He was twenty-two and had a job at the co-op that paid him just enough money to buy beer and lotto tickets. He was good-looking but sleazy, and Rob and Sue were adamant that their daughter wouldn't date him.

Unfortunately, Charlotte no longer obeyed them. She wore seduc-tive clothes, dyed her hair Madonna blond and did whatever she pleased. With guys she was quiet and docile, eager to please—exactly the kind of girlfriend Mel wanted. The harder Rob and Sue fought, the more appealing the forbidden fruit became, and eventually they lost this battle too.

When Charlotte talked about Mel, I was surprised by how realistic her perceptions were. She knew he was a loser and disapproved of his heavy drinking and gambling. She even admitted that sometimes she was bored with him. All they did was rent movies and drink at his place. Now and then they fished for catfish and carp, but as Charlotte said, "Those trips are really an excuse to stay out drinking all night."

Mel didn't even like to have sex that often. But Charlotte was fiercely loyal. Mel was the first guy she dated who wanted a relation-ship with her. As she put it, "With him, it wasn't wham, bam, thank you ma'am."

Mel had confided to her about his own difficult family situation. His father was the town drunk in the town just west of them on the highway. Once Mel came home from school to find all their furniture had been sold to buy booze. He had memories of Christmases without presents, of food baskets from churches delivered by his classmates and of nice kids not being permitted to play with him.

Charlotte's eyes softened when she talked about Mel. She had a mission—to save him and to make him happier than he'd ever been before. She conceded that, so far, Mel didn't seem that happy, but she thought that in time they could get their lives together.

Mel was the only person she trusted—she hated high school boys, who "only wanted one thing." Most of the girls at her school were "snobs." Her friends who had babies were okay, but they were busy now with their own problems and not "there for her." Rob and Sue argued a lot and "weren't as sweetie-sweet as they acted in therapy."

She particularly hated the school and her teachers. She felt her math teacher, Mr. Jenson, deliberately humiliated her. Her Spanish teacher looked at her breasts whenever he could. None of the courses had anything to do with real life. The kids who brownnosed got the good grades. The lunches were "slop." When I asked her if there was anything she liked about school, Charlotte thought for a while. "I'd like sewing class if the teacher weren't such a bitch."

One day Charlotte brought up sex. "Before Mel, I needed to be drunk to have sex. Otherwise, I remembered things from the past. When I was high, it didn't matter."

"Have you been raped?" I asked softly.

Charlotte pushed her brown hair off her face and said in a flat voice, "I've had trouble you can't imagine."

She looked younger and more vulnerable as we sat quietly with her words. I didn't push for more information. It would come out in future sessions. I thought about William Faulkner's line "The past isn't dead. It isn't even past."

Even though Charlotte was from a small, sleepy town, she exemplifies the problems of girls in the 1990s. She had an abusive, alcoholic father. Her mother divorced when Charlotte was young, and the family was poor and overburdened for many years. As a teenager, Charlotte is in all kinds of trouble—she drinks, smokes pot and cigarettes, diets and is flunking school. She has run away from home and she has been raped. She's distanced from her parents and is alone except for an older, chemically addicted boyfriend. Especially with men, she's docile and other-directed. She does what she thinks she should do in order to be accepted.

Charlotte has made many choices that sacrifice her true self and support a false self. Her choices show in her face. There's deadness to her demeanor that comes from inauthenticity, from giving away too much. Charlotte is evidence of a childhood lost. And what has replaced childhood glitters but is not gold. I hope the therapy can help her find herself. It will be reclamation work.

LORI (12)—ON THE CUSP

Last month Lori, whom I had known since her birth, started junior high at a large school known for its wealthy, competitive students. I visited her home to see how she was taking to junior high. We met in her newly redecorated bedroom. Lori was proud of her Elvis stamp poster and Elvis bedspread and curtains. She had a white desk neatly arranged with paper, pens and a dictionary, pink beanbag chairs and a large glass cage for her gerbil, Molasses, "Mo" for short.

I was struck by how fresh and cheerful she was. She was dressed in green sweats. Her short brown hair curled over silver star earrings. She bounced around her room showing me a book she liked, her swim team trophies and Mo's tricks. Lori made me feel I was in another place and time, back in the fifties in a home with plenty of money, happily married parents, and children who were not afraid or stressed. The cynical part of me wondered, Where's the skeleton in the closet? If I hadn't known this family for twenty years, I would have been even more cynical about so much happiness.

Lori is highly gifted, which in our school system means her IQ is higher than 145. She qualified for a special tutor, but she felt that this would isolate her from friends. She preferred a combination of regular and accelerated classes. Lori loved junior high. She liked elementary school as well, but said that by the end she had outgrown it. Junior high was exciting, with its hallways full of kids, nine different teachers, a tableful of friends at lunch and a swimming pool in the gym.

She was busy in and out of school. She swam and danced several nights a week and sang and acted whenever she had the chance. This year she was taking voice lessons at the university. Her mom was a stay-at-home mom who could run her to all these lessons, rehearsals and swim meets. Her dad was an attorney who could pay for these activities and who showed up for her meets and performances.

Her younger sister, Lisa, also swam and danced. Lisa was gifted in piano, which gave her a unique talent. Lori was social and bubbly, Lisa quieter and more introverted. While Lisa curled up with a book or played piano in the living room, Lori talked on the phone for hours.

Lori kept most of her old friends and made many new friends at junior high. She said, "I have friends, and I'm moderately popular. To be super popular you have to look like a model and wear expensive clothes." She described her closest friends as like herself—good students, happy and involved in activities.

Lori said she was known for being independent and funny. She said, "I know who I am, and I don't always think like other people think." She was also unusual in that she's relaxed about her appearance. Unlike most of her friends, who awaken early so they will have time to get ready for school, Lori gets up ten minutes before it's time to leave and throws on anything she can find. Unlike her friends, she eats whatever she wants and doesn't worry about weight. She said, "Lots of my friends wish they could be like me about appearance."

I asked about alcohol and drugs.

"I think they're stupid. I would never consider them."

"What if you were pressured to use them at a party?"

"I'd say, 'You do what you want, I'll do what I want.' " She laughed. "And then I'd leave the party."

She knew some kids who drank, but none of her close friends did yet. I asked about sexual harassment. Lori scratched the top of her head. "Some of my friends have been hassled, but I haven't yet. I know who to avoid. There's this certain hall that I don't walk down."

We talked about dating, a subject Lori had carefully considered. She didn't want to date until she was in high school and even then, not seriously. She believed that sex comes with marriage. I asked her how she felt about the music and movies that show teenagers having casual sex. Lori said, "I turn that stuff off. I don't have time for TV anyway. With music, I don't pay attention to the words."

I said, "It sounds like you screen out things that upset you."

Lori agreed. "Not everything, but things I can't change."

Lori lit up when we talked about dance. She was proud that her teacher had recently moved her into an advanced class. She liked swimming too, and believed that all the exercise helped her manage stress. "I work out almost every day."

Although she admitted that they could be embarrassing in public, she loved her parents. She felt her dad was too skinny and her mom was overly friendly. She said that just lately her mom had been getting on her nerves. She wanted more privacy than she used to. But still she loved Sunday nights when the family had Cokes, apples and popcorn, and played cards or watched a movie.

I asked about career goals. She liked dance but suspected it was not a practical career. Lori was proud of her writing and thought she'd like a career in journalism. She had already had an article published in her school's newsletter, and she'd interviewed a reporter for a class project.

Lori showed me out, her star earrings flashing. Lisa was practicing on the new grand piano as we left. Her mother sat beside her turning the pages of a Clementi sonatina. Her dad read the newspaper nearby.

I thought about Lori as I drove home. She seemed to be holding on to her true self miraculously well. She was social, but not overly awed by popularity. She chose to be with friends rather than have a mentor, but she still made straight As. She had kept all her prepuberty interests: singing, dancing, swimming and acting. She was relaxed about her appearance and didn't worry about her weight. Even though she was slightly embarrassed by her parents, she still loved them and enjoyed spending time with them.

Lori was independent and funny. She made conscious choices about sex, drugs and alcohol. In fact, she made conscious choices about everything. She looked within herself for guidance and answers. Lori already had sorted her experience into what she could and couldn't control, and she knew how to screen out what was beyond her control. She had a sense of who she was and an orientation toward the future. Though she certainly might change her mind about journalism, the fact that she had a goal demonstrated that her life was not all lived in the moment.

Lori was so well rounded and mentally healthy that I pondered how to explain it. She was extraordinarily lucky. She inherited a cheerful, energetic personality. She was pretty, smart, musical and athletic. Her parents were loving and protective, but not overly protective or demanding. She lived in a relatively safe and prosperous neighborhood surrounded by stable families. And she'd managed to escape being assaulted or traumatized.

She may have more trouble in the next few years than she anticipates. The social scene will get tougher, her emotions more turbulent, and the time may come when she thinks family night is dumb. She is just moving into the time when adolescent girls really struggle. But I think she is much more likely than most girls to hold on to her true self. She has a strong inner focus and self-confidence that I think will hold. I wished I could protect her, wrap a magic cloak around her that would keep her safe. I thought of the last line of a poem that a mother wrote about her child: "I hurl you into the universe and pray."

My horticulturist friend says that the environment is the richest and most diverse at borders, where trees meet fields, desert meets mountains or rivers cross prairies. Adolescence is a border between adulthood and childhood, and as such it has a richness and diversity unmatched by any other life stage. It's impossible to capture the complexity and intensity of adolescent girls. I think of one client at twelve, wanting to be a fashion model or a corporate attorney—whichever made more money. And another, an Amerasian girl who escaped Vietnam, shyly explaining that she wants to go to medical school. I think of Sara pouring forth songs from *Guys and Dolls* as I drive her to school. I think of the awkward movements and downcast eyes of a girl who works in her parents' deli or the self-assured way that a neighbor girl walks back from the mound after pitching a no-hit inning.

Adolescents are travelers, far from home with no native land, neither children nor adults. They are jet-setters who fly from one country to another with amazing speed. Sometimes they are four years old, an hour later they are twenty-five. They don't really fit anywhere. There's a yearning for place, a search for solid ground.

Adolescence is a time of intense preoccupation with the self, which is growing and changing daily. Everything feels new. I remember the impulse to hit my mother when she woke me one morning for school. Even as I felt that rage, I was appalled by my weirdness. I remember going weak-kneed when certain boys walked by me in the halls. These moments took my breath away and left me wondering who I was becoming. I was as surprised by my reactions as I would have been by a stranger's.

Sara, at twelve, needed to be reminded to brush her teeth, but she wanted to rent R-rated movies and get a job. She flew all over the map. One minute she was arguing with us about politics and the next she was begging for a stuffed animal. She wouldn't be seen with us in public, but was upset if we missed her school programs. She no longer let us hug or kiss her. One night during this time of constant declarations of independence, Sara woke me in the night. She had a fever and wanted me to get a cold cloth and sit by her. I was pleased by this temporary reprieve from her ban on touching.

With adolescence, many kinds of development occur—physical, emotional, intellectual, academic, social and spiritual—and they don't always occur in tandem. Tall, physically well-developed girls can have the emotions of children. Abstract thinkers can have the social skills of first-graders. These differences in developmental levels within the same girl confound adults. Should adults relate to the fifteen-year-old or the four-year-old part of the girl?

Generally, puberty is defined as a biological process while adolescence is defined as the social and personal experience of that process. But even puberty is influenced by culture. Girls are menstruating much earlier now than during the colonial era, and even earlier than in the 1950s. There are many theories about why puberty comes earlier— changes in nutrition (girls get bigger at a younger age because they are better nourished), hormones added to beef and chicken (growth hormones that are known to affect humans may trigger early puberty) and electricity (bodies are programmed to enter puberty after exposure to a certain amount of light, which comes much earlier in a woman's lifetime in an age of electricity). The point is that girls enter adolescence earlier than they did forty years ago. Some girls menstruate at age nine.

Early puberty actually slows down many aspects of girls' development. Early development and the more difficult culture of the 1990s increase the stress on adolescents. Girls who have recently learned to bake cookies and swan-dive aren't ready to handle offers for diet pills. Girls who are reading about Pippi Longstocking aren't ready for the sexual harassment they'll encounter in school. Girls who love to practice piano and visit their grandmothers aren't ready for the shunning by cliques. And at the same time girls must face events prematurely, they are encouraged by our culture to move away from parents and depend on friends for guidance. No wonder they suffer and make so many mistakes.

Girls stay in adolescence longer now. In the fifties and sixties, most teens left home as soon as they graduated from high school, never to return. Increasingly in the 1980s and 1990s young adults do not want to leave home, or they leave home for a while and return to live with their parents in their twenties. Partly children stay because of economics, partly they stay because home seems a safe haven in an increasingly dangerous world. Now adolescence may begin around age ten and may last until around age twenty-two. It can take twelve years to make it through the crucible.

There is an enormous gap between the surface structure of behaviors and the deep structure of meaning. Surface structure is what is visible to the naked eye—awkwardness, energy, anger, moodiness and restlessness. Deep structure is the internal work—the struggle to find a self, the attempt to integrate the past and present and to find a place in the larger culture. Surface behaviors convey little of the struggle within and in fact are often designed to obscure that struggle.

By definition, the deep-structure questions are not articulated clearly to adults. Rather, the surface questions are coded to speak to larger issues. "Can I dye my hair purple?" may mean "Will you allow me to develop as a creative person?" "Can I watch R movies?" may mean "Am I someone who can handle sexual experiences?" "Can I go to a different church?" may mean "Do I have the freedom to explore my own spirituality?"

The deep-structure questions are processed in a serpentine manner with friends. Endlessly girls discuss the smallest details of conversations and events—who wore what, who said what, did he smile at her, did she look mad when I did that? The surface is endlessly combed for information about the depths.

This deep structure–surface structure split is one reason why girls experience so much failure in relationships. Communication is confused and confusing. Relationships between friends are so coded that misunderstandings abound. Parents who attend to the surface structure often miss the point.

Because the deep-structure work is so serious, the surface behavior is often tension-releasing, a way of dispelling internal energy that must escape somehow. This marked difference in behaviors reminds me of my first few years as a therapist. I spent long days being serious, talking about problems and analyzing situations. Then after work I craved goofing off with my kids, telling stupid jokes and watching W.C. Fields movies. The harder my day, the more I wanted comic relief. Teenage girls are doing therapy all day too, only it's inside their own heads. They need the time off whenever they can get it.

When I work with adolescent girls I try to understand what their surface behavior is telling me about their deep-structure issues. I try to ascertain when their behavior is connected to their true selves and when it is the result of pressure to be a false self. Which thinking should I respect and nurture? Which should I challenge?

PHYSICAL SELVES

The body is changing in size, shape and hormonal structure. Just as pregnant women focus on their bodies, so adolescent girls focus on their changing bodies. They feel, look and move differently. These changes must be absorbed, the new body must become part of the self.

The preoccupation with bodies at this age cannot be overstated. The body is a compelling mystery, a constant focus of attention. At thirteen, I thought more about my acne than I did about God or world peace. At thirteen, many girls spend more time in front of a mirror than they do on their studies. Small flaws become obsessions. Bad hair can ruin a day. A broken fingernail can feel tragic.

Generally girls have strong bodies when they enter puberty. But these bodies soften and spread out in ways that our culture calls fat. Just at the point that their bodies are becoming rounder, girls are told that thin is beautiful, even imperative. Girls hate the required gym classes in which other girls talk about their fat thighs and stomachs. One girl told me of showering next to an eighty-five-pound dancer who was on a radical diet. For the first time in her life she looked at her body and was displeased. One client talked about wishing she could cut off the roll of fat around her waist. Another thought her behind was "hideous."

Geena was a chubby clarinet player who liked to read and play chess. She was more interested in computers than makeup and in stuffed animals than designer clothes. She walked to her first day of junior high with her pencils sharpened and her notebooks neatly labeled. She was ready to learn Spanish and algebra and to audition for the school orchestra. She came home sullen and shaken. The boy who had his locker next to hers had smashed into her with his locker door and sneered, "Move your fat ass."

That night she told her mother, "I hate my looks. I need to go on a diet."

Her mother thought, Is that what this boy saw? When he looked at my musical, idealistic Geena, did he see only her behind?

Girls feel an enormous pressure to be beautiful and are aware of constant evaluations of their appearance. In an art exhibit on the theme of women and appearance, Wendy Bantam put it this way: "Every day in the life of a woman is a walking Miss America Contest." Sadly, girls lose if they are either too plain or too pretty. Our cultural stereotypes of the beautiful include negative ideas about their brains—think of the blonde jokes. Girls who are too attractive are seen primarily as sex objects. Their appearance overdetermines their identity. They know that boys like to be seen with them, but doubt that they are liked for reasons other than their packaging. Being beautiful can be a

Pyrrhic victory. The battle for popularity is won, but the war for respect as a whole person is lost.

Girls who are plain are left out of social life and miss the developmental experiences they most need at this stage of their lives. They internalize our culture's scorn of the plain.

The luckiest girls are neither too plain nor too beautiful. They will eventually date, and they'll be more likely to date boys who genuinely like them. They'll have an identity based on other factors, such as sense of humor, intelligence or strength of character. But they don't feel lucky in junior high. A college girl told me, "In junior high I wanted to kill myself because I was too tall. I could not conceive of happiness at that height." Another told of watching a cute blonde in her eighth-grade class flirt with boys. "The same boys who tripped over themselves to open doors for her would look away if I walked by."

Appearance was important when I was in junior high, but it's even more important today. Girls who lived in smaller communities were judged more holistically—for their character, family background, behavior and talents. Now, when more girls live in cities full of strangers, they are judged exclusively by their appearance. Often the only information teenagers have about each other is how they look.

The right look has always mattered, but now it's harder to obtain. Designer clothes, leather jackets, name-brand tennis shoes and expensive makeup shut more girls out of the competition. The standards of beauty are more stringent. Miss Americas have become taller and slimmer over the years. In 1951, Miss Sweden was 5 feet 7 inches tall and weighed 151 pounds. In 1983, Miss Sweden was 5 feet 9 inches tall and 109 pounds. While beautiful women are slimmer, average women are heavier than they were in the 1950s. Thus the discrepancy between the real and the ideal is greater. This discrepancy creates our plague of eating disorders.

What is culturally accepted as beautiful is achieved only with great artifice—photo croppings, camera angles and composite bodies are necessary to get the pictures we now see of beautiful women. Even the stars cannot meet our cultural ideals without great cost. Dolly Parton dieted until she looked ill. Jamie Lee Curtis, who worked months to get in shape for the movie *Perfect,* felt her body was not right for the part. Jane Fonda and Princess Di have both had eating disorders.

I'm struck by how intense and damaging these issues are every time I speak in a high school or college class. I ask, "How many of you know someone with an eating disorder?" Usually every hand goes up.

After my talk girls come up to ask about their friends, their sisters or themselves. They all have horror stories of girls who are miserable because they don't quite meet our cultural ideals.

With early adolescence, girls surrender their relaxed attitudes about their bodies and take up the burden of self-criticism. Just at the point their hips are becoming rounder and they are gaining fat cells, they see magazines and movies or hear remarks by peers that suggest to them that their bodies are all wrong. Many girls scorn their true bodies and work for a false body. They allow the culture to define who they should be. They diet, exercise compulsively and wear makeup and expensive clothes. Charlotte thought of her body as something other people would examine and judge. How her body appeared to others, not how it felt to her, was what mattered.

A girl who remains true to herself will accept her body as hers and resist others' attempts to evaluate and define her by her appearance. She's much more likely to think of her body in terms of function than form. What does her body do for her? Lori, for example, was proud of her body's ability to dance and swim. Her self-esteem didn't revolve around her appearance. She eschewed diets and time spent in front of a mirror. Interestingly, even as her friends primped and dieted, they envied her her casual attitudes about beauty. Lori cared more about being than seeming. She was lucky because, as De Beauvoir writes, "to lose confidence in one's body is to lose confidence in oneself."

EMOTIONAL SELVES

A friend once told me that the best way to understand teenagers was to think of them as constantly on LSD. It was good advice. People on acid are intense, changeable, internal, often cryptic or uncommunicative and, of course, dealing with a different reality. That's all true for adolescent girls.

The emotional system is immature in early adolescence. Emotions are extreme and changeable. Small events can trigger enormous reactions. A negative comment about appearance or a bad mark on a test can hurl a teenager into despair. Not only are feelings chaotic, but girls often lose perspective. Girls have tried to kill themselves because they were grounded for a weekend or didn't get asked to the prom.

Despair and anger are the hardest emotions to deal with, but other emotions are equally intense. Just as sorrow is unmodulated, so is joy.

A snowstorm or a new dress can produce bliss. There's still a childlike capacity to be swept away. One girl told me of wandering about in woods reading poetry and feeling in touch with the central core of the universe. She was elated by the sunlight dappling the leaves, the smells of wild plum blossoms, the blueness of the sky and the trills of meadowlarks. The feeling of the moment is all that exists.

I teach girls to rate their stress as a way to modulate their emotions. I'll say, "If one is a broken shoestring and ten is a terminal brain tumor, rate things that upset you on this one-to-ten scale." Then I'll ask, "What would you rate your argument with your boyfriend today?" The girl will say, "A fifteen."

The instability of feelings leads to unpredictable behavior in adolescents. A wildly energetic teen will be frenetic one moment and lethargic the next. A sentence or a look from a parent can start a crying spell or World War III. A girl who is incredibly focused when it's time to plan a skit for prom night is totally disorganized about her social studies project due the same day.

It's hard for adults to keep up with the changes and intensity of adolescent emotions. When Sara was in junior high I called her after school. Some days she was full of laughter and confidence. ("School rocks my world.") Other days she needed crisis intervention over the phone. ("It sucks to be me.")

Girls' emotional immaturity makes it hard for them to hold on to their true selves as they experience the incredible pressures of adolescence in the 1990s. They are whipped about by their emotions and misled by them. At a developmental time when even small events are overwhelming, big events such as date rape or a friend who tests positive for the HIV virus can be cataclysmic.

Girls deal with intense emotions in ways that are true or false to the self. A girl who operates out of her false self will be overwhelmed by her emotional experiences and do what she can to stop having these painful emotions. She may do this by denial of her feelings or by projection onto others. Charlotte did this by running away, by using alcohol and drugs and by losing herself in a relationship in which she thought only of her boyfriend's feelings. When girls fail to acknowledge their own feelings, they further the development of a false self. Only by staying connected to their emotions and by slowly working through the turbulence can young women emerge from adolescence strong and whole.

Lori is still remarkably stable emotionally. I predict that she may have a rough time ahead, and that like most girls she may feel anxiety, confusion and despair. But I suspect she will manage to acknowledge these emotional experiences. She'll be able to rage, cry, talk and write about her emotions. She'll process them and gradually sort them out. Lori will emerge from adolescence somewhat tattered emotionally but intact. She will be an authentic person who owns all her emotional experiences. She'll possess what Alice Miller calls "vibrancy."

THINKING SELVES

Most early adolescents are unable to think abstractly. The brightest are just moving into formal operational thought or the ability to think abstractly and flexibly. The immaturity of their thinking makes it difficult to reason with them. They read deep meaning into casual remarks and overanalyze glances.

The concreteness of girls' thinking can be seen in their need to categorize others. People are assigned to groups such as geeks, preps and jocks. One girl's categories included "deeper than thou," a derogatory term for the sophisticated artists at her school. Another divided the world into Christian and non-Christian, and another into alternative, non-alternative and wannabe alternative.

Teenage girls are extremists who see the world in black-and-white terms, missing shades of gray. Life is either marvelous or not worth living. School is either pure torment or is going fantastically. Other people are either great or horrible, and they themselves are wonderful or pathetic failures. One day a girl will refer to herself as "the goddess of social life" and the next day she'll regret that she's the "ultimate in nerdosity."

This fluctuation in sense of self would suggest severe disturbance in an adult, but in teenage girls it's common. Psychological tests, like the MMPI, need different norms for female adolescents. Their thoughts are chaotic and scrambled. Compared to stable adults, they all look crazy.

Girls also overgeneralize in their thinking from one incident to all cases. One affront means "I have no friends." One good grade means "I am an academic diva." Offhand remarks can be taken as a prophecy, an indictment or a diagnosis. One client decided to become a nurse because her uncle told her she would be a good one. When I was in eighth grade, my teacher returned my first poem with the word "trite" scribbled across the top of the page. I gave up my plans to be a writer for almost twenty years.

This tendency to overgeneralize makes it difficult to reason with adolescent girls. Because they know of one example, they'll argue, "Everyone else gets to stay out till two," or "Everyone I know gets a new car for their sixteenth birthday." They'll believe that because the girl next door gets a ride to school, every girl in the universe gets a ride to school. They aren't being manipulative as much as they earnestly believe that one case represents the whole.

Teenage girls have what one psychologist called the "imaginary audience syndrome." They think they are being watched by others who are preoccupied with the smallest details of their lives. For example, a niece was most upset that her mother wanted to take binoculars to her soccer game. She told her mom, "All the other kids will know you are watching my every move." A friend told me how anxious her daughter was when she wore jeans and a sweatshirt to her daughter's school conference. A twelve-year-old told me how embarrassing it was to go to performances with her mother, who had a way of clapping with hands high in the air. Sometimes when her mother was particularly pleased, she shouted bravo. My client said, "I can't believe she does this. Everyone in the place knows she's a total dork."

Teenage girls engage in emotional reasoning, which is the belief that if you feel something is true, it must be true. If a teenager feels like a nerd, she is a nerd. If she feels her parents are unfair, they are unfair. If she feels she'll get invited to homecoming, then she will be invited. There is limited ability to sort facts from feelings. Thinking is still magical in the sense that thinking something makes it so.

Young girls are egocentric in their thinking. That is, they are unable to focus on anyone's experience but their own. Parents often experience this egocentrism as selfishness. But it's not a character flaw, only a developmental stage. Parents complain that their daughters do only a few chores and yet claim, "I do all the work around here." A mother reports that her daughter expects her to spend hours chauffeuring to save the daughter a few minutes of walking.

At one time I would have said that teenage girls think they are invulnerable. And I could have cited many examples, such as girls refusing to wear seat belts or to deal with the possibilities of pregnancy. I still see glimpses of that sense of invulnerability. For example, one of my clients who volunteered at a rehabilitation center came in with stories of head-injured patients. One day, after a particularly sad story about a boy her age, I blurted out, "Well, at least now you are wearing your seat belt." She gave me a surprised look and said, "Not really. I won't get in a wreck."

But I do see this sense of invulnerability much less frequently. It is shattered by trauma in the lives of girls or their friends. Most twelve-year-olds know they can be hurt. They read the papers and watch television. Psychiatrist Robert Coles writes that children in some parts of America are more frightened than children in Lebanon or Northern Ireland. Girls talk more about death, have more violent dreams, more spooky fantasies and more fears about the future. As one client put it, "With all these shootings, all the people will disappear."

It's important not to oversimplify this topic. Some children feel much safer than others. Lori, for example, with her lovely neighborhood and stable family, feels much safer than Charlotte, with her history of trauma. Even traumatized children sometimes forget to be scared, while protected children have nightmares about being shot. But experience largely determines whether or not a girl feels invulnerable. Becoming conscious of the dangerous world can happen overnight or be a gradual process. The same girl can be of two minds depending on the week. One week she'll lock doors and worry aloud about danger, the next she'll believe that she can fight off any attacker. But generally, adolescents no longer feel invulnerable in the ways they did in my childhood, or even ten years ago.

Girls deal with painful thoughts, discrepant information and cognitive confusion in ways that are true or false to the self. The temptation is to shut down, to oversimplify, to avoid the hard work of examining and integrating experiences. Girls who operate from a false self often reduce the world to a more manageable place by distorting reality. Some girls join cults in which others do all their thinking for them. Some girls become anorexic and reduce all the complexity in life to just one issue—weight.

Some girls, like Charlotte, work hard not to think about their lives. They run from any kind of processing and seek out companions who are also on the run. They avoid parents who push them to consider what they are doing. Charlotte was heavily swayed by peers in her decision making. She was a sailboat with no centerboard, blowing whichever way the winds blew. She had no North Star to keep her focused on her own true needs.

Girls who stay connected to their true selves are also confused and sometimes overwhelmed. But they have made some commitment to understanding their lives. They think about their experiences. They do not give up on trying to resolve contradictions and make connections between events. They may seek out a parent, teacher or therapist to help them. They may read or write in a journal. They will make many mistakes and misinterpret much of reality, but girls with true selves make a commitment to process and understand their experiences.

Lori was particularly good at looking within herself to make decisions. She thought through issues and decided what was best for her. After that, she was relatively immune to peer pressure. She was steering, not drifting, determined to behave in ways that made sense to her.

ACADEMIC SELVES

Schools have always treated girls and boys differently. What is new in the nineties is that we have much more documentation of this phenomenon. Public awareness of the discrimination is increasing. This is due in part to the American Association of University Women (AAUW), which released a study in 1992 entitled "How Schools Shortchange Girls."

In classes, boys are twice as likely to be seen as role models, five times as likely to receive teachers' attention and twelve times as likely to speak up in class. In textbooks, one-seventh of all illustrations of children are of girls. Teachers chose many more classroom activities that appeal to boys than to girls. Girls are exposed to almost three times as many boy-centered stories as girl-centered stories. Boys tend to be portrayed as clever, brave, creative and resourceful, while girls are depicted as kind, dependent and docile. Girls read six times as many biographies of males as of females. Even in animal stories, the animals are twice as likely to be males. (I know of one teacher who, when she reads to her classes, routinely changes the sex of the characters in the stories so that girls will have stronger role models.)

Analysis of classroom videos shows that boys receive more classroom attention and detailed instruction than girls. They are called on more often than girls and are asked more abstract, open-ended and complex questions. Boys are more likely to be praised for academics and intellectual work, while girls are more likely to be praised for their clothing, behaving properly and obeying rules. Boys are likely to be criticized for their behavior, while girls are criticized for intellectual inadequacy. The message to boys tends to be: "You're smart, if you would just settle down and get to work." The message to girls is often: "Perhaps you're just not good at this. You've followed the rules and haven't succeeded."

Because with boys failure is attributed to external factors and success is attributed to ability, they keep their confidence, even with failure. With girls it's just the opposite. Because their success is attributed to good luck or hard work and failure to lack of ability, with every failure, girls' confidence is eroded. All this works in subtle ways to stop girls from wanting to be astronauts and brain surgeons. Girls can't say why they ditch their dreams, they just "mysteriously" lose interest.

Some girls do well in math and continue to like it, but many who were once good at math complain that they are stupid in math. Girl after girl tells me, "I'm not good in math." My observations suggest that girls have trouble with math because math requires exactly the qualities that many junior-high girls lack—confidence, trust in one's own judgment and the ability to tolerate frustration without becoming overwhelmed. Anxiety interferes with problem solving in math. A vicious circle develops—girls get anxious, which interferes with problem solving, and so they fail and are even more anxious and prone to self-doubt the next time around.

When boys have trouble with a math problem, they are more likely to think the problem is hard but stay with it. When girls have trouble, they think they are stupid and tend to give up. This difference in attribution speaks to girls' precipitous decline in math. Girls need to be encouraged to persevere in the face of difficulty, to calm down and believe in themselves. They need permission to take their time and to make many mistakes before solving the problem. They need to learn relaxation skills to deal with the math anxiety so many experience.

The AAUW study found that as children go through school, boys do better and feel better about themselves and girls' self-esteem, opinions of their sex and scores on standardized achievement tests all decline. Girls are more likely than boys to say that they are not smart enough for their dream careers. They emerge from adolescence with a diminished sense of their worth as individuals.

Gifted girls seem to suffer particularly with adolescence. Lois Murphy found that they lose IQ points as they become feminized. In the 1920s Psychologist Louis Terman studied gifted children in California.

Among the children, the seven best writers were girls and all the best artists were girls, but by adulthood all the eminent artists and writers were men.

Junior high is when girls begin to fade academically. Partly this comes from the very structure of the schools, which tend to be large and impersonal. Girls, who tend to do better in relationship-based, cooperative learning situations, get lost academically in these settings. Partly it comes from a shift girls make at this time from a focus on achievement to a focus on affiliation. In junior high girls feel enormous pressure to be popular. They learn that good grades can even interfere with popularity. Lori learned to keep quiet about grades. She said, "Either way I lose. If I make a good grade, they are mad. If I make a bad grade, they spread it around that even I can screw up." Another girl said, "When I started junior high I figured out that I'd have more friends if I focused on sports. Smart girls were nerds." Another, who almost flunked seventh grade, told me, "All I care about is my friends. Grades don't matter to me."

I saw a seventh-grader who was failing everything. I asked her why and she said, "My friends and I decided that making good grades wasn't cool." Her story has a happy ending, not because of my work, but because the next year, in eighth grade, she and her friends had another meeting and decided that it was now "cool" to make good grades. My client's academic situation improved enormously.

This tendency for girls to hide their academic accomplishments is an old one. Once on a date I was particularly untrue to myself. Denny and I went to the A&W Root Beer Drive-In on Highway 81, and he asked me what I would like. Even though I was famished I ordered only a small Coke. (Nice girls didn't eat too much.) Then he asked about my six-weeks grades. I had made As, but I said I had two Cs and was worried my parents would be mad. I can still remember his look of visible relief.

As Charlotte got lost in junior high, her grades fell. Partly this was because she didn't work, and partly it was because she lost the confidence in herself that a student needs to tackle increasingly difficult material. She expected to fail and gave up at the first sign of frustration. Lori, on the other hand, liked challenges. She had found that by trusting herself and working hard, she could succeed. She was aware that her good grades didn't help her socially, but she wasn't willing to sacrifice her academic career for the short-term goal of pleasing her easily threatened peers.

SOCIAL SELVES—FAMILY

Adolescence in America is the psychological equivalent of toddler-hood. Just as toddlers move away from their parents physically, so adolescents move away from their parents emotionally. There are continuous negotiations between parents and children about distance. Children want to explore and parents want to keep them safe. And both toddlers and adolescents are outraged when their parents don't agree with them about the ideal balance of freedom and security.

Of course, since the fifties, families have changed. Divorce, which was uncommon in my childhood, is a fact of life in the 1990s. One in every two marriages ends in divorce, and the most common family is now a blended family. The average adult has at least one divorce, and half of all children spend some of their childhood in single-parent homes. There are many families in which the adults cannot or do not protect their children. Adults who are struggling with their own problems such as depression, drug or alcohol addiction or crippling poverty often have no energy to parent. There are families in which parents are abusive or neglectful. Many children are homeless or in foster care or institutions. Still the majority of parents are motivated to do their best for their children.

Adolescence is currently scripted in a way that builds in conflict between teenagers and their parents. Conflict occurs when parents try to protect daughters who are trying to be independent in ways that are dangerous. Teenagers are under great social pressure to abandon their families, to be accepted by peer culture and to be autonomous individuals.

Girls this age often no longer want to be touched by their parents. They grimace and pull away with a look of alarm when their parents approach. Partly that's a reaction to their new awareness of their bodies, partly that's a way of asserting their grown-upness. But it's more than that. It's a way of stating, "I need space to be my own person."

At the same time, girls want to stay close to their parents. They may even argue as a way to maintain a connection. Fights are a way of staying close and asserting distance at the same time. Baffled parents, especially mothers, report that their daughters go out of their way to pick fights. "We can argue over whether the sky is blue." Another said,

"We fight ten times a day, over the most ridiculous stuff. It's like being nibbled to death by minnows."

Much of girls' behavior is not what parents think. The surface behavior is not all there is. The deep structure is on a quest for an autonomous self. The distancing and hostility are not personal. On the other hand, understanding why girls act the way they do doesn't take away all parental stress. It's hard when loving daughters refuse to be seen with their parents in public. It's hard when a daughter storms off in response to the question "How was your day?" It's painful for parents to be criticized for the way they yawn or peel potatoes.

Because parents often are ignorant of how much the world has changed, further misunderstandings arise. Parents wrongly assume that their daughters live in a world similar to the one they experienced as adolescents. They are dead wrong. Their daughters live in a media-drenched world flooded with junk values. As girls turn from their parents, they turn to this world for guidance about how to be an adult. They cling to the new, reject the old.

Music is important to most girls at this time. It catapults them out of the world of their family and into the world of their peers. It expresses the intensity of their emotions in a way that words cannot. Music is a place where love is a life-and-death matter, where small events are dramatized and memorialized. Music fits the emotional experience of girls much more closely than ordinary adult speech. Unfortunately, much of the music girls hear offers them McSex. As Tipper Gore noticed some time ago, in much of teen music girls are treated as sexual machines. There's a big difference between Elvis Presley and 2 Live Crew.

A friend told me about talking to her eleven-year-old daughter about sex. She was embarrassed, but wanted to give her daughter more information than she had received. She struggled through the mechanics of sex and then shared her values about healthy relationships. She confessed that she had had sex before marriage. The daughter listened as her mother shared her sexual values.

An hour later she went into her daughter's room. MTV was showing a nubile young woman clad in a leather bikini crawling all over a muscular young man. She mouthed song lyrics in praise of their sexual experience the night before. The young man had been too drunk to remember, so she was refreshing his memory with salacious details. My friend said, "I realized then that we were in different worlds with different languages. My daughter could no more understand my shame at being sexual before marriage than I could understand this girl in a leather bikini. It was a hard discovery."

Girls tell me how radically their relationships with their parents changed when they hit puberty. Many said that they had once been "good little kids" but that with puberty they stopped being good. They lied, sneaked around, drank, smoked, yelled and disobeyed. These girls realized the choices they made were self-destructive, but they were in terrible binds. They believed that only nerds stayed close to their parents.

Girls, like Charlotte, who operate from a false self are more likely to break emotionally from their families. They are vulnerable to peer pressure to reject all parental advice. They are more likely to do things that cause great conflict in the family. Because they are operating from false selves, they have no way of keeping peer culture in perspective. They give up the relationship they most need, the relationship with people who would protect them from girl-diminishing experiences.

Girls who hold on to their true selves are more likely to keep their relationship with their families alive. Although they distance some, they do not totally abandon their families. Lori still loves and trusts her parents even though she has typical teenage reactions, such as wanting more time away from her parents and being embarrassed by their smallest flaws.

The role of parents has changed radically in the 1990s. Parents used to help their children fit into the culture. Now many parents fight against the cultural influences that they know will harm their daughters. This was true of both Lori's and Charlotte's parents. They wanted their daughters to have more time to grow and develop, time without sex, drugs, alcohol and trauma. They fought to preserve their daughters' androgyny and wholeness in girl-destructive environments. Most parents today are not the agents of culture, but rather the enemies of the cultural indoctrination that their daughters face with puberty. They battle to save their daughters' true selves.

SOCIAL SELVES—PEERS

As girls pull away from parents, peers are everything. Teens who hardly speak to their parents talk all night with friends. Peers validate their decisions and support their new independent selves. This is a time of deep searching for the self in relationships. There is a constant experimenting—What reaction will I get from others? Talking to friends is a way of checking the important question—Am I okay? The talk is endless, as any parent who shares a phone line with their teenager can attest. Cutting teens off from their friends is incredibly punishing. As one girl explained it, "Grounding teenagers drives them crazy."

While peers can be satisfying and growth-producing, they can also be growth-destroying, especially in early adolescence. Many girls can describe a universal American phenomenon—the scapegoating of girls by one another. Many girls become good haters of those who do not conform sufficiently to our culture's ideas about femininity.

Like any recent converts to an ideology, girls are at risk of becoming the biggest enforcers and proselytizers for the culture. Girls punish other girls for failing to achieve the same impossible goals that they are failing to achieve. They rush to set standards in order to ward off the imposition of others' standards on them. The content of the standards is variable—designer jeans or leather jackets, smoking cigarettes or the heavy use of eye shadow. What's important is the message that not pleasing others is social suicide.

This scapegoating functions as the ultimate form of social control for girls who are not sufficiently attentive to social pressures. Scapegoats are shunned, teased, bullied and harassed in a hundred different ways. Girls who are smart, assertive, confident, too pretty or not pretty enough are likely to be scapegoated.

Girls do not learn to express anger directly. Unlike boys, they are not permitted to fight physically with their enemies. They express anger by cattiness and teasing. They punish by calling a girl on the phone to say that there's a party and she's not invited. They punish by walking up to girls with insults about their clothes or bodies. They punish by nicknames and derogatory labels. They punish by picking a certain girl, usually one who is relatively happy, and making her life miserable.

Of course this shunning takes its toll. The pain often drives adolescent girls to despair. As one girl put it, "You can only go so long with people putting you down before you begin to believe it."

In junior high I was a big awkward girl with wild yellow hair. One day a girl approached me and said sweetly, "Promise you won't get mad if I ask you a question?" Now this should have been a tip-off, but I was only twelve. I promised, and she said, "Do you ever brush your hair?"

My classmate Patty was obese and slow-moving. She suffered the most. Her nickname was "Mammoth," and girls called her this to her face. Anything she did was scorned. One year her mother brought in lovely red popcorn balls for Halloween. No one would eat them even though just looking at the bowl made our mouths water. Everyone was afraid that if we ate popcorn balls made by "Mammoth's mother" we'd be "germed."

My school had the "germs" method of shunning. Girls who were unpopular were considered to have germs, and anyone who touched them would be infected unless they immediately passed them along to another girl. Lots of between-class time was spent getting rid of germs from contact with undesirables. To my credit I never played, but I hated the days when I was labeled as the person with germs. I have since learned how common that game was in towns all over the country. Even today it's played. In my town now, the germs are called shigellae.

The peer culture is much tougher now than when I was a girl. Chemicals are more available and more widely utilized. Teenagers drink earlier and more heavily. A speaker in my college class told about his life in a small Nebraska town in the early sixties. He said that in high school his buddies would buy a six-pack and cruise on a Saturday night after they dropped off their dates. After his talk, a young woman in the class said that she lived in his hometown in the 1990s. He asked how it was different. She said, "Kids buy cases, not six-packs, and the girls get drunk too."

Most teenagers are offered drugs by seventh grade. Marijuana wafts through the air at rock concerts and midnight movies. Gangs operate along the interstate, and crack is sold in the suburbs.

Many girls complain about sexual harassment in the schools. While junior-high boys have always teased girls about sex, the level of the teasing is different. Girls are taunted about everything from oral sex to pubic hair, from periods to the imagined appearance of their genitals. The harassment that girls experience in the 1990s is much different in both quality and intensity. The remarks are more graphic and mean-spirited. Although the content is sexual, the intent is aggressive, to be rude and controlling.

Recently the American Association of University Women released a study, "Hostile Hallways," that documents what girls are experiencing. It reports that 70 percent of girls experience harassment and 50 percent experience unwanted sexual touching in their schools. One-third of all girls report sexual rumors being spread about them, and one-fourth report being cornered and molested. The study says that the classrooms and hallways of our schools are the most common sites for sexual harassment. Many girls are afraid to speak up for fear of worse harassment.

Often harassment extends beyond remarks to touching. It's usually from students, although girls also report harassment from male teachers. Generally girls do not tell school authorities about these incidents. More and more I see girls who are school refusers. They tell me they simply cannot face what happens to them at school. Charlotte had trouble returning to school, where she was called a slut when she walked through the halls. Another client complained that boys slapped her behind and grabbed her breasts when she walked to her locker. Another wouldn't ride the school bus because boys teased her about oral sex.

Girls are also harassed on the streets, in the parks and in swimming pools. In the summer of 1993 New York police reported making arrests at different pools and different times for "the whirlpool." This was a phenomenon in which bands of young men locked arms and churned through the water, surrounded a girl and then harassed her.

What is sexual harassment in junior high can turn into sexual assaults later. In Lakewood, California, fourteen high school athletes, called the Spur Posse, were on trial for raping many girls, one of whom was ten years old. The gang used threats and persuasion to score points in a long-running game of conquest. Even more alarming than the assaults are the reactions of many of the adults and students in the community to the assaults.

The boys claimed they were innocent of wrongdoing. One said, "The schools pass out condoms and teach us about pregnancy, but they don't teach us any rules." Another said, "It's not illegal to hook up with sluts."

After their arrests the boys returned to their school for a heroes' welcome, their status enhanced by all the media coverage of their assaults. Students wore black armbands to protest their arrests and called the girls "sluts" who got what they asked for. Some of the boys' parents were bewildered, others boastful. One father said that his son was "all man" and added, "There wouldn't be enough jails in America if boys were imprisoned for doing what he has done." Another father said that his son had acted no differently from Wilt Chamberlain, who claimed to have had sex with 20,000 women.

This case and others all over the country speak to the craziness of the peer culture that teenage girls now enter. Especially with sexuality, things are tough. Adolescents are exposed, via music, television, movies and pornography, to models of sexuality that are brutal and callous. Girls are caught in the cross fire of our culture's mixed sexual messages. Sex is considered both a sacred act between two people united by God and the best way to sell suntan lotion.

Girls who maintain their true selves resist peer pressure to be a certain way. Lori, for example, knew she wouldn't drink or smoke just because other kids pressured her at a party. She also had her own position about sexuality and wouldn't be pressured to be sexually active before she was ready. She wanted to be liked, but was unwilling to make the concessions necessary to be super popular. She could see clearly that to be accepted by everyone she would have to give up too much of herself.

Charlotte, on the other hand, tried very hard to win peer approval. She was sexually active with boys at her school. Her attempts to be popular with boys backfired. She made choices based not on her own true needs but on her sense of what other people, especially her boyfriend, Mel, wanted from her. Because she was so dependent on peer approval, she got into a great deal of trouble and was utterly lost to herself when I first met her.

SPIRITUAL SELVES

Many of the great idealists of history, such as Anne Frank and Joan of Arc, were adolescent girls. This is a time when girls actively search for meaning and order in the universe. Often this is the time of religious crisis and of exploring universal questions such as what happens after death and the purpose of suffering. Some girls become deeply religious and will sacrifice everything for their beliefs. Others have a crisis in faith.

At thirteen I was a loyal Methodist. Then I read Mark Twain's story "Captain Stormfield's Visit to Heaven," in which he pokes fun at heaven as a place where people sit around and play harps all day. That story catapulted me into an examination of my faith. At fifteen I read Ayn Rand's *The Fountainhead* and Bertrand Russell's *Why I Am Not a Christian* and debated with my minister and my friends about the existence of God.

One client at thirteen accepted Christ as her personal savior. She committed herself to a Christian life and evaluated her behavior daily. She believed that her most important relationship was with God, and that her most important time was the time she spent in prayer. She became the spiritual leader of her family and chided her parents when they acted in un-Christian ways. She led her younger siblings in daily Bible study.

This is a time of great idealism—many girls this age become environmentalists or advocates for the poor or sick. Another student organized recycling for her neighborhood. One friend of Sara's spent part of her allowance on sandwiches for homeless people. She carried food to their street corners and visited about their lives while they ate. Soon she knew most of the homeless people in town by name. Still another friend monitored canned tuna to make sure it was caught in dolphin-free nets, and she protested fur sales at downtown stores.

Many girls become vegetarians. They love animals and actively work for animal rights. I think this cause is popular with girls because they so easily identify with the lack of speech and powerlessness of animals. One girl I know wore a button that said "If animals are to talk, we must be their voices." Girls identify with gentle, defenseless creatures. And they will work with great idealism and energy to save them.

The sixties were a great time to be an adolescent girl. That was an era of optimism and idealism, and many girls say they wished they had lived in those times. It's much harder to be idealistic and optimistic in the 1990s. Girls who stay true to themselves manage to find some way to respect the parts of themselves that are spiritual. They work for the betterment of the world. Girls who act from their false selves are often cynical about making the world a better place. They have given up hope. Only when they reconnect with the parts of themselves that are alive and true will they again have the energy to take on the culture and fight to save the planet.

Adolescence is an intense time of change. All kinds of development—physical, emotional, intellectual, academic, social and spiritual—are happening at once. Adolescence is the most formative time in the lives of women. Girls are making choices that will preserve their true selves or install false selves. These choices have many implications for the rest of their lives.

Of course, the above generalizations about adolescence don't hold true for all girls. Some girls have had tough lives as children and don't experience their elementary school years as happy. Other girls who are stable and protected seem to slide through junior high. The intensity of the problems varies, as does the timing—from age nine to around age sixteen.

Another caveat: Much of what I know about junior-high girls I learned from high school girls. Junior-high girls do not confide in me nearly as often or as articulately as do slightly older girls. I hear what happened in junior high a few years later, after "the statute of limitations has run out." In junior high the thoughts, feelings and experiences are too jumbled to be clearly articulated. The trust level for adults is just too low. Girls are in the midst of a hurricane and there's not much communication with the outside world.

While the world has changed a great deal in the last three decades, the developmental needs of teenage girls have changed very little. I needed, and girls today need, loving parents, decent values, useful information, friends, physical safety, freedom to move about independently, respect for their own uniqueness and encouragement to grow into productive adults.

Girls like Lori, who are the happiest, manage against great odds to stay true to themselves. But all girls feel pain and confusion. None can easily master the painful and complicated problems of this time. All are aware of the suffering of friends, of the pressure to be beautiful and of the dangers of being female. All are pressured to sacrifice their wholeness in order to be loved. Like Ophelia, all are in danger of drowning.

Chapter 4

FAMILIES—
THE ROOT SYSTEMS

■

FRANCHESCA (14)

Betty and Lloyd came to discuss their daughter, who was born Lakota Sioux on an Indian reservation. When Franchesca was three months old, she was placed with Catholic Social Services, who offered her to Betty and Lloyd. Betty showed me a picture of Franchesca in an infant swing. "We loved her from the moment we saw her. She had shiny hair and eyes the color of black olives."

Lloyd said, "There was some feeling against the adoption in Betty's family. They didn't call it prejudice, but they worried about bad genes and wondered if Francie would fit in."

Betty apologized for her family. "They were small-town people. It took us a while to teach them to say 'Native American' instead of 'Indian,' but once they saw Francie they loved her."

Lloyd clasped his hands over his ample stomach and looked sober. "Everyone's done their best really. We don't blame them for what's happened."

"What's happened exactly?"

Lloyd and Betty explained that Franchesca had a typical childhood. Lloyd was a pharmacist who ran his own store. Betty stayed with Franchesca until first grade, then she worked part-time with Lloyd. Franchesca fell off her bike in second grade and broke her leg. She had a slight speech impediment that was corrected with speech therapy in third grade. They lived in a quiet neighborhood with lots of kids. Franchesca had birthday parties, summer vacations, Girl Scouts and pottery lessons.

Lloyd added, "In elementary school her grades were good and she was popular with her classmates. She had a sweet disposition—always smiling."

Betty agreed. "We never treated her differently because she was adopted or Sioux. At the time, we felt that was the right thing to do. Now I wonder if we didn't gloss over things that needed to be discussed."

Lloyd looked surprised. "What do you mean?"

"Francie got teased at school about being a Native American. When we knew about it, we stopped it, but I wonder if we always knew. We told her that being adopted didn't matter, that we were just like other families. But we weren't really. She was brown and we were white."

I thought about how adoptions were handled fourteen years ago. Social service agencies reassured parents that adopted children would be just like their own. This was more true for the parents than for the children. Parents tended to bond immediately, but children almost always felt that adoption made them different.

In particular teenagers, who are focused on identity issues, struggle with the meaning of adoption in their lives. Often they are silent about their struggles because they don't want to be disloyal. When adoption involves mixing races, the issues become even more formidable. Racial issues are difficult for Americans to discuss. We have so few examples of good discussions about ethnic differences that even to acknowledge differences makes most of us feel guilty. So differences tend to be ignored and feelings about them become shameful, individual secrets.

Betty continued. "In seventh grade, Francie started her periods and was cranky all the time. I thought it was hormonal. Before, she'd always told us everything, but in seventh grade she hid in her room. I talked to my sister and we agreed that teenagers go through stages like this. In fact, her girls were giving her fits at the time. So we let it slide.

"Her grades dropped and that worried us." She sighed. "We called the counselor and he said lots of kids have trouble their first year. We made her study two hours a night and her grades picked up a little. She wasn't seeing her old friends, but we let that slide too."

"We let too much stuff slide," Lloyd said.

Betty continued. "This year has been horrible. Lloyd is the main disciplinarian. He's not that strict really, only the ordinary rules—let us know where she's going, no alcohol and passing grades—but you'd think he was beating her. She hardly speaks to him and it's breaking his heart. She'll talk to me a little more, but not much. She won't go to church with us."

Lloyd twisted in his seat. "She's running with a rough crowd and drinking some. We've smelled it on her. She's lying and sneaking around."

Betty added, "Last week we let her go to a ball game with friends and she didn't come home. We were worried sick. Lloyd drove around until sunrise. The next day when she came home, she wouldn't tell us where she'd been."

I said, "I'd like to meet Franchesca."

Lloyd said, "She doesn't want to come, but we'll make her."

"Just one time," I said. "I let teenagers decide whether to return."

The next week Franchesca sat stiffly in my office. She was dressed in green jeans and a SIX FLAGS OVER TEXAS T-shirt. Her long black hair was pulled back into a ponytail and her eyes were filled with tears. At first she was quiet, almost sullen. She looked over my head at the various diplomas on the walls and answered my questions by nodding.

I searched for an issue on which we could connect—school, friends, books or her parents. She barely acknowledged my questions. I asked her about adoption and noticed that her breathing changed. At that point I sat still and waited.

Franchesca raised her eyes and looked me over. She inhaled deeply and said, "I'm living with nice people, but they are not my family."

She paused to see how I was taking this.

"Every morning when I wake up I wonder what my real mother and father are doing. Are they getting ready for work? Are they looking in the mirror and seeing faces that look like mine? What are their jobs? Do they talk about me and wonder if I am happy?"

Big tears dropped onto her shirt and I handed her the Kleenex box. She wiped her cheeks and chin and continued. "I can't stop feeling that I'm in the wrong family. I know it would kill Mom and Dad to hear me say this, but I can't make it go away."

I asked Franchesca what she knew about her real mother.

"She gave me up when I was three months old. Maybe she was poor or unmarried. I'm sure she never hurt me. I feel in my heart that she loved me."

Outside flakes of snow floated by. We watched the snow.

"How does it feel to be Native American?"

Franchesca sighed. "For a long time I pretended that it didn't matter, but all of a sudden it's the most important thing in the world.

"I've been teased since I was little about being a Native American and my tribe doesn't even know I exist." Franchesca talked of the years of teasing, the names—Redskin and Squaw—and the remarks about Indian drunks, welfare cheats, and Indian giving. She ended by saying, "The worst is that line—the only good Indian is a dead Indian."

I asked what Franchesca knew about Native Americans.

"I saw *The Last of the Mohicans* and *Dances With Wolves.* Before that, the movies about Native Americans made me sick. Have you ever seen *The Lone Ranger?* Do you remember his pal Tonto? Do you know that Tonto in Spanish means 'fool'?"

She paused. "Sometimes I see Native Americans among the homeless downtown. I don't even know if they are Sioux. My mother might be one of them."

I asked, "Would you like to know more about your people?"

Franchesca looked out at the snow. "In a way no and in a way yes. It will make me madder and sadder, but I feel like I can't know myself until I know."

I wrote down the name of a Native American writer, Zitkala-Sa. "Maybe you could check out some of her books."

"Do you think I am being disloyal?"

I thought how to answer. "Your interest in your past is as natural as that snowfall." Franchesca rewarded me with a smile, her first that hour.

Franchesca loved the books of Zitkala-Sa, who was a Sioux of the Yankton band, born in 1896. She wrote of being ripped from her family on the reservation and being sent to Indian School. After reading about Zitkala-Sa's experiences, Franchesca asked Betty and Lloyd to take her to visit Genoa, a now abandoned Native American school.

The trip went well. They walked around the three-story brick building and peeked through its dusty windows at the old sewing machines and work benches. Later they ate roast beef sandwiches in the main street café and talked about other places to visit. They traveled to powwows and to a conference for Plains tribes entitled Healing the Sacred Hoop.

Over the next few months Franchesca visited the Native American Center and volunteered to work part-time. She was assigned the job of making coffee and serving cookies to the senior citizens. She joked with them and listened to their stories. From them, she learned many things about the Sioux nation and reservation life. She learned to make fry bread.

Some of our sessions were family sessions. We distinguished between adoption, race and adolescent issues and talked about the adolescent concerns first. Francie thought her father was too strict and her mother too intrusive. She felt that Lloyd and Betty still saw her as a little girl, and Lloyd struck her as rigid and inflexible. Betty got on Franchesca's nerves. "For no reason, I just want to yell at her."

Lloyd compromised with curfews, but remained firm about knowing where Francie was. Betty agreed to stay out of Francie's room and respect her meditation time. After these talks, Francie began to joke with Lloyd again. After school, she sat in the kitchen and told Betty about her day.

We stopped pretending that the family had no feelings about adoption. Everyone had feelings. Lloyd worried that Franchesca might be more vulnerable to alcoholism the way so many Native Americans are. Betty was fearful that someday Franchesca might find her real mother and abandon them. Franchesca felt she lived in between a brown and a white world and wasn't totally accepted by either. She loved Lloyd and Betty, but she could not look to them for clues about her identity. As we talked about these issues I remembered something Wendell Berry said: "If you don't know where you are from, it's hard to know who you are."

Franchesca told Betty and Lloyd that she wanted information about her biological mother. They were ambivalent, but agreed to allow Franchesca to look into her health and tribal background. Franchesca was glad to have some information, but she wanted more. She told Betty and Lloyd, "Someday I will have to find her."

In our individual sessions Franchesca grappled with many issues. She was uncertain who to befriend. "My old friends are shallow, but my new friends are getting into trouble."

I suggested she consider making one or two close friends and not worry about belonging to a crowd. I reminded her that the people at the Indian Center were her friends.

Franchesca learned to center herself by meditating. She prayed to the Great Spirit for guidance before she began. She had two worlds to combine, two histories to integrate. She made conscious choices about what she would keep for herself from both worlds. She would keep her home with Betty and Lloyd, but she would visit the reservation and learn more about the Sioux. She would return to her parents' church, but she would worship the Great Father as well.

As she worked on her issues, Franchesca became an advocate for the Native American students at her mostly white junior high. She decided to challenge all racist remarks. She pushed for more Native American literature and history.

At our last meeting Franchesca was dressed in blue jeans and a woven Native American blouse. Betty and Lloyd sat proudly on either side of her, Lloyd in his white pharmacist jacket and Betty in a polyester pants suit. Lloyd said, "I've learned to speak a few words of Lakota." Betty said, "This research has opened a new world for us."

Franchesca said, "I belong to two families, one white and one brown. But there is room in the sacred hoop for all my relatives."

Franchesca is an example of how complicated family life can be in the 1990s. At fourteen she was dealing with race and adoption issues as well as issues around alcohol, sex, religion and school. She was searching for an identity and distancing from her parents by rebelling and keeping secrets. Yet she loved her parents and needed their support. She looked mildly delinquent, but her behavior was really a signal about the struggle within to find herself.

So Franchesca and her family were "up to their ears in alligators," as Lloyd put it. Fortunately the family sought help. They turned out to be an affectionate family with about the right mix of structure and flexibility. The parents had rules and expectations and the energy to enforce them, but they also had the ability to grow and change as their daughter changed. When they realized that Franchesca needed more contact with her people, they developed an interest in Native American customs. They had some tolerance for diversity, even of religious beliefs. With time and effort on everyone's part, things settled down. Franchesca was on her way to having her own identity and yet she remained connected to her parents. She explored who she was, but not in ways that were self-destructive.

At the Whitney Biennial Art Show, I stood before a tableau entitled "Family Romance." Four figures—a mother, father, son and daughter—stood naked in a row. They were baby-doll shapes of spongy tan material and real hair. They were all the same height and the same level of sexual development. I interpreted this work as a comment on life in the 1990s. To me it said: "There is no childhood anymore and no adulthood either. Kids aren't safe and adults don't know what they are doing."

When we think of families, most of us think of the traditional family, with a working father and a mother who stays home with the children, at least until they go to school. In reality, only 14 percent of our families are this way. Family demographics have changed radically since the 1970s, when less than 13 percent of all families were headed by single parents. In 1990, 30 percent of all families were headed by single parents. (Mothers are the parents in 90 percent of single-parent homes.)

Our culture has yet to acknowledge the reality of these figures. In the 1990s a family can be a lesbian couple and their children from previous marriages, a fourteen-year-old and her baby in a city apartment, a gay man and his son, two adults recently married and their teenagers from other relationships, a grandmother with twin toddlers of a daughter who has died of AIDS, a foster mother and a crack baby, a multigenerational family from an Asian culture or unrelated people who are together because they love each other.

Whatever the composition of families, in this last half of the twentieth century, families are under siege. Parents are more likely to be overworked, overcommitted, tired and poor. They are less likely to have outside support.

Money is a problem. We have become an increasingly stratified society with some children living in a luxurious world of designer clothes, computer games, private schools and camps, while other children walk dangerous streets to inadequate schools.

Time is a problem. Studies show that the average couple talks to each other twenty-nine minutes a week; the average mother talks seven minutes a day to her teenager, while the average father talks only five minutes. Supervision is a problem. The small tight-knit communities that helped families rear children are increasingly extinct. Instead television is the baby-sitter in many homes.

The great respect that Americans have for independence creates certain difficulties in families. A philosopher friend said to me recently, "Aren't you proud of your daughter? She's turning out so differently from you and your husband. What better definition could you have of successful parenting?" When I bemoaned the distance between Sara and me, another friend said, "Would you want it any other way?"

Our nation began with a Declaration and a War of Independence. We admire feisty individualists, and our heroes are explorers, pioneers and iconoclasts. We respect Rambo, Jack Kerouac, Clint Eastwood and Amelia Earhart. We love Walt Whitman with his famous dictum "Resist much, obey little."

The freedom that we value in our culture we also value in our families. Americans believe adolescence is the time when children emotionally separate from their parents, and this assumption becomes a self-fulfilling prophecy. Daughters behave as they are expected to behave, and ironically, if they are expected to rebel, they will rebel. They distance from their parents, criticize parental behavior, reject parental information and keep secrets.

This distancing creates a great deal of tension in families. Parents set limits to keep their daughters safe, while daughters talk about their rights and resent what they see as their parents' efforts to keep them young. Parents are fearful and angry when their daughters take enormous risks to prove they are independent. For most families, the heavy battles begin in junior high.

Parents who grew up in a different time with a different set of values are unhappy with what their daughters are learning. They feel like they are trying harder than their parents tried, and yet their daughters are more troubled. The things that worked when they were teenagers are no longer working. They see their daughters' drinking, early sexualization and rebelliousness as evidence of parental inadequacy. They see their own families as dysfunctional. Instead I believe what we have is a dysfunctional culture.

My experience is that most parents want their daughters to develop into healthy, interesting people. They are hindered in their efforts to help their daughters by the dangerous culture in which we live, by the messages that our culture sends young women and by our ethic that to grow up one must break from parents, even loving parents.

My family lives in a neighborhood filled with three-story houses and lovely oak and maple trees. Most of the parents have worked hard at parenting, yet their teenagers are driving them crazy. As an attorney said to me at a block party, "Parenthood is the one area of my life where I can feel incompetent, out of control and like a total failure all of the time."

At a New Year's Eve party, I asked another couple how their teenage daughters were. The husband said without a smile, "I wish they'd never been born."

Another thing that separates girls from their parents is their own unhappiness. With junior high, many girls lose their childhood gaiety and zest. Because of their developmental level, girls hold parents responsible for this. They are still young enough that they expect their parents to protect them and keep them happy. When they crash into larger forces and find themselves miserable, they blame their parents, not the culture.

Parents are not the primary influence on adolescent girls. Instead girls are heavily swayed by their friends, whose ideas come from the mass media. The average teen watches twenty-one hours of TV each week, compared to 5.8 hours spent on homework and 1.8 hours reading. The adolescent community is an electronic community of rock music, television, videos and movies. The rites of passage into this community are risky. Adulthood, as presented by the media, implies drinking, spending money and being sexually active.

The mass media has the goal of making money from teenagers, while parents have the goal of producing happy, well-adjusted adults. These two goals are not compatible. Most parents resist their daughters' media-induced values. Girls find themselves in conflict with their parents and with their own common sense.

For example, Jana was the petite only child of older, professional parents. Until junior high, she had loved and felt loved by them. But in junior high she faced the choice of being the good daughter her parents expected or being popular and having a boyfriend. She said, "All through junior high, I'd do anything to fit in. I tried out friends like flavors of ice cream, but eventually I settled in with the popular crowd. I went to a Catholic school where the nuns told us that we would go to hell if we swore. But to be cool I had to swear. So I had the choice of eternal damnation or being unpopular."

We laughed at her rueful tone. "In junior high this guy in math class liked me and I liked him. But he wasn't popular, so I didn't go out with him."

Once her dad caught her sneaking out late at night to meet her friends. Jana said, "He sat on the couch and cried. He lectured me about rape and all that stuff." Another time she came home drunk on "purple passion." As our interview ended she whispered to me, "My parents have no idea all the trouble I've been in. They'd be blown away."

Adolescents and their families are a challenge to mental-health professionals. We need a balance between respecting parents' responsibility to protect their children and supporting adolescents' need to develop as individuals and move into a broader world. Not every girl who is suffering comes from a troubled family. In my experience, parents are often desperately fighting to protect the authenticity of their daughters.

Psychologists who study what kinds of families produce what kinds of children have focused on two broad dimensions. The first has to do with affection. At one end are parents who are accepting, responsive and child-centered; at the other end are parents who are rejecting, unresponsive and parent-centered. The second dimension has to do with control strategies. At one end are parents who are undemanding and low in control, and at the other end are parents who are demanding and high in control.

These two dimensions interact to produce different outcomes for teenagers. Low-control and low-acceptance parents produce teens with a variety of problems, including delinquency and chemical dependency. Parents who are high in control and low in acceptance (authoritarian parents) have children who are socially inadequate and lacking in confidence. Parents who are low in control and high in acceptance (indulgent parents) have teenagers with high impulsivity, low responsibility and low independence. Parents who are high in control and high in acceptance (strict but loving parents) have teenagers who are independent, socially responsible and confident. According to this research, the ideal family is one in which the message children receive from parents is: "We love you, but you must do as we say."

LUCY (15)

As a teenager, Lucy was recovering from leukemia. She, like many young people who have been ill, was close to her parents in ways that were adaptive when she was fighting the disease. Now that she had recovered, the closeness was keeping her from developing her own sense of self. Doing exactly what her parents and doctors said had kept her alive. With her recovery, she needed to learn that it was okay to make decisions independent of the well-meaning advice of adults.

Lucy was chubby, with the soft, pale skin of the chronically sick. Her radiation and chemotherapies had caused her hair to fall out and just now she was growing stubby new hair. When she went to school or shopping she covered her head with a knitted purple cap, but today in my office I could see her scalp.

Lucy sat placidly between her parents as they explained her medical history. Two years ago she had been diagnosed with leukemia and had been through a series of hospitalizations. The doctors were optimistic about her long-term prognosis and felt that with good follow-up, she would recover completely.

I asked how all this medical turmoil had affected the family. Sylvia said, "We did what we needed to do to save Lucy's life. I never left her side when she was in the hospital. Frank came every night after work."

She looked at her husband. "Frank's a policeman. He was passed over for promotion this year. I'm sure his captain thought he had his hands full. But there will be other years. I am sick to death of hospitals, but Lucy is alive; I'm not complaining."

Frank spoke carefully. "Our boy had the toughest time. He stayed with my sister. Lucy came first."

"Mark's been a brat since I came home," Lucy interrupted.

I asked Lucy about the hospital time. "It wasn't so bad except when I was sick from the chemo. Mom read to me; we played games. I know the answers to all the Trivial Pursuit questions."

It had been hard for her to return to school. Everyone was nice to Lucy, almost too nice, like she was a visitor from another planet, but she was left out of so many things. Her old friends had boyfriends and were involved in new activities. When she was in the hospital they would visit with flowers and magazines, but now that she was better, they didn't seem to know what to do with her.

Frank said, "Lucy's personality has changed. She's quieter. She used to clown around. Now she is more serious. In some ways she seems older; she's suffered more and seen other children suffer. In some ways she's younger; she's missed a lot."

Lucy had missed a great deal: ninth-grade graduation, the beginning of high school, parties, dating, sports, school activities and even puberty (the leukemia had delayed her periods and physical development). She had lots of catching up to do. She'd been so vulnerable that her parents were protective. They didn't want her to become tired, to eat junk food, to forget to take her medicines or to take any chances. Her immune system was weak and she could be in trouble with the slightest injury. Lucy, unlike most teens, didn't grimace at her parents' worries. She associated them with staying alive.

The first time I saw Lucy alone, she was shy and tongue-tied. She sat looking out the window, her forehead wrinkled with worry. She was good at quoting what her mother or the doctors thought she should think or do. Lucy volunteered that when she watched television she marveled at the energy of the characters. "They move around so much and sound so perky. I get tired and jealous just watching them."

I began by asking her what she thought was fun. She drew a blank. So I suggested that by the next session perhaps she would know. Lucy agreed to sit alone for ten minutes a day and think about what she enjoyed.

Lucy came in the next time rather discouraged. She had religiously followed my instructions and the main thing she had discovered was that she had no thoughts of her own. "All I think is what I'm supposed to."

I said that realizing this was the beginning of the process of finding her private thoughts. We talked about how Lucy was different from Sylvia, Frank and Mark. At first this was difficult, but as we talked she became interested and animated for the first time since we'd met. Her differences were small: "I like candy and Mom doesn't. I like rock music and Mark likes country. I am short and Dad is tall." But later they became more important. "Mom suffers without complaining, while I like to tell others. I cry when I'm upset and Mark gets mad. I like people around when I'm worried and Dad likes to be alone." We discussed these differences without judging and Lucy seemed pleased that she could be different from her family and still be close to them.

The next week Lucy came in with a jubilant smile on her face. "I know what I like," she said. "Last Thursday my family went to a Cub Scout meeting and I stayed home. I thought, 'How should I spend this evening?' I realized that what I wanted to do was watch an old movie on television. *Duck Soup* was on and I loved it."

Lucy said proudly, "No one told me to do this or cares whether I like movies or not. I just did it for myself."

I congratulated Lucy on her illumination. Even though the content of her self-discovery was small, the process was critical. Lucy had managed to discover something about herself and to respect that discovery. She had an original thought.

After this first thought, Lucy slowly built a more independent personality. She wrote about her time in the hospital. At first she wrote her polite feelings—she was grateful to the doctors and nurses, grateful to her parents for sticking so close. Later she was able to write about her fear of death, her anger at being a cancer patient, her rage at the painful treatments and her sadness about the children who didn't make it.

Lucy worked her way back into the world of friends and school. She joined Spanish Club. She invited her old friend to spend the night with her. Sylvia worried these activities would tire Lucy. Her worrying, which had been so adaptive during the fight against leukemia, was less adaptive now that Lucy was recovering. After five sessions, Lucy reported that she and her mother had argued over a late-night phone call. I laughed in relief.

The family therapy became a posttraumatic stress debriefing. Lucy's leukemia had affected everyone's life. Sylvia told of coming home from the hospital after a night when Lucy had thrown up every fifteen minutes from the chemotherapy. She walked into Lucy's empty bedroom, lay down on her canopy bed, still decorated with unicorns. She'd picked up Lucy's My Little Pony and cried till she felt her body had no more tears.

Frank talked about how hard it was to work. He'd be ticketing speeders and thinking of Lucy in her hospital bed. "Sometimes a speeder would be rude or argumentative," Frank said. "I'd just want to punch him in the mouth."

Mark was mad at Lucy for getting sick. "I thought she did it to get attention. Sometimes I thought she was faking it, and other times I was sure she would die. She got lots of presents and Mom and Dad did whatever she wanted. I wanted to get sick too."

After eight months, Lucy was ready to stop therapy. Her voice had become firmer and more animated. Her hair had grown into a sleek brown cap. She had begun an exercise program and her body had slimmed down and firmed up. Her periods had started. She'd reconnected with some old friends and made some new ones. She was losing the ultraserious personality of the sick. She had learned that she could disagree with her parents and no one dropped dead. She could say what she thought and develop into the person she wanted to become.

LEAH (18)

Leah was born into a culture with very different assumptions about families. In Vietnamese culture, families are seen as shelter from the storm. Adolescents don't rebel, but rather are nested in extended families that they will be with forever. Also, because Leah grew up in an impoverished communist country, she missed the information explosion of the Western world.

I interviewed Leah at her high school during her junior year. She was dressed casually in a Garfield sweatshirt and jeans, but she was carefully groomed with long ice-blue nails and an elaborate hairstyle. Only her crooked, brown teeth betrayed the poverty she must have experienced in Vietnam.

Leah was born in Vietnam in 1975. She was the daughter of a Marine and a Vietnamese woman who had lost her husband to the war and was struggling to support her four children. The Marine left without knowing that Leah's mother was pregnant, and Leah never met her father. He gave his home address to Leah's mother and she wistfully wrote it out for me. She read the words aloud like a mantra, but added, "I would never bother him. Perhaps my father is married and would be embarrassed by me."

Leah grew up in Vietnam, the beloved baby of the family. Her mother worked long hours to support her children. She said, "I sat by the window and cried as I waited for my mother to come home from work. When she arrived home, I followed her everywhere and begged to sit on her lap."

She described her childhood as happy. The family lived in one house, and when her brothers married they brought their wives home to live. Leah never had to work and had all the toys she wanted. "My brothers and sisters protected me and competed to hold me."

When I asked her if she fought with her mother, she said, "Why would I fight with my mother? She gave me the gift of life."

I asked her if she ever disobeyed her mother's rules and she said no. She explained, "She is my mother and I owe her obedience, but it's more than that. She knows what is good for me. Her rules will help me."

Three years ago, because of Leah's parentage, she and her mother were able to come to America. They would miss her siblings but felt they must move. Leah explained, "Vietnam is a communist country. There is no freedom and no money. I couldn't even go to school beyond ninth grade."

At first she and her mother lived in a small apartment with no furniture and wore clothes from Goodwill. The Refugee Center helped Leah's mother find work at a local cannery, and now they have an adequate income, even enough to send money back to Vietnam.

At night, after her mother goes to bed, Leah writes letters to her brothers and sisters. Holidays, especially the Vietnamese New Year, are lonely for her. Still she is happy to be here. The high school is much better than the schools in Vietnam. She has made friends with some of the Vietnamese students. "The teachers are kinder and we have computers."

I asked her about her days here. "I wake early so I can cook breakfast for my mother. It makes me sad to see her work, so I try to help her. Then I walk to school. After school I clean house and fix dinner. In the evenings I study and help my mother learn English."

I asked about hobbies. "I like to listen to Vietnamese music, especially sad music. I write poems about my country."

Leah considers herself too young to date. She told me, "I would never have sex until I was married. That would bring great shame on my family."

When she is in her twenties she plans to date only Vietnamese men who promise that her mother will always be able to live with her. She showed me a class ring and a silver bracelet. "Mother bought me this. I begged her not to, but she wanted me to look like an American teenager. I could never leave my mother. My mother has given me everything and kept nothing for herself. I am all she has now."

She and her friends speak mostly Vietnamese or French, and American teenagers leave them alone. She has yet to see an American movie. When we discussed American teenagers, Leah hesitated, clearly concerned not to appear rude. Then she said, "I don't like how American children leave home when they are eighteen. They abandon their parents, and they get in a lot of trouble. I don't think that's right."

Leah likes the freedom and the prosperity of America. She said, "It's easier to earn a living here. I can hardly wait to finish school and get a job so I can support my mother."

In Leah's culture, autonomy and independence are not virtues. Vietnamese families are expected to be harmonious and loyal. The good of the family is more important than the individual satisfaction of its members. Children are expected to live at home all their lives (sons with their parents and daughters with their husbands' parents). No one anticipates that children will rebel or disagree with their parents, and children rarely do disagree. Authority is not questioned, which may be tolerable when authority is wise and benevolent, but can be tragic when authority is malevolent or misguided.

These beliefs in obedience and loyalty allowed Leah to have a less turbulent adolescence. She didn't need to distance from her family or reject family beliefs in order to grow up. On the other hand, she didn't differentiate into her own person. She was unlikely to develop in ways different from her family. If she tried, she would have been discouraged.

JODY (16)

Jody was the oldest daughter of a conservative, fundamentalist family. They lived in an old farmhouse that had managed to survive as elegant suburban homes were built around it. The front porch was piled high with boxes of *National Geographic*s, sleds, snow shovels and work boots. The small living room reminded me of my grandparents' home in the fifties. It was cramped but cozy, with worn overstuffed furniture. Doilies perched on the television and pots of Swedish ivy hung from macramé cords. Every available space was occupied by family pictures, trophies and knickknacks.

I'd heard about Jody from her teachers and wanted to interview her. This afternoon she was home alone. Her sisters were at ball practice and her mother and brothers were at a church bazaar. Her dad was at work in the family tree-trimming and firewood business.

I'd seen a photo of Jody in the paper when she was homecoming queen, but today I wouldn't have recognized her. She wore no makeup and her long black hair was pulled back in a ponytail. She was dressed in gray sweats and glowed with good health and wholesomeness. I knew she had a softball scholarship and I asked first about sports.

Jody said, "Everyone plays ball in my family. All my uncles coach and my cousins play. We start as soon as we're old enough to catch a ball. The family business sponsors several softball teams. My grandmother has a master calendar she uses in the summer to keep track of all the games. In a record week she attended seventeen games."

I asked what role her father had played in her life as an athlete.

"Dad has a great philosophy of sports," Jody said. "He taught us to play for fun. He thinks that we learn more from losing than winning, and that our goal should be to improve with every game."

I asked, "How does he deal with your mistakes?"

"Sometimes he might show us something we did wrong, but he doesn't say much." She laughed. "Dad does get upset about bad sportsmanship. He never lets us get aggressive or blame other players."

Jody had great respect for her father. Her church taught her that men were in charge of decisions. Her father decided where the family would go on vacations and how they spent money. He led the family prayers and made the rules and punishments.

"How are you disciplined?" I asked.

"Until sixth grade we got spankings, after that, groundings. There was no back talk. If we did something wrong, we got punished. Dad didn't let us off when we cried or apologized."

I asked how she would discipline her kids. Jody said carefully, "I know it's not popular to say, but I would spank my kids too. I think it taught us right from wrong."

"Does your family discuss problems as they come up?"

"Not as a family. I talk to my mom, and my brothers and sisters talk to me. Mom talks to Dad, and he doesn't talk to anyone."

She paused. "I've only seen Dad cry one time—when his mom died. That scared me."

Jody sipped her tea. "Dad is hard to get along with sometimes. If he's had a tough day at work he can be impatient. I wish he spent more time with the family."

She brushed her hair from her face and said quickly, "I know he loves us, though. He takes care of our family. When we do something that makes him proud, he doesn't compliment us directly, but maybe he'll punch us in the arm or give us a noogie."

Jody answered the phone. It was her aunt inviting them over to Sunday dinner. Jody's family spent most Sundays with this aunt's family. The parents played cards on Saturday nights. They all played ball together and attended the same church.

I asked about Jody's mom. She smiled. "Mom's a total sweetheart. She'll do anything for us kids. She won't buy anything for herself until we have what we need. She dropped out of high school to get married, but she wants us to go to college."

"How do your parents get along with each other?"

Jody shook her head. "They fight quite a bit. Mom tries to do what Dad says, but sometimes she gets mad at him. He's picky about housework and that bugs her."

"How has it been being the oldest in the family?"

"I take care of my sisters and brothers when Mom is doing the bookkeeping for Dad. I cook most nights. My parents were strictest with me because they wanted me to set a good example."

She rubbed her upper arm. "They made me take vaccinations first in front of the little ones. I was expected to be brave and announce that the shots didn't hurt. I'm not complaining, though. I am close to my family, much closer than any of my friends."

We talked about junior high, which was a big change for Jody. She got teased about her hand-me-down clothes and cheap tennis shoes. Her dad wouldn't let her wear makeup.

Jody looked at me. "Do you have any idea how much drinking goes on?" I nodded and she continued. "I was thrown in with kids from all over town. Kids tried to talk me into drinking and smoking. They swore all the time to prove they were tough. I got left out of things. I'm glad I had sports to keep me busy."

I asked about difficult times and Jody looked sad for the first time in our interview. "In tenth grade I started dating Jeff. He was a caring person, very sensitive. But after a few months Dad told me I had to stop dating him. At first I was mad. Jeff made me happy and I thought, Why would Dad take this away from me? We even sneaked around for a few dates, but I couldn't take it. I gave up trying to see him. I still see Jeff in the halls at school and feel bad."

I asked Jody if she was angry. "I wish Dad would have let me decide, but I'm not mad. He was worried I'd have sex before marriage, and I don't want to do that. Also, he wanted me to keep my options open and not get serious too young. I can accept that."

Jody looked out the window. "My locker is in the area where hard-core kids hang out. When I go to my locker I hear a lot of sexual talk. Guys hassle girls and girls come on to guys. I'm sorry that they value themselves so little."

I could hear Jody's sisters returning from ball practice. I asked her what else she wanted to tell me. "I want to follow God's plan for me. Maybe I'll be a phys. ed. teacher. I want to marry and have a close family like mine."

She thought for a while. "Sometimes I wonder if I'm too close to my family. I try so hard to be like my aunt and my mom. I wonder if there is a different side of me that I don't allow myself to look at. Sometimes I feel myself thinking thoughts I'm sure no one in my family ever had."

"What might that different side of you be like?"

Jody shook her head. "I don't know. There are so many things I haven't tried: drama, music, things my family isn't interested in. Would I like those things?"

Jody's sisters burst into the room. We greeted them and then I said good-bye to Jody. She hugged me. "I liked this interview," she said. "It made me think."

For a high school girl, Jody had a lot of responsibility that she shouldered without complaint. Her life seemed all of one piece. She loved her family and believed as they did in the importance of God and softball. Her appreciative and respectful attitude toward her parents, her lack of self-pity and her industriousness reminded me of Vietnamese girls like Leah.

Psychologists would condemn many of the elements in Jody's background—the traditional sex roles of the parents; the physical punishments; the lack of lessons, camps and other enrichment experiences; the strict religion and the conformity of family members. They would note that this wasn't a family that talked much about feelings. Particularly the father's injunction against dating seems harsh by 1990s standards. Psychologists would question the family's rigid beliefs. Interest in philosophical questions and self-examination were not encouraged. The parts of Jody that were different from her family would not flower.

I struggled with the questions this interview raised for me. Why would a girl raised in such an authoritarian, even sexist, family be so well liked, outgoing and self-confident? Why did she have less anger and more respect for adults? Why was she so relaxed when many girls are so angst-filled and angry?

I remembered some facts from sociology. There are fewer suicides in authoritarian countries than in more liberal ones. Those facts seem somehow related to Jody's strength and happiness. In neither authoritarian countries nor Jody's family are there many opportunities for existential crises. Someone else is making the important decisions. The world is black and white and there is a right way and a wrong way to do everything. The rules are clear, consistent and enforced. There simply aren't enough choices to precipitate despair.

The diversity of mainstream culture puts pressure on teens to make complicated choices. Adolescents don't yet have the cognitive equipment. Young adolescents do not deal well with ambiguity. If the parents are affectionate and child-centered, teenagers are comforted by clarity and reassured by rules. Teens like Jody are protected from some of the experiences of their peers. Jody had challenges that she could be expected to meet—challenges that had to do with work, family responsibility and sports.

But there were costs. Jody's family had limited tolerance for diversity. Obedience was valued more than autonomy. Jody hadn't been encouraged to think for herself and develop as an individual. As an adolescent, Jody looks stronger than her peers, who are at odds with their families and overwhelmed by all the choices they must make. I wonder how she'll look in her mid-twenties. By then teens raised in more liberal homes may look as strong as Jody and they may have even more creative and independent spirits.

ABBY AND ELIZABETH

One of my favorite families was the Boyds. Bill was a warmhearted man who played the ukulele and had formed our state's chapter of Men Against Rape. Nan was an organic gardener who brought extraordinary dishes to political potluck dinners. Once she brought a casserole made of nettles, once a salad of morel mushrooms and wild onions, and another time a mulberry cheesecake.

Bill and Nan were community organizers and political activists who drove a beat-up pickup and spent their money on good causes. I saw them at marches for human rights or the environment, at peace workshops and at tree plantings. They had lots of company—foreign exchange students, friends of friends driving through our state, relatives and political allies. Every summer they took their daughters on month-long camping vacations.

Bill could make anyone laugh. He could cut the tension in a room of angry people with a joke or a song. He gave everyone nicknames they wanted to keep forever. Even though he was a socialist, Republicans liked him.

Nan's vegetables took over the neighborhood in late July. She traveled door to door begging neighbors to take her zucchini and bell peppers. Once their cat Panther had a litter of six black kittens whom they named after their friends in order to entice them to adopt. Not surprisingly, it worked.

Abby was blonde and willowy, the most serious member of the family. In elementary school she won the statewide spelling bee. Elizabeth was shorter and red-haired. As a girl, she was the leader of a pack of adventurous pranksters we called the Crazy Kids. Abby and Elizabeth were involved in everything—politics, drama, music, sports, camps and their church. The family had parties—for the first snowfall, the first day of spring, a straight A report card or May Day. Their parents were loving and low-key. Problems were handled by discussion. Neither girl had ever been spanked. The parents trusted Abby and Elizabeth to make their own choices. They had the freedom to grow into whomever they wanted to be.

Both girls had trouble with adolescence. Abby got depressed in eighth grade. She missed weeks of school because of allergies and stomach ailments. Her grades fell and she dropped out of activities. She skipped the family parties and no longer marched beside her parents at demonstrations.

Much to her parents' consternation, Abby dropped her neighborhood friends and joined a group of "druggies." She became secretive about her whereabouts and locked the door to her room. Her parents wondered if she'd been drinking or smoking. Once she came home red-eyed and confused and they took her to an emergency room for a drug test. It was negative and they never tried that again. It was too traumatic for everyone.

During Abby's adolescent years, Bill would suggest a bike ride and Abby would give him a withering look. Nan would bake a gooseberry pie and she'd refuse to eat it. She quit coming to meals with the family. When they tried to talk to her about the changes, she clammed up or attacked them for being unreasonable.

Nan and Bill couldn't understand what was going wrong. Nan had some family history of depression, but she'd never worried about it. Abby had seemed calm and stable. They took her to a therapist, but Abby wouldn't talk. She claimed she could work her life out on her own.

Two years later Elizabeth was in trouble. She dropped the Crazy Kids and stayed in her room, which she turned into a dark cave. She listened to her radio and read science fiction. Elizabeth also hated school and managed to flunk three courses in her eighth-grade year. Her only friend was Colin, who shared her interest in science fiction.

Elizabeth managed to pull her grades up and by high school she was again an honor roll student But she remained distant from the other students. She and Colin formed a small world of their own. She argued with Bill and Nan, who tried to push her back into the world of her school. Unlike Abby, she never used chemicals, but she was an angrier daughter. She hurled insults at her parents and told them nothing about her life.

When Elizabeth first had trouble, Nan and Bill again found a therapist. This one talked to Elizabeth alone and then assured Nan and Bill that they were doing everything right. She said, "I've never seen quite so much trouble in such a healthy family." Nan told me later that she wasn't sure whether to feel good or bad about that remark.

The therapy may have helped some, but both girls remained in trouble. They blamed Bill and Nan for the difficulties they were having, as if somehow perfect parents would have protected them from the chaotic world they were entering. In spite of her intelligence, Abby barely graduated from high school and never attended college. Elizabeth got pregnant her junior year and decided to keep the baby.

At first I was baffled by this family's trouble. I wondered if there were problems I didn't know about, if Nan or Bill had secret vices or if the girls had been assaulted by a relative or family friend. Reading the research on families with different control strategies and levels of affection helped me understand this family.

The Boyds were an affectionate family but had minimal controls. Their daughters turned out much as the research would have predicted. They had low self-esteem and problems with impulsivity. Clearly in their early adolescent years they would have benefited from more structure.

The Boyds believed in autonomy, tolerance and curiosity. They wanted their girls to experience the world in all its messiness and glory. They raised daughters who were open to experience, eager to try new things, socially aware and independent. Because girls like this are so open and aware, when they reach junior high they are hit full force by the gales of the hurricane. When all that force hits, they are temporarily overwhelmed. It's too much to handle too fast. Often they handle it in the way Abby and Elizabeth did, by withdrawal and depression. They screen out the world to give themselves time to process all the complexity.

Abby and Elizabeth are now in their early twenties. They are both "in recovery" from their adolescent experiences. Abby works at a food co-op as produce manager and is active in Ecology Now. She hates drugs, even caffeine, and allows herself only herbal teas. She loves the community of like-minded people who work at the co-op. She and Nan shop together for herbs and vegetables to plant in the spring. Together they concoct natural-food recipes for the co-op deli. She and Bill just returned from a bike ride across Iowa.

Elizabeth is a good mother for her lovely red-headed daughter. She, Colin and the baby live on a rented farm outside of town. Neighbor kids follow her around as she feeds the goats and chickens on her farm. When her daughter is older, she intends to go back to school and study biology.

ROSEMARY (14)

Gary ran a silk-screening business and Carol gave violin lessons to children after school. They had three children: Rosemary, in eighth grade, and twin boys three years younger, who were stars of their neighborhood soccer team.

Carol and Gary were New Age parents. Gary wore beads and had a ponytail. Carol collected crystals and spent time in the brain wave room at our New Age bookstore. They had raised Rosemary to be her own person. They hadn't tried to mold her in any way, but rather believed in letting her character unfurl. Gary said, "Our biggest fear was damaging her spirit."

They tried to model equality in their relationship and to raise their children free of gender role constraints. Rosemary mowed the lawn and the twins did the dishes and set the table. Gary taught Rosemary to pitch and draw. Carol taught her to read tarot cards and to throw the I Ching.

This was a child-centered home, very democratic, with an emphasis on freedom and responsibility rather than conformity and control. The parents didn't believe in setting many limits for the children. Rather they felt they would learn their own limits through trial and error. They both liked to describe themselves as friends of their kids. They taught Rosemary to stand up for herself and had many stories of her assertiveness with adults and peers.

Carol and Gary spared no expense to offer their children enrichment opportunities. Rosemary took art lessons from the best teacher in town and attended baseball camp every summer. The boys had ball teams, YMCA camps and yoga classes.

At our first appointment Carol and Gary seemed vulnerable and shaken.

Carol said, "I want my daughter back." She talked about how happy and confident Rosemary had been in elementary school. She'd been a good student and student council president in her sixth-grade year. She was interested in everything and everybody. They had trouble slowing her down enough to get rest and food. She once said to her art teacher, "I'm your best student, aren't I?"

With puberty she changed. She hated the way her wiry body "turned to dough." She was still assertive with her parents, even mouthy and aggressive much of the time, but with peers she was quiet and conforming. She worried about pleasing everyone and was devastated by small rejections. Many days she came home in tears because she sat alone at lunch or because someone criticized her looks.

She stopped making good grades because she felt grades didn't matter. Popularity was all that counted. She obsessed about her weight and her looks. She exercised, dieted and spent hours in front of the mirror.

Suddenly she cared more about being liked by athletes than about being an athlete. She became what her parents called "boy crazy." They found notes she'd written filled with sexual innuendos. She talked about boys all the time, called boys on the phone and hurled herself at any boy within reach. She was asked to parties by ninth-grade boys who were experimenting with sex and alcohol.

Gary said, "We're in over our heads with Rosemary. She's doing stuff now that we thought she'd do in college. We're not sure that we can protect her."

Carol said, "I wish we could find a nice safe place and put her there for about six years until she matures." We all laughed.

"We're both from small towns," Carol continued. "When we were Rosie's age, we didn't have these kind of temptations. We don't know what to do."

Carol handed me a CD they'd found in her room. "Look at what she's listening to—'Reckon You Should Shut the Fuck Up and Play Some Music,' 'Crackhouse' and 'You Suck' by the Yeastie Girls."

Gary said, "We had a family rule that anyone who swore put a quarter in the jar, and when it filled we'd all go out to eat. After listening to that CD, we realized that we were in a new ballpark."

Gary stared at his hands. "We taught her to be assertive and take care of herself, but it seems like she uses all her assertiveness against us. She keeps things stirred up all the time. She has a real flair for the dramatic and her timing's great. She'll blow just during my meditation time or when I have a customer on the phone."

They worried about Rosemary all last year. Then the previous Saturday night she had stayed with a boy in a hotel room after a Jelly-

fish concert. She lied and claimed to be at a sleep-over with girlfriends.

I agreed to visit with Rosemary. She was petite, with dark hair
and dramatic eyes. She wore designer jeans and Nikes to the session
and carried a paperback copy of *The Anarchist's Cookbook*. She immediately told me that she wanted my help in getting her parents to
lighten up.

I was careful to listen rather than talk. I knew that any advice would
sound parental, and hence unacceptable. I asked about her concerns.
She was worried about her weight and her physical flaws. She felt she
needed to lose ten pounds; her left profile was "hideous" and her skin
too splotchy. She had tried dieting but hated it. She felt crabby and
depressed and eventually would cave in and eat.

I gently introduced the concept of lookism. Rosemary felt her
friends were lookist and so was she. She was frightened of not being
pretty enough. She said, "Wherever I go, I look around and there's
always someone prettier than me. That drives me nuts."

We talked about how sexualized and unnatural models looked and
about the way women were depicted on MTV and in the movies. A
part of Rosemary hated the pressure and another part was obsessed
with looking right. A part of her scorned lookism and a part of her
evaluated everyone on the basis of appearance.

We talked about how her life had changed since elementary school.
Rosemary had been happier then. She smiled when she talked about
baseball and drawing with her dad. She had loved her parents and felt
close to them then, but now she didn't. "They don't understand what
I'm going through. They always give me stupid advice. They don't
want their little baby girl to grow up."

Rosemary felt close to her friends, but she admitted that friendships
were difficult. She worried about betrayal and rejections. The social
scene changed from day to day. She felt uneasy standing up for herself
with boys. She did things she didn't agree with to fit into the popular
crowd.

We talked about her friends' experiences more than her own. She
had friends who were dumped after they had sex with their boyfriends.
Other friends were raped or had abortions. Generally she felt that she
wouldn't get in the same kind of trouble, but she admitted she had
experienced a few close calls.

When we talked about guys, she was surprisingly insightful. She had
wanted a boyfriend so badly that she had done anything to win favor.

She said, "I don't feel good about myself unless a guy likes me. I do whatever it takes."

Our work proceeded erratically. It's hard to do therapy with an anarchist. Like her parents, I wanted to keep her safe while she grew up, and like them, I had to be careful or I might say the wrong thing. If she folded her arms over her chest and looked out my window, I knew it was over for that session.

Rosemary saw the world in rigid categories. She overgeneralized, simplified or denied what she couldn't understand. Her feelings were chaotic and often out of control, and her need for peer approval, particularly male approval, placed her in dangerous situations. She had a hard time saying no to boys who pushed for sex. Furthermore, she was determined to figure everything out for herself. She literally flinched on those rare occasions when I offered advice.

I thought of the many ironies in this family. These New Age spiritual parents had a daughter whose main concern was weight. The parents' laissez-faire approach didn't work well in a time of AIDS and addictions. Carol and Gary were careful to raise Rosemary in an androgynous environment, and she was now ultrafeminine so that she could attract and hold boys. They taught her to be assertive, but she used those skills only with grown-ups. Most ironic of all, Rosemary, who had grown up in a home with a meditation room, needed centering.

All of the families in this chapter are high in the affection dimension, but they vary on the control dimension. Jody and Leah come from families that are high in control. Franchesca and Lucy come from families that are moderate in control, and Rosemary, Abby and Elizabeth are from families that are low in control.

Jody's and Leah's families believed that the best defense against bad ideas was censorship. Development was carefully channeled so that it fit the family's values. Sheltered from the storms, Jody and Leah experienced challenges at a rate they could handle. But their protection had a cost. Their growth was circumscribed and thwarted, like that of bonsai trees. In adolescence these girls looked strong, but their life choices were restricted.

Lucy and Franchesca came from homes that believed that the best defense against bad ideas was some censorship and some freedom. Both families were reasonably protective and yet allowed the daughters freedom to grow in their own directions. Not surprisingly, their daughters were less stressed than Abby, Elizabeth and Rosemary and less well behaved than Jody and Leah.

Abby's, Elizabeth's and Rosemary's families believed that the best defense against bad ideas was better ideas. They were more liberal, democratic and prone to negotiating. They valued experience more than structure, autonomy more than obedience. These families had many strengths—respect for individual differences and commitment to the developing potential of their daughters. But the daughters weren't ready for existential choices, and often they made bad decisions. These girls looked miserable and out of control in early adolescence. Later, however, they settled down into interesting and unique adults.

In a perfect universe, all girls would be loved. Adolescent girls would be protected by their families and yet allowed to blossom and flower as individuals. Families would provide moral clarity without sacrificing too much personal freedom. But in reality, this perfection is impossible. Families have choices. With less structure comes more risk to girls in the short term and more potential for individual growth over time. With more structure comes less short-term risk but more risk of later conformity and blandness. Families of adolescent girls struggle to find a balance between security and freedom, conformity to family values and autonomy. Finding this balance involves numerous judgment calls. The issues are complex and mistakes can be costly. Parents can be overwhelmed by the intensity of the issues. The perfect balance, like the golden mean, exists only in the abstract.

Chapter 5

MOTHERS

■

My mother was a general practitioner in small Kansas and Nebraska towns. This was when most people died at home and much of what a doctor did was sit with the patient and family.

Mother told me, "Just before old people die, they get addled. They leave this reality and go some other place. The men become farmers again, driving their horses home through a blizzard. They'll call out, 'Giddy up, go on. It's not far.' They'll see a light in the window and their breathing will relax. They'll see their wives watching for them and laugh in relief. 'I'm coming,' they will shout. They'll flail at their bedclothes, whipping their team on through the snow. 'Giddy up, now. We're almost home.' "

"What do women say?" I asked.

"Women call out for their mothers."

When I was ten, my mother often didn't make it home till late at night. She wore a tailored dark suit, red lipstick and black high heels. Her hair was short and curly and her eyes were always tired. When she walked in with her doctor bag and trench coat, I ran to her side and stayed there till bedtime. I watched her eat warmed-over stew, look through her mail, read my brothers a story and change into her housecoat and slippers. I rubbed her sore feet and asked about her day.

I accompanied her on house calls and on her trips to the hospital sixteen miles from our town. She told me stories about her childhood on a ranch. She'd killed rattlesnakes, found fossils in the creek bed, buried herself in a haystack during a hailstorm and played on a championship high school basketball team. She'd gathered cow chips for fuel during the Depression. I asked for more. "Tell me about when you ate watermelons right from the patch; tell me about the gypsies who came through; tell me about the twins who died from drinking the water in the chicken coop; tell me about the time the stunt pilot crashed at the county fair."

In junior high I grew irritated with her. She had a big stomach, thin hair and wasn't as pretty as my friends' mothers. I wanted her to stay home, bake tuna fish casseroles and teach me to sew. I wanted the phone to stop ringing for her.

For a high school graduation gift, she took me to San Francisco. We went to a coffeehouse in North Beach where beat poets read. I was sure that everyone was staring at my mother, and even though I liked the poetry, I insisted we leave early.

As an adult, I traveled with my family to her house for holiday dinners. She fixed my favorite foods—crab cocktails, vegetable soup and pecan pie. She gave my children too many sweets and presents. At midnight when I tried to go to bed, she offered to fry me a steak, go for a walk, anything to keep me talking for another hour. When it was time to go, she walked me to the car and held on to the door handle. "When are you coming back?" she asked.

The last month of her life, I sat by her in the hospital. She liked me to read and tell her stories. I brushed her hair and her teeth for her and fed her grapes one at a time. One night when she was out of her head from all the medicines, she imagined she was fixing spaghetti for twelve. "Hand me those tomatoes. Chop that onion quick. They'll be here soon." Another night she was delivering babies. "Push, push now," she said. "Wrap that baby up." When I slept beside her, she could sleep.

My relationship with my mother, like all relationships with mothers, was extraordinarily complex, filled with love, longing, a need for closeness and distance, separation and fusion. I respected her and mocked her, felt ashamed and proud of her, laughed with her and felt irritated by her smallest flaws. I felt crabby after twenty-four hours in her house, and yet nothing made me happier than making her happy.

Western civilization has a history of unrealistic expectations about mothers. They are held responsible for their children's happiness and for the social and emotional well-being of their families. Mothers are either idealized like the Virgin Mary or bashed in fairy tales and modern American novels. We all think of our mothers with what Freud called primary process thought, the thinking style of young children. We have trouble growing up enough to see our mothers as people.

Western civilization has a double standard about parenting. Relationships with fathers are portrayed as productive and growth-oriented, while relationships with mothers are depicted as regressive and dependent. Fathers are praised for their involvement with children. Mothers, on the other hand, are criticized unless their involvement is precisely the right amount. Distant mothers are scorned, but mothers who are too close are accused of smothering and overprotecting.

Nowhere are the messages to mothers so contradictory as with their adolescent daughters. Mothers are expected to protect their daughters from the culture even as they help them fit into it. They are to encourage their daughters to grow into adults and yet to keep them from being hurt. They are to be devoted to their daughters and yet encourage them to leave. Mothers are asked to love completely and yet know exactly when to distance emotionally and physically.

Daughters are as confused as mothers by our culture's expectations. Girls are encouraged to separate from their mothers and to devalue their relationships to them. They are expected to respect their mothers but not to be like them. In our culture, loving one's mother is linked with dependency, passivity and regression, while rejecting one's mother implies individuation, activity and independence. Distancing from one's mother is viewed as a necessary step toward adult development.

When Sara was fifteen she made a joke that was funny in a painful way. I liked to take her swimming, walking or out to lunch. Tongue in cheek, we labeled those outings mother-daughter bonding experiences. Then one day she began calling them mother-daughter "bondage" experiences. We both had tears in our eyes from laughing. To this day, we call our outings "mother-daughter bondage."

Growing up requires adolescent girls to reject the person with whom they are most closely identified. Daughters are socialized to have a tremendous fear of becoming like their mothers. There is no greater insult for most women than to say, "You are just like your mother." And yet to hate one's mother is to hate oneself.

The experience of American girls is so different from that of Leah, who was reared in a culture that respected the mother-daughter bond. In Western culture, mother-daughter tensions spring from the daughter's attempt to become an adult, to be an individual different from and not dependent on her mother. Because of mixed messages within the culture, conflict between mothers and daughters is inevitable. To have a self, daughters must reject parts of their mothers. Always mothers and daughters must struggle with distance—too close and there is engulfment, too distant and there's abandonment.

These age-old tensions are exacerbated by the problems of the 1990s. Mothers and daughters have even more turbulent relationships today. My office is filled with mother-daughter pairs who are struggling to define their relationships in positive ways. Part of the problem is that mothers don't understand the world that their daughters now live in. Their experiences were different. For example, most mothers were teased by boys in junior high about their bodies and their sexuality. They hear their daughters complain about what happens to them at school and they think it's the same thing, but it's not. The "teasing" is more graphic, mean-spirited and unremitting. It's no longer teasing, it's sexual harassment, and it keeps many girls from wanting to go to school.

Mothers are often unprepared for how their daughters behave. Their daughters may swear at them, call them bitches or tell them to shut up. This shocks them because they never swore at their own mothers. Their daughters may be sexually active at a much younger age. They struggled with sexual issues in committed relationships, and their daughters' casual attitudes floor them. Today's mothers kept secrets from their mothers, but they have no idea how different their daughters' secrets are.

Most mothers do their best to raise healthy daughters, but they are often unsure how to operate. For example, a neighbor raised her daughter to fight for her rights and to resist anyone's efforts to control her. Now at eleven, her daughter is often in trouble at school. She starts fights with teachers who she thinks are unfair and hits kids who pick on other kids. While her scrappiness is admirable from a feminist perspective, it's getting her in trouble. Other children have realized that she's a fighter and they set her up for trouble. The mother wonders if she has done the right thing.

A friend actively encouraged her daughters to keep up with sports, to eschew makeup, eat hearty meals and speak up in class when they knew the answers. During adolescence, her daughters were hurt and rejected by more sex-typed peers. They didn't conform to the feminine norms and suffered dreadfully.

My cousin's common sense told her that her daughter shouldn't have a two-hundred-dollar low-cut dress for her eighth-grade graduation. But all her daughter's friends had such dresses. Her daughter begged her to buy it because she was afraid that she would feel like a geek at her graduation party.

This same cousin had strong beliefs about alcohol and teenagers. She said no to parties where alcohol was served. But her daughter insisted that all the popular kids went to the parties and that she'd be left out of her crowd. My cousin was torn between her fear of alcohol and her desire for her daughter to be accepted at her school.

Mothers want their daughters to date, but are terrified of date rape, teenage pregnancy, AIDS and other diseases. They want their daughters to be independent, but are aware of how dangerous the world is for women. They want their daughters to be relaxed about their appearance, but know that girls suffer socially if they aren't attractive.

Daughters struggle to individuate, but also need their mothers' guidance and love. They resist their mothers' protection even as they move into dangerous waters. And they are angry when their mothers warn them of dangers that they understand even better than their mothers.

Most girls are close to their mothers when they are young, and many return to that closeness as adults. But few girls manage to stay close to their mothers during junior high and high school. Girls at their most vulnerable time reject the help of the one person who wants most to understand their needs. The stories I tell focus on the mother-daughter struggle for the right amount of closeness. Jessica and Brenda have been so close that, with adolescence, Jessica rejects everything her mother offers. Sorrel and Fay have a good working relationship that's neither too close nor too distant. Whitney and Evelyn have too much distance.

JESSICA (15) AND BRENDA

Jessica and Brenda were a study in contrasts. Brenda was a social worker in her late thirties. She was casually dressed and pudgy with wild, blond-gray flyaway hair. She talked earnestly and rapidly, using her hands to punctuate her expressive speech. She had words for every feeling and a sophisticated theory about every problem that she and Jessica were having. Around her blue eyes were deep laugh lines. Beside her sat Jessica, as still and distant as an ice sculpture. She was thin with long dark hair and a pale complexion, and she was dressed in a black silk shirt and pants.

Brenda said, "I'm at my wit's end with Jessie. She won't go to school and the authorities are on my case. Since I'm a social worker, this really embarrasses me. But I can't physically force her to go."

She sighed. "I can't make her do anything. All she does is sleep, watch MTV and read magazines. She's not doing chores or going out with friends. She's throwing her life away."

I asked Jessica how she spent her time. She looked away and Brenda answered. "She likes the television in my bedroom. All day while I'm at work she lies on my bed and generally messes things up. I bought her a television, but she still goes into my room. She claims my bed is more comfortable."

Jessica sniffed dramatically and Brenda continued. "I wasn't married when Jessie was born. She missed having a father. That's affected her self-image."

Jessica scowled when her mother talked about her, but refused to speak for herself.

"Jessie and I used to do everything together. She was a wonderful, enthusiastic girl. I'm amazed by what's happening." She sighed. "I can't do anything right with her. If I ask her a question, she thinks it's stupid. If I'm quiet, she accuses me of glaring. If I talk to her, I'm lecturing. I have to brace myself to deal with her. She yells at me constantly."

Brenda patted her daughter's leg. "I know she has low self-esteem, but I can't figure out how to help her. What more can I do?"

I asked Jessica to leave the room. For someone so apparently disgusted by the conversation, she seemed surprisingly reluctant to go. For the next thirty minutes Brenda gave me a history of Jessica's life. Then Jessica knocked on the door. "I'm sick. I need to go home."

I handed Jessica an appointment card. "I'll see you alone on Tuesday."

I was glad this mother-daughter pair had come to counseling. Brenda, perhaps because she was a social worker, was reluctant to judge her daughter. She was so afraid of rejecting Jessica that she wasn't being firm. She had parenting confused with abuse, and she was trying so hard to be good to her daughter that she was denying Jessica a chance to grow up. Brenda was in danger of "understanding" Jessica all the way into juvenile court.

On Tuesday Jessica came dressed in black jeans and a black turtleneck. She sat silently on the couch, waiting for me to begin. I wrestled with my own feelings of pessimism about what the hour would bring. Already, after three minutes with her, I felt I was dragging a barge across a desert.

"How do you feel about being here?"

"Okay."

"Do you really feel okay?"

"I don't see any need for it, but morning television isn't that thrilling anyway."

"How are you different from your mom?"

Jessica arched one black eyebrow. "What do you mean?"

"Do you have different values, ideas about life?"

She smirked. "I totally disagree with her about everything. I hate school, she likes school. I hate to work and she loves it. I like MTV and she hates it. I wear black and she never does. She wants me to live up to my potential and I think she's full of shit."

I considered saying that her life goal seemed to be to frustrate her mother, but instead I asked, "What have you wanted to do?"

Her eyes widened. "Modeling. Mom hates the idea. She thinks it is sexist and shallow."

I suggested that she look into modeling for herself. She could do some research on the profession: What should she be studying now to prepare herself? Where would she get training? Are there jobs locally? How much does it pay?

After Jessica left I thought about this family. Brenda had devoted her life to Jessica's happiness, and with adolescence all this closeness became a problem. Jessica tried to get distance by rebelling, but Brenda was too understanding. She forgave her and continued to be loving. So Jessica would be even more difficult and Brenda would be even more understanding. By now Jessica felt so engulfed that she would do anything to separate herself from Brenda. She was defining herself almost exclusively as "not Brenda."

I saw Brenda later that day and warned her. "Whatever you do, don't express any interest in Jessica's research on modeling. Don't offer to help or tell her that you're glad she's doing something productive."

I asked Brenda about her life. "My life is Jessie and my work. I haven't had time for anything else. I hoped that when she was a teenager I'd have more time, but it hasn't worked out that way. I need to be around constantly. I wake her up every morning, go home at lunch to fix her something to eat. Otherwise she won't eat, and you can see how thin she is. At night I keep her company. The poor kid doesn't have anyone else."

"You need a life of your own."

She nodded. "I know you're right, but . . ."

I said, "Let's plan some fun for you."

I continued to work separately with Brenda and Jessica. They were terribly connected to each other and resistant to outsiders. Our therapy reminded me of the old joke—Question: "How many therapists does it take to change a light bulb? Answer: "One, if the light bulb wants to change."

With Brenda, I pushed for some life apart from her daughter. Could she occasionally go for lunch with a friend or go for a walk in the evening with a neighbor? Did she like to read, listen to music or work with her hands? She decided to work on a school bond issue and once a week she left Jessica alone and went to a meeting. The first time she did this, Jessica called and said she was sick. But the second time Jessica made it through the evening in fine shape. When Brenda returned, she'd actually made them some popcorn and lemonade.

At first Brenda's concerns were all about Jessica. Would she be sick, lonely or get into trouble? She felt guilty and anxious leaving her daughter in the evenings. Later she admitted that she had her own concerns: She was uneasy socially after all these years of no practice and she worried that a man might ask her out.

She said dramatically, "I am not ever going to date."

"That's one way that you and Jessica are alike," I said. "Neither of you wants to deal with the opposite sex."

With Jessica, I asked questions that I hoped would help her define herself as separate from her mother. She considered her mother's views stupid, but she knew exactly what they were. We had our most success with the modeling research, which Jessica pursued throughout our time together. She sent off for information about clinics and schools. She read the autobiography of a famous model and a book with tips on becoming a professional model. She experimented with her hair and makeup. One day she came to our session dressed in royal blue. I looked surprised and she said, "Black is just not me."

She returned to school and after much discussion decided to join the photography club. All my work with Jessica was funneled through her desire to be a model. I encouraged her to exercise by noting that models with muscles were popular. As she exercised, she became less depressed and more energetic.

I suggested that models needed self-confidence to cope with all the competition. Jessica agreed and worked on this. She kept a record of three things she was proud of each day. She recorded: "I'm proud I fed the cats, went to school and didn't yell at Mom." "I'm proud I washed my hair, turned in my homework and smiled at a girl in my gym class." Later she bought a counter at Ben Franklin's and clicked it every time she did the smallest thing that pleased her. This put Jessica on a positive search for what she liked about herself. Also she, not her mother or anyone else, determined what was valuable about her. Her feelings of self-worth were coming from within. Soon Jessica was able to click fifty or sixty times a day. We defined victories as times when she made an effort to accomplish her long-term goals. Jessica began reporting regular victories. She signed up for an aerobics class at the YWCA. She talked to a friend who was also interested in modeling, and they agreed to exchange information about local competitions and shows. She developed a portfolio of pictures of herself.

I encouraged Jessica to write down her thoughts and feelings and to sort out which values of her mother's she wanted to keep or reject. Gradually Jessica had thoughts that were not simply reactions to Brenda. She discovered the joy of developing her own ideas rather than rebelling against Brenda's.

One day Jessica said, "I hate it when Mom doesn't respect my choices. That's worse than her not loving me." That led to a discussion of how important her mother's regard for her really was. She desperately wanted her mother to acknowledge that she was growing up into her own person.

This case was one in which I needed to set aside my own judgments and stay humble. I shared much of Brenda's antipathy toward modeling, and I generally work to minimize appearance and develop other qualities in my clients. But I needed to trust Jessica to do what was right for her. Jessica's interest in modeling helped her reenter the world and develop a self.

At our last joint session, Jessica was dressed in a silky green shirt and neon-yellow tights. Her eyes were lively and she talked easily. She had an opportunity to model clothes for a local store. Her grades were just average, but she was proud of her Bs in business math and merchandising.

Brenda said, "I'm not nuts about modeling, but I'm happy that Jess is happy. She doesn't have to choose something I would choose. I am trying to acknowledge that Jess is growing up and becoming her own person. I want that for her."

"You need your own life too," Jessica said.

Brenda nodded. "I'm working on that."

I quoted the old saying "Velvet chains are the hardest to break."

SORREL (16) AND FAY

Fay and Sorrel sat in my office late one winter afternoon. A week earlier Sorrel had told Fay that she was a lesbian, and Fay urged her to seek help in understanding what this meant to her life. Mother and daughter both wore jeans, dark sweaters and old hiking boots. I asked Sorrel how she felt about being a lesbian.

"I have known I was different for a long time, but I couldn't say exactly how. When I was in sixth grade, I imagined kissing cheerleaders and pretty teachers. But I didn't know any lesbians and I'd heard the word only as a put-down. So even though I was attracted to girls, I refused to label myself lesbian."

She looked at her mother and Fay nodded encouragement to continue. Sorrel exhaled deeply. "I found some old books written by psychologists about homosexuality, but they didn't help at all. I wanted stories about girls like me that were okay. There was nothing like that. I was happy when k.d. lang announced she was a lesbian. She was talented and pretty, someone I wouldn't mind knowing."

Fay said, "Sorrel has always been unique."

"I made life hell for Mom when I was little and she was married to Howard." Sorrel laughed. "Howard was a jerk. He tried to control me and make me into a little lady."

Fay agreed. "Howard wanted her to wear dresses and she refused. He insisted that we teach Sorrel who was boss, and we fought about that. I never have tried to control Sorrel. I have loved her uniqueness and wanted her to be exactly who she is."

"Mom and Howard divorced when I was seven," Sorrel said. "I don't plan on ever living with a man again."

Fay continued. "Even as an elementary student, Sorrel was different. She spent a lot of time alone reading or sketching. She collected rocks and leaves."

Sorrel interrupted. "I liked things that humans hadn't touched. I liked things orderly and regular."

I asked how other children treated Sorrel. Sorrel answered, "I didn't have many friends unless you count imaginary ones. I preferred boys to girls. Girls were catty and superficial."

"I couldn't protect her," Fay said. "At least I had the sense to not try and change her. I knew she was fine the way she was. I tried to make our home a safe haven for her."

Sorrel said, "Junior high was the pits. I felt like I was on a different planet from the other kids. I was the untouchable of my school."

She looked at Fay and said softly, "Mom doesn't like to hear this, but I thought some about killing myself. I didn't fit anywhere. I didn't dare admit even to myself why I was different."

Fay winced at the mention of suicide, but she held her peace and let Sorrel continue with her story.

"I survived by living in my own world. The real world was too hostile so I made new ones. I drew lots of fantasy pictures."

Fay beamed. "Sorrel had her own vision of the world."

Sorrel said, "Drawing saved me."

I asked Sorrel how I could help.

"I need to meet other lesbians. I need to know that I'm not the only one. I want to read more about girls like me."

We talked about the local Women's Resource Center and a nearby women's bookstore. I told her about the gay/lesbian support group for teenagers.

Fay reminded us that Sorrel was different in many ways besides her sexual orientation. She was more self-sufficient that other girls. She had acute sensibilities, sometimes so acute Fay worried they would destroy her.

Sorrel said, "I want to compliment Mom on her support. She's stood by me through all my weirdness."

Fay smiled. "I have tried to teach her that intelligent resistance is a good thing. Sorrel has wonderful things to offer the world, and I've tried to protect her gifts. As a girl, I was fearful. I wanted to fit in and be popular. I lost a lot by being such a conformist. As an adult, I have spent years sorting out the mess I became in high school. I was determined to help Sorrel resist."

Sorrel didn't fit into our cultural categories for young women. She belonged to an invisible population: lesbian adolescents. Particularly in junior high, she had suffered for the sin of being different. Luckily

Fay possessed an uncommon ability to give her daughter uncondi-
tional love. She accepted Sorrel as she was and valued her daughter
when others didn't. She resisted the temptation to urge Sorrel to conform and fit in. She made their own home a safe house.

WHITNEY (16) AND EVELYN

Whitney and Evelyn resembled each other with their blond hair and
round freckled faces, but stylistically they were different. Whitney was
relaxed and wholesome-looking in jeans and a turtleneck sweater,
while Evelyn was dressed in an elegant suit with matching shoes.
Clearly Evelyn had been a knockout when she was younger, and she
still spent a great deal of time on having the perfect look. Today in my
office she held herself stiffly and seemed uncomfortable.

Whitney was open and flexible while Evelyn was quiet and cautious.
She grimaced when I asked why they were in my office. "Sam insisted.
He's fed up with our fighting. He's worried about both of us, but
particularly Whitney. She doesn't want to go to school."

Whitney said, "I wanted to come. I asked Mom a year ago if we
could see a therapist, but she said it cost too much."

Evelyn said, "I don't think it will help, but I'm willing to try. I
promised Sam."

First I talked with Evelyn, who told me that she had had trouble
with Whitney since the day she was born. She had a difficult labor and
suffered a major postpartum depression. Immediately after Whitney's
birth, she made Sam promise no more children. Evelyn had been a shy,
well-behaved girl and Whitney was boisterous and outgoing. From the
moment of her birth, Whitney had stolen the show.

Evelyn clearly resented Sam's relationship with Whitney. "He thinks
she walks on water. He doesn't see her sneakiness and self-centered-
ness. She's got him snowed."

I asked about Evelyn's relationship with Sam. She said it was good
when he was around. Sam ran an international business and spent lots
of time abroad. Evelyn felt they would get along fine if it weren't for
Whitney. They fought about her constantly. Evelyn felt he spoiled her,
and Sam felt Evelyn was cold and uncaring.

As Evelyn talked, I was impressed by how lonely she was. If she had
any affection for her daughter, I could not find it. She had no close
friends and seemed utterly dependent on Sam for companionship and

support. And Sam was a scarce commodity. She was devoted to him and resented that his devotion was divided between her and Whitney.

Evelyn said, "Sam doesn't know Whitney like I do. She drinks and she's had sex. I wasn't raised that way. I was a virgin when I married."

I asked about her relationship with Whitney. Evelyn said, "She's mouthy. I never, ever yelled at my mother. I don't want her to touch me or talk to me. I'm counting the days until she moves out."

In fact, Whitney was pretty well behaved for the nineties. She worked part-time at a sporting-goods store, and until recently she was an honor roll student. She was on student council and active in the Young Republicans. She was sexually involved with her boyfriend of a year, but she'd been honest with her parents about this. She'd made her own arrangements for birth control pills.

I suspected that Evelyn's antipathy came from deep within herself—perhaps from her own unsatisfied needs for love or her disappointment that Whitney was not a replica of herself. Evelyn wasn't able to change with the times and appreciate that Whitney lived in a different world from the one she inhabited as a girl. She seemed stuck on the idea that things should stay the same.

When I met with Whitney alone, she was surprisingly positive about her mother. She clearly respected her mother's talents—as a home-maker, an expert on grooming and a seamstress. She yearned for more connection and less competition between them, but she was baffled about how to make that happen. She said, "I can't be someone I'm not just to please her."

Whitney felt closer to her father, who she knew loved her. But he was gone so much, and when he was home he had to be careful not to side with Whitney. She said, "Mom notices who Dad hugs first. She tells him stories so he'll be angry with me.

"Mom calls me a slut because I've had sex," Whitney said. "Nothing I do is right for her. She gives me the silent treatment, and sometimes I can't even figure out what she's mad about."

She began to cry as we talked. "I need Mom. Things happen that I wish I could tell her, but I'm afraid to."

I asked for an example. "Right now, I'm being bugged by these guys in the parking lot after school. They gawk at me and call me names, and one of them tried to pull my blouse off. If I told Mom, she'd say it was my own fault, that I deserve what I get. That's one reason I hate school now."

Whitney had other problems too. She was working too many hours and worried about balancing her time. She loved her boyfriend, but they fought almost daily and Whitney wanted to talk about improving that relationship. She didn't bring these things up with her mother because she was certain she'd be blamed for her troubles.

At the end of that first session we all met together. Evelyn said, "The basic problem is I don't respect Whitney's morals."

Whitney said, "No. We need to communicate more. I need you to understand me."

Evelyn was white-lipped as she talked. "I'll never approve of what you're doing. That's not the way things were done in my family."

I thought to myself, But Whitney is not you and the world isn't the same. I searched for a way to end the session on a positive note. This was an unusual case because the mother had broken her bonds with the daughter. Evelyn seemed more fragile than Whitney and more rigid in her thinking. Until Evelyn felt better about herself, she couldn't care for Whitney. Evelyn needed more friends and interests, a life besides waiting for Sam to come home. I asked if Sam could come with them next time, and I complimented Evelyn on her honesty. I would have to nurture her before she would nurture her daughter.

Chapter 6

FATHERS

■

My father grew up in the Ozarks during the Depression. He was a good-looking, slow-talking Southerner. He left the South for World War Two, and his military service took him to Hawaii, Japan and, later, Korea. In San Francisco he met and married my mother, who was in the Navy. When I was young, he attended college on the GI Bill and developed a taste for big-band music and trips to Mexico. But he remained Southern in his beliefs about race and women until he died in 1973.

I was his first child and he insisted I be named Mary after the Blessed Virgin and Elizabeth after the English queen. He woke in the night to check on my breathing. By the time I was six months old, he had a Benny Goodman record that he played when he came home from work. I would hear that record and flail in my crib. He would pick me up and dance me around our small living room.

When I was five he taught me to fish. We walked to a pond filled with bluegill and sun perch. He hooked a worm on my line, sat beside me waiting for a hit, and then he helped me take the fish off the hook. He untangled line, chased away snakes and picked off the ticks I acquired en route to the pond. We could sit all afternoon along the bank, listening to frogs, watching turtles and filling a gunnysack with keepers.

He taught me to drive a blue 1950 Mercury on the back roads of Cloud County. Smoking Chesterfields and drinking Dr Pepper, he sat beside me, his black curly hair blowing in the breeze. He was an anxious teacher, always grabbing the wheel and shouting, "Steer, steer, goddammit."

When I was twelve I told him I loved the smell of new books. I said I loved to hold them to my face and breathe in their aroma. He looked alarmed and said, "Don't tell anyone that. They'll think you are a pervert."

When he and my mother drove me down to the state university, he was full of advice. "Don't date anybody but freshmen and don't get serious with them. Don't get in with a crowd that smokes or drinks. Stay away from foreigners. Don't get behind in your studies." When he left he hugged me, his first hug in years, and he said, "I'll miss you. I talk more to you than to anyone else."

I had my last conversation with my father the day before he died. Much to his relief, I was married. He called to see if I had passed my comprehensive exams in psychology. I told him yes and he was pleased. Then I begged off—people were coming to dinner and I needed to fix a salad. He said, "I'm proud of you." The next day he had a stroke and went into a coma. I was with him in the ICU when the machines bleeped to a stop.

My father was the best and worst of fathers. He would have given his life to save mine. He was embarrassingly proud of my accomplishments and naively certain that I would succeed. But he had a double standard about sex and rigid views about women. In short, we had a typical complicated father-daughter relationship, probably closer than most such relationships in the 1950s because both of us were big talkers.

All fathers are products of their times. The rules for fathers have changed a great deal since the 1950s, when to be a good father, a man should stay sober, earn a living, remain faithful to his wife and not beat the kids. Men weren't expected to hug their daughters, tell them they loved them or talk to them about personal matters. Now fathers are expected to do all the things they did in the 1950s, plus be emotionally involved. Many fathers didn't learn how to do this from their own fathers. Because they missed their training, they feel lost.

Most fathers also received a big dose of misogyny training as boys, and nowhere does this hurt them more than in parenting their daughters. They are in the awkward position of loving a gender that they have been taught to devalue, of caring for females whom they have been taught to discount. And yet in our culture, the main job of fathers is to teach their children to fit into broader society.

Americans tend to have a double standard on parenting. Mothers are seen as having great power to do harm with their mistakes. Fathers are viewed as having great power to do good with their attention. In our society when daughters are strong, credit is often given to fathers. But in my experience, strong daughters often come from families with strong mothers.

While most girls are connected to their mothers by close if often conflicting ties, with fathers they have varied relationships. Some girls barely speak to their fathers, while others have warm, close relationships and common interests. One client said, "I hardly know my dad exists. We have nothing in common." Another said, "My favorite thing about Dad is that he plays duets with me every night after dinner. We both love the violin and have had this time together since I was three years old."

Fathers also have great power to do harm. If they act as socializing agents for the culture, they can crush their daughters' spirits. Rigid fathers limit their daughters' dreams and destroy their self-confidence. Sexist fathers teach their daughters that their value lies in pleasing men. Sexist jokes, misogynistic cracks and negative attitudes about assertive women hurt girls. Sexist fathers teach their daughters to relinquish power and control to men. In their own relations with women they model a power differential between the sexes. Some fathers, in their eagerness to have their daughters accepted by the culture, encourage their daughters to be attractive or lose weight. They produce daughters who believe their only value is their physical attractiveness to men. These fathers undervalue intelligence in women and teach their daughters to undervalue it too.

On the other hand, nonsexist fathers can be tremendously helpful in teaching their daughters healthy rebellion. They can encourage daughters to protect themselves and even to fight back. They can encourage their daughters' androgyny, particularly in sports and academics. They can teach daughters skills, such as how to change tires, throw a baseball or build a patio. They can help them understand the male point of view and the forces that act on men in this culture.

The best fathers confront their own lookism and sexism. Fathers can model good male-female relationships and respect for women in a wide variety of roles. Fathers can fight narrow definitions of their daughters' worth and support their wholeness. They can teach their daughters that it's okay to be smart, bold and independent.

In the 1970s, I did research on father-daughter relationships. I interviewed high school girls, one-fourth of whose fathers had died, one-fourth of whose parents were divorced and one-half of whose parents were together. I was interested in how daughters' relationships to fathers affected their self-esteem, sense of well-being and reactions to males.

I quickly found that the physical presence of the father had little to do with the quality of the relationship. Some girls whose fathers lived in the home rarely spoke to them, while other girls who never saw their fathers were sustained by memories of warmth and acceptance. Emotional availability, not physical presence, was the critical variable. I found three kinds of relationships: supportive, distant and abusive.

Supportive fathers had daughters with high self-esteem and a sense of well-being. These girls were more apt to like men, to feel confident in relationships with the opposite sex and to predict their own future happiness. They described fathers as fun, deeply involved and companionable.

In my study, the majority of fathers fell in the distant relationship category. They may have wanted relationships, but they didn't have the skills. Girls with distant fathers said they liked the income their fathers brought home, but they appreciated little else. Besides being the breadwinner, often the father had only one other role: rule enforcer. Distant fathers were generally perceived as more rigid than mothers, less understanding and less willing to listen. As one girl put it, "If Dad moved out, we'd be poorer, but there'd be more peace around here."

These distant fathers were often well-meaning but inept. They were likely to work long hours outside the home and have less time and energy for the hard work of connecting with adolescents. Distant fathers didn't know how to stay emotionally involved with their complicated teenage daughters. They hadn't learned to maneuver the intricacies of relationships with empathy, flexibility, patience and negotiation. They had counted on women to do this for them.

Some distant fathers had more than a skill or time deficit. Because of their socialization to the male role, they did not value the qualities necessary to stay in close long-term relationships. They labeled nurturing and empathizing as wimpy behavior and related to their daughters in cold, mechanical ways.

The third category was the emotionally, physically or sexually abusive father. These were the fathers who called their daughters names, who ridiculed and shamed them for mistakes and who physically hurt or molested their daughters.

Katie's father was a supportive father. However, because of his illness, Katie had taken too much responsibility for him. Holly's father lacked the skills necessary to help his daughter. Dale was well-meaning but distant. Klara's father also fell into the distant category. He was a rigidly sex-typed father who imposed his definitions of femaleness on his daughter. These fathers all played important roles in the lives of their daughters, for good or ill.

KATIE (16) AND PETE

Pete was a single parent whose wife had died in a car accident when Katie was three. An invalid, homebound with muscular dystrophy, Pete managed to support himself and Katie with a computer consulting business.

When Katie was in high school, he insisted she come to therapy. He was concerned that she was letting her love for him keep her from living her own life. Katie came in under duress, claiming that she could share all her thoughts and feelings with Pete.

Katie was so loving and insightful that she seemed too good to be true. Unlike most teenagers, she had a sense that her work was important to others. She took care of Pete, worked at a nearby drugstore and studied. Time after time she managed to make good decisions about a life filled with problems.

I asked about her relationship to Pete. "He's always trusted me. When I have a problem, he insists I figure it out for myself. He says that I'll make the right decision. We can talk about everything: sex, boys, drugs, menstruation, you name it. He's the best listener in the world."

I asked her if she missed having a mother. "I don't remember my mother. Of course I wish she were with us, but I'm happier than most of my friends. I have more of a father than anyone I know."

Only when I asked about Pete's health did her tone change. Her face darkened and she said softly, "He's getting worse and I hate to leave him for long. I'm worried about his future."

While she detailed his health problems and his poor prognosis, I listened. Her voice was clear and firm but filled with pain. She had thought a great deal about what she wanted to give to Pete, but less about what she needed to keep for herself. I worried that she had few other relationships to sustain her when her father died. I wanted to be careful and not fix what wasn't broken, but on the other hand, Katie needed to think more about her own life. Pete was right—she needed more friends and more fun.

I shared my thoughts with her at the end of the session. Katie said, "Dad is so great that I don't miss friends. I know that sounds weird, but I like my life just like it is."

I wanted to meet this great dad, so I drove to their small suburban home one Saturday afternoon. Pete lay on a daybed covered with quilts and three Siamese cats. Nearby were his computer and telephone. He was thin and frail with a big smile and an outgoing manner.

Pete and Katie joked about my black coat and the white cat hairs. We talked about the ice storm that had frozen our city over the weekend and Katie's skills as a cook. No one seemed eager to broach the topic of Pete's health.

I complimented Pete on the wonderful job he had done raising Katie. He laughed. "She raised me. She's tons more mature than I am."

I agreed with him that Katie was mature, but I noted that she needed more social life. I thought to myself she needed friendships and Saturday-night dates. I suspected that some of her reluctance came from worry about her father, but some probably stemmed from ordinary teenage social anxiety.

Pete said, "Usually I respect Katie's judgment, but she needs to look at herself in this area. She's more comfortable with me than she is with kids her age. She hates to fail and she knows she can succeed with me."

I offered to be Katie's "social-life consultant," and she agreed to come in for a while. But I could tell she was humoring us. I changed the subject. "How will things go when Katie graduates from high school?"

Pete and Katie exchanged looks and Pete laughed. "We have a big difference of opinion there. We have my wife's insurance money. Katie can go to school anywhere she wants. She can get into Harvard, Yale, her grades are first-rate."

Katie interrupted, "I want to go here."

Pete continued, "Katie has things all planned out. She wants to live at home and care for her sick old pa. I won't let her do that."

"You've never told me what to do and you can't start now," Katie said.

We all laughed.

But then Katie's eyes filled with tears and she said, "You are all the family I've got and I won't leave you. I couldn't enjoy being anywhere else. I'm not staying to take care of you. I'm staying because I want to."

Pete shook his head no.

"I'll live in the dorms if I can come home every day for a visit."

"What do you think I'll be doing?" Pete joked. "Snorting coke, losing my money in crap games?"

Katie stood up for her position. "I think you'll be doing what you do now and you need my help to do it. You can hire someone for some things, like shopping and cleaning, but I'm going to visit daily and that's that."

"You've raised a stubborn daughter," I said. "I suggest you accept Katie's offer. It's not unhealthy or wrong for families to stick together."

Pete said, "I don't have any choice. I don't think Katie will start taking orders now."

Katie wouldn't take orders, but I sensed that she was healthy enough to respond to conversation and encouragement. I knew that at some level she was aware that she was hiding from peers. On the other hand, I admired the closeness of Pete and Katie and was determined not to pathologize a loving relationship. I said, "There are many ways to compromise. Katie could perhaps study abroad one year or attend an out-of-state school for a summer session. We can talk about this when she comes to my office."

"I think Katie will do what she wants." He smiled at her. "She's my cross to bear."

HOLLY (14) AND DALE

Holly's mother had fallen in love with a neighbor and slipped away one day while Holly was at kindergarten and Dale was at work. They never saw her again. Dale worked as a supervisor at the Goodyear plant. His wife and daughter had been his life, and he was devastated by the abandonment and the responsibilities of single parenting. He arranged for Holly's physical care and supervision, but he had neither the energy nor the understanding to deliver much emotional support and companionship.

After his wife left, Dale's days were all the same. He came home, fixed dinner, did the dishes and parked himself in his recliner in front of the television. Many nights he fell asleep before the ten o'clock news. He rarely made it to Holly's school programs and had no outside interests of his own. Once a coworker tried to set him up for a date, but Dale refused. He wasn't taking that kind of chance again.

Holly quickly learned to care for herself. She kept her bedroom neat and washed and ironed her own clothes. She was only vaguely aware that other girls had more friends and activities and parents who read to them and took them on outings. She never studied, but she was well behaved and her report card was a dull list of "satisfactories."

In elementary school, she watched television with Dale, but by junior high she dropped TV in favor of music. Holly became obsessed with the music of Prince. She papered her walls with his posters and record covers. She joined his fan club, and once a week she wrote long letters to her idol. She played his music until she had all the lyrics memorized, and because Prince wore purple, Holly dressed exclusively in purple. She dyed her hair red and spiked it because Prince claimed he liked red hair.

Dale hardly noticed this until the school counselor called to say that students were teasing Holly about her purple clothes and outrageous hair. She also was worried that Holly had few friends and no interests except Prince. She encouraged Dale to sign Holly up for a club, sports or drama classes.

Dale asked Holly if she would join a club and she said no. He offered her lessons in whatever she wanted and she declined. Dale bought her new brightly colored T-shirts and Holly put them in a drawer unopened. Dale sensed Holly's problem might be related to her home life, but he was unsure what else to do. He gave up and returned to his television.

Then Holly met Lyle, a skinny eighth-grader who had a studded black leather jacket and a tattoo that read "Live fast, die young." Lyle, like Holly, had chosen music as his way of dealing with his aloneness. He listened to music virtually every waking minute that he was not in class. He was in trouble at school for blasting music during lunch break. They met in the back row of English class. Holly noticed that

Lyle had slipped a Sony Walkman into the school and shyly asked him if he liked Prince. Lyle, unlike most of the boys, didn't think that Holly's teased hair and purple outfits were a liability. He said yes, he liked Prince.

He asked Holly to come to his house after school and listen to music. By the weekend they were going steady. Holly transferred much of the devotion she'd lavished on Prince to Lyle. She called him first thing in the morning to wake him and met him at the corner south of school for a cigarette. She wrote notes to him during classes, ate lunch with him in the school cafeteria and then, after school, went to his house. In the evenings she spent hours on the phone to Lyle.

Dale was relieved that Holly had a friend. He told me, "Lyle was a strange agent, but he had good manners." Dale sensed that so much closeness so fast might not be healthy, but he was unsure what to do about it. He brought up sex to Holly and she angrily told him that she could handle it. He doubted that, but was uncertain what to say or do next.

For three months Holly lived for Lyle. Then Lyle broke off the relationship abruptly. He told Holly that he wasn't ready for a serious relationship and wanted more time to practice his guitar and hang out with musicians. Lyle's mother called Dale to warn him about the effect this news would have on Holly. She said that while they liked Holly, she and her husband felt that things were moving way too fast and that Lyle needed to slow down. After all, these were eighth-graders. They talked to Lyle about their concerns and he agreed to cool it. Before she hung up, she told Dale that Holly and Lyle had been sexually active.

Dale was stunned by the news. He suggested a pregnancy test but Holly refused. In fact, she refused to discuss Lyle with him at all. When he came home at night she fled to her room and slammed the door. For a few days Holly cried nonstop, refusing to eat or go to school. Her eyes were red and her face puffy from grief. She called Lyle daily but the talks didn't go well. Her pleading made him even more determined to break up. Then one day Holly swallowed all the pills in the house.

Fortunately, Dale came home at lunch to check on Holly. He found her asleep in a pool of vomit and called 911.

I met Holly at the hospital after this suicide attempt. Alone in a white room, she was dressed in the regulation hospital gown, but with her hair properly spiked and a *Rolling Stone* magazine by her side. When I introduced myself, she was polite but distant. I asked her about the suicide attempt. Holly stared out the window at the harsh November day and said, "My life is over." The rest of our time she answered questions in noncommittal monosyllables.

Things were not much better at the office. Dale came the first time and filled me in on his life with Holly. He knew almost nothing about her thoughts and feelings. Clearly he cared about his daughter, but he had no ideas about how to express his caring in helpful ways. He and Holly had talked so rarely that now that Holly was in a crisis, they had no foundation for working things through. I was struck by the little pleasure his own life had. His parents were dead. He didn't believe in socializing with his coworkers. His only interest was television.

I called the school counselor, who said, "Holly doesn't really have a life. She's living in a fantasy world that she's constructed around Prince. She tried to substitute Lyle for Prince, but real people are too complicated for her."

Slowly I began to build a relationship with Holly. Once a week she showed up in a different purple outfit and we talked about Prince. I encouraged her to bring a tape and we listened together. To test me, she played "sexy" Prince songs. Afterward I commented on whatever I could praise.

"I like the line about staying until the morning light."

She shrugged and said, "That's his old stuff. Listen to this."

I asked, "What does this song mean to you?"

Holly said, "It's two against the world. Undying love."

"You haven't had that—undying love, I mean," I said.

"Are you bringing up my mother?"

Holly often answered my questions by quoting Prince's songs. I listened and pulled themes from the lyrics for further consideration. I waited for Holly to use her own words. Finally I suggested that she write a Prince-style song about her feelings.

The next week Holly handed me a song. It was Prince-like with themes of loneliness and abandonment. She grinned when I praised it. After that Holly and I communicated mostly via her songs. She brought a fresh one each week—a song about her mother's leaving, another about her anger over the divorce, a song wondering where her mother was and why she didn't call and a song about how cruel kids could be. I listened, discussed the writing, asked what meaning the songs had in her life.

Otherwise, I gently encouraged her to make a friend. Because of her mother's abandonment and because of teasing by girls, Holly didn't trust females. She shook her head no to my suggestions about talking to girls. I suggested music lessons and maybe a band.

After many months I felt we had a strong enough relationship that I could bring up sex. I suggested a doctor's appointment for an examination. I told her basic facts about sexuality that "all girls wonder about and are afraid to ask."

We talked about how vulnerable she'd been to the first person who said "I love you." Lyle was a decent guy, lonely and naive like Holly, but the next person might be different. I pointed out that "I love you" are the first words that psychopaths say to girls.

Holly was vulnerable to a common adolescent girl's mistake—using her sexuality to get love. She needed affection, not sex, and most of all she needed affection from her father. We discussed how she and her father were strangers to each other, and I invited Dale in for a visit. That first joint session he was even more awkward than Holly. He sat stiffly with his arms folded across his chest and said "yes, ma'am" to my questions.

"We don't talk," Holly said accusingly.

Dale said, "Your mother was better at that. I never had much experience talking to kids."

I asked if they wanted to be closer. Holly twirled her hair around her little finger and nodded shyly. Dale choked up but finally said, "That's all I want. What else am I alive for?"

I recommended that they go slowly. Neither had many skills and both would be overwhelmed by failure. They could cook a meal together or drive around and look at Christmas lights. When I suggested they attend a holiday concert, both looked alarmed. I backed down and suggested they talk ten minutes each evening about how their day had gone.

The next session they reported that the talks were difficult at first but easier with practice. Dale asked about Holly's school. She told him about lunchtime in the loud cafeteria. Holly asked what her dad did at work, and after all these years he explained it to her.

In therapy we gingerly approached their long-buried feelings about Holly's mother leaving. Dale said, "I tried to put it behind me. I couldn't change it, so what was the point crying about it?"

Holly said, "I was afraid to bring it up because Dad always looked so sad. After the first month I didn't mention Mom anymore. For a long time I cried myself to sleep."

I asked both Holly and Dale to write letters to the absent mother in which they expressed their true feelings about her leaving. These letters were not for sending (indeed, we didn't even know where to send them) but for Holly and Dale's reworking of the painful events.

The next week Holly and Dale read their letters aloud. At first Dale's letter was formal and emotionally constricted, but later more passionate. Years of pent-up anger came tumbling out, and after the anger, sadness, and after the sadness, bad feelings about himself. He was a failure as a husband, he wasn't able to communicate clearly or to show affection. He blamed himself for his wife's leaving.

Holly listened closely to her Dad's letter and handed him Kleenex for the tears. She patted his arm and said, "It wasn't your fault, it was mine."

She read her letter, which, like Dale's, began in a formal, polite way and built up steam over time. Her first and strongest emotion was loss—her mother had chosen to leave and never see her again. She suspected that something must be wrong with her, some secret flaw she couldn't identify. She had grieved since it happened, unsure how to express or even acknowledge such painful feelings.

Ever since her mother left, she hated to be touched or praised by women. If a teacher patted her, she cringed. Instead of moving toward women for support, she tried to toughen herself so she wouldn't need it. She didn't like to visit girls at their homes. She got too jealous watching them with their mothers.

She blamed herself for her mother's abandonment. She was "a mouthy little kid." After her mother left, Holly stopped being mouthy, she almost stopped talking. She no longer trusted that words could help her.

Since her mother's abandonment, Lyle was the first person she let in emotionally. He gave her hope that she was lovable. He listened to her, held her and told her she was beautiful. When he left, the pain was horrible. It reminded her of her mother's leaving and convinced her that she was unworthy of the love of another human being.

At the end of that session, both Holly and Dale were crying. I realized that Holly and Dale desperately needed each other. They could sink or swim together. Neither of them felt lovable, and the only person who was close enough to change that basic feeling about themselves was the other. By making their relationship a loving one, they could prove to themselves that they were capable and worthy of love. In what I hoped would be a self-fulfilling prophecy, I said, "You two can teach each other how to show love."

That's what we worked on. Dale had been distant because of his own unprocessed pain and because of a lack of relationship skills. Indeed, this same lack of skills had probably cost him his marriage. Holly had been distant because she was abandoned. Her dad made it easy to stay distant. Prince was the perfect love object since he was a thousand miles away and totally inaccessible. She could love him without taking any risks.

Gradually Holly and Dale formed a caring relationship. They talked more about personal topics. For example, Holly asked about Dale's friends at work and he said he avoided them. He told her they read *Playboy* and talked about women in a way that made him uncomfortable. Holly told him about the way boys teased her at school and about her discomfort when boys touched her in the halls. That led them into a philosophical discussion of the relations between the sexes. They both had things to learn and teach.

Dale became a more involved parent. He limited himself to an hour of television a night and spent the rest of his time talking to Holly, looking at her homework or working on a hobby. He asked to see Holly's school papers and wanted reports on her day. Most teenagers would fight involvement at this late stage, but Holly was so lonely that she welcomed his attention. He wasn't a harsh critic and she learned to trust her dad with her failures as well as her successes. He turned out to be always on her side, supportive of whatever she did.

They went to a rock-and-roll concert at the city auditorium. Holly shared her songs with Dale and he offered to pay for guitar lessons. Her mother had a good voice and he hoped Holly had inherited that from her. Holly set her songs to music and began sharing them with a local band called Power Peach.

KLARA (15) AND KURT

The school counselor called me about Klara, who was flunking math. She said, "Klara has been falling through the cracks in our system for years. She's the kind of kid we tend to miss—well behaved, quiet and depressed. I noticed how thin she was last week when she came in with a truancy slip. I asked about her health and heard she hadn't been to a doctor in years. That's when I decided that she needed attention. She's not in a crisis, just a slow slide down. If we don't stop it, she'll drop out of school next year when she turns sixteen."

Klara came in with her father, Kurt. She was as the counselor had described—passive and demure. Kurt, a large bald man dressed in his work uniform, was an outspoken critic of psychotherapy. Since his wife died of cancer, he hated doctors. As he put it, "They take all your money and leave you with shit." Besides, he didn't think Klara needed help. "Hell, she keeps the house up fine. She does what she's told. She's not mouthy."

We talked about Klara's mother's death, when Klara was four. Klara could hardly remember her. She had a few of her things: her mother's wedding ring, her Bible and a fur cape that Kurt had given his wife as a fifth-year anniversary gift. She kept her picture on her dresser and had a letter her mother wrote to her that was to be read on her wedding day. In spite of being tempted, Klara hadn't read it yet.

On the topic of his wife's death, Kurt was originally gruff, but soon softened. His wife had been a "beautiful lady" who loved him and Klara "one hundred percent." He visited her grave regularly. He had no interest in dating other women as there was no one like her. As Kurt talked, his eyes grew moist, but he stopped himself from crying. He balled up his fists and got mad instead. "Why are we talking about this? Isn't school the issue today?"

I sensed that if Kurt cried in front of me he would be so humiliated that he'd never return. So I asked about grades. Kurt said, "Her grades aren't great, but so what? She'll get married and have a husband to support her."

I asked Klara why she agreed to come. She looked hesitantly at her father and said, "The counselor thought it would be a good idea."

I asked what she thought and she said, "I don't know really."

Klara admitted that she didn't like school. She never spoke in class because she was afraid she'd be teased if she said something stupid. She didn't think she was smart and didn't believe that studying would help. She had no extra-curricular activities. Aside from caring for her dad, she spent most of her time with her boyfriend.

"And primping," Kurt interrupted. "Klara spends hours in the bathroom getting herself fixed up for school."

The one subject she liked to discuss was her boyfriend, Phil, whom she had dated since eighth grade. She described their relationship as close. They didn't talk much or do much outside their homes; mostly he watched television. Both Phil and Kurt were sports fans and Klara would bring them popcorn and Cokes while they watched ball games.

I asked what Phil liked about her. She thought for a minute and said,

"He would say I'm the nicest girl he ever met. And he thinks I'm pretty. He can't stand fat girls and he thinks I have a good figure. He likes to be seen with me."

I felt pessimistic about this case. Already Kurt had announced he wouldn't pay for more than four sessions. I didn't have much time to help Klara fight her depression. She reminded me of a mannequin. She looked the way women are taught to look, and she acted the way she'd been taught to act. Devoid of liveliness, she was overly socialized in feminine behavior.

I wanted Klara to talk about her mother's death. I wanted to explore what she wanted, what she valued in herself and others, who she was. I hoped I could broaden her sense of possibilities. I hoped we could talk about her preoccupation with looking good rather than feeling good. I wanted her to stay in school.

I would need to be careful and not set her up for her dad's anger. He expected her to do as she was told. We would have to discuss when it was safe for her to be assertive. She would still have her chores to do, but perhaps Klara could formulate some new goals for herself.

I asked Klara to do one thing a day to make herself happy. She looked skeptical but agreed. As they left, Kurt said, "This wasn't as stupid as I thought it would be. I might come back, but don't get your hopes up."

I wished Kurt would come in alone. I wanted him to examine his assumptions about feminine and masculine behavior. His views of women were hurting his daughter, and his views of men were keeping him from dealing with his own grief and moving on. He looked frightened of losing control, which for him meant crying or admitting he was scared about Klara. Even though Kurt seemed set in his ways, I suspected that he might be willing to examine his life if properly approached. He loved his daughter even though he had a very limited sense of who she was or could be. I thought of his earlier experiences with doctors and I wanted this time to be different. Last time he lost his wife. This time I wanted to introduce him to his whole daughter.

As Kurt saw progress he relented and let Klara come beyond the four sessions. Klara was a shy, humble person, but like most people, she responded quickly to respect and interest in her opinions. We worked on a variety of issues. Klara managed pain the way her father did, by denial and repression, and my first goal was to teach her some new coping strategies.

I encouraged her to face rather than avoid things that scared her and to talk about rather than bury upset feelings. Like many oversocialized females, Klara had a hard time expressing anger. I asked her about times she was angry or upset and she talked in a low-key, tentative way. Little by little, Klara learned she could talk about feelings and neither of us died of shock.

As often happens, once negative feelings are expressed, clients recover their capacity for joy. Klara laughed some in sessions now, a lovely musical laugh. She reported enjoying experiences at school, with her dad and with Phil. Her grades didn't pick up, but the quality of her relationships improved. She talked more. One day she told me that she insisted that every other Sunday Phil take her out to eat or to the movies instead of watching televised sports with her dad.

Klara continued to care about her appearance, but our talks about lookism gave her a new perspective. She wanted to be valued for more than her appearance and she no longer let Phil make negative comments about heavy women.

Klara loved her bald, sexist dad and remained fiercely protective of him. I was careful not to say anything critical about Kurt, who was Klara's shelter from the storm. She wasn't ready, and maybe never would be, to examine her relationship with her father.

Kurt came in for one more session at the end of my work with his daughter. He said to me, "I thought this was a racket at first, but the proof's in the pudding. Klara's a hell of a lot better. No doubt about that."

He paused and said softly, "She laughs like her mother used to."

I offered to see him again, but he adamantly refused. "That's girl stuff. I'm fine." He thanked me for helping his daughter and gallantly ended our session by saying, "Not all doctors are money-grubbing quacks."

Chapter 7

DIVORCE

■

JULIA (14)

Jean, an animated woman dressed in a business suit, reported that her daughter had been arrested for being a minor in possession of alcohol. Julia, dressed in pink stretch pants, an oversized sweater and shark earrings, groaned and folded her arms across her chest. "I had one beer."

I listened as Jean explained their complicated family. Julia's parents had divorced two years ago after her father became involved with a younger woman. He had since married the younger woman and moved to a nearby town. They had a baby girl born three months ago. Since the birth of his new daughter, Julia's father hadn't seen Julia. He called a couple of times, but was busy with the new baby and his new wife. Jean hadn't even told him about Julia's arrest.

Jean had been the custodial parent since the divorce. She worked at an accounting firm and they'd scraped by on her earnings. Jean, Julia and Reynold, Julia's ten-year-old brother, had moved to a smaller house in a less expensive part of town. The children had to change schools and Julia had been cut off from her closest friends.

A year ago in Parents Without Partners, Jean had met Al, the owner of a small printing company. Right away she had liked his kindness and sense of humor. He liked her efficiency and common sense. For several months they met on Saturday nights for dinner and a movie.

They combined their children for some family picnics and miniature-golf outings. Three months ago they were married.

Jean, Julia and Reynold had moved again, into Al's home with his three boys. This fall Julia attended her third junior high in two years. Jean said, "Reynold hasn't had much trouble. He's a jock who found friends right away on the softball team. But the divorce hit at a bad time for Julia. She was just beginning seventh grade. At her first new school she was shy and didn't make friends. At her next school she made friends with the kids who were smoking and drinking. I'm sure her arrest is connected to all the changes."

I thought to myself that most teenagers, like plants, don't do well with moves.

Julia curled her feet under her and nestled into the couch. "I know Mom and Dad weren't getting along, but I was fine. I haven't been happy since the divorce."

She looked at her mother. "Al's not a bad guy—he's good to Mom—but I hate his sons. They're spoiled rotten. I have to pick up after them and do their dishes. Al lets them get away with murder. They're jerks."

"It's true that Julia does more than her share. Al's boys never have had chores. Al's a softy," Jean said.

"Most step-families need some counseling, especially if there are teenagers," I said. "Making a new family is so difficult that everyone needs a consultant."

Julia said, "For a long time I wished my parents would get back together. Now I just wish that Reynold and I could live alone with Mom. I don't like all the noise and mess at Al's."

Jean touched her daughter's arm. "You're not home very much."

"I try not to be," Julia said.

Jean said, "Last week Julia was busted at a party. Afterwards one of the mothers suggested we parents get together and make rules. We all work and no one is home after school to supervise. There are always empty houses available."

Julia said, "Mrs. Snyder's a creep. Don't you dare get involved in that. Everyone drinks. You don't know anything about it."

Jean sighed. "Kids are different now. I had a roller-skating party for Julia's eighth-grade birthday and it was an eye-opener. The kids talked filth. The rink had security people to check for drugs. Believe me, the rinks were different when I was a kid."

Julia said, "Of course things are different. Why do you treat me like they aren't? You have the same stupid rules for me that your mother had for you. Don't you understand that I can't live by those rules and have any friends?"

Jean looked hopelessly at me. "I want her to be safe."

Clearly Julia had too much to handle—her parents' divorce, the loss of her father, the new house, the new schools and the new stepfather and stepbrothers. Plus, she had all the issues that hit girls with puberty. Like many adolescent girls whose parents divorce, she turned to friends. She found a crowd who kept her away from home and gave her a sense of belonging. She used alcohol to forget.

Julia needed a place to talk about all of her losses. She needed to reconnect with her father. I suspected that she needed some guidance about sexuality, a drug and alcohol evaluation and maybe a support group for teen users. If she could sort through the pain she wouldn't need to medicate it away.

I recommended family therapy. The rules regarding housework should be fair. Al's boys could use more discipline. Jean agreed to discuss this with Al.

I asked Julia if she would like to come in alone. Julia uncurled her legs and looked hard at me. "Yes, as long as you don't lecture me."

I promised I wouldn't.

My own thinking about divorce has changed in the twenty years I've been a therapist. In the late 1970s I believed that children were better off with happy single parents rather than unhappy married parents. I thought divorce was a better option than struggling with a bad marriage. Now I realize that, in many families, children may not notice if their parents are unhappy or happy. On the other hand, divorce shatters many children. As one girl said when I asked her how she felt living with her dad and seeing her mother once a month, "I try not to think of it; it hurts too much. I try not to feel anything."

A Peruvian friend of mine who is studying in the United States commented on the number of children she knew in America whose parents were divorced. She said, "They are needier than Peruvian children. They have more material goods, but they all cry out for adult touch and attention."

Of course, some marriages are unworkable. Especially if there is abuse or addiction involved, sometimes the best way out of an impossible situation is the door. Adults have rights, and sometimes they must take care of themselves, even when it hurts their children. Living in homes with unhappy parents who have stayed together for the sake of the children is by no means ideal for anyone. But divorce often doesn't make parents happier. Certainly it overwhelms mothers and fathers, and it cuts many parents off from relationships with their children.

Many times marriages don't work because people lack relationship skills. Partners need lessons in negotiating, communicating, expressing affection and doing their share. With these lessons many marriages can be saved. And if these lessons aren't learned in the first marriage, they will have to be learned later or the next marriage will be doomed as well. So in the 1990s I try harder than I did in the 1970s to keep couples together and to teach them what they need to know to live a lifetime with another human being.

These last decades have been rough on families, and many have broken under the stress. Most adults experience at least one divorce, and many children spend some time in single-parent homes. Single-parent households are tough on everyone. Often the parents are chronically tired from "double shifts." They have no time for themselves—for exercise, friends, intellectual life or even sleep—and they often complain that their lives are not in balance. They are alone when it's time to make tough decisions about their children. When they must enforce rules and consequences, there's no one to back them up. Children in single-parent homes have no court of appeal when their one parent is tired, cranky or arbitrary. They miss the chance to observe in close quarters how couples function in relationships.

Divorces almost always make women poorer. Often families must move and teenagers find themselves in new schools surrounded by strangers. They have left their longtime friends, who could have helped them through this. Often they worry about money for clothes, cars and college.

Divorce is particularly tough for adolescents. Partly that's because of their developmental level and partly it's because teenagers require so much energy from parents. Teenagers need parents who will talk to them, supervise them, help them stay organized and support them when they are down. Divorcing parents often just don't have the energy to give. Adolescents feel an enormous sense of loss—of their parents, their families and their childhoods. And, unlike younger children, when they express their pain, they are likely to do it in dangerous ways.

Adolescents' immature thinking makes it difficult for them to process the divorce. They tend to see things in black-and-white terms and have trouble putting events into perspective. They are absolute in their judgments and expect perfection in parents. They are likely to be self-conscious about their parents' failures and critical of their every move. They have the expectation that parents will keep them safe and happy and are shocked by the broken covenant. Adolescents are unforgiving.

Just at a time when feeling different means feeling wrong, divorce makes teenagers feel different. If a parent wearing the wrong kind of shoes can humiliate a teenager, a parent who is divorcing causes utter shame. Teenagers are so egocentric that they think everyone knows about the divorce in all its details. They are ashamed of their families, which they see as uniquely dysfunctional.

Adolescence is a time when children are supposed to move away from parents who are holding firm and protective behind them. When the parents disconnect, the children have no base to move away from or return to. They aren't ready to face the world alone. With divorce, adolescents feel abandoned, and they are outraged at that abandonment. They are angry at both parents for letting them down. Often they feel that their parents broke the rules and so now they can too. They no longer give their parents moral authority. Instead they say, "How dare you tell me what to do when you've screwed up so badly."

Until late adolescence, children don't think of their parents as people with needs separate from their own. Rather they are seen as providers of care. Most teens aren't able to empathize with their parents and prefer their parents to be married even if they are unhappy. They find it frightening that parents can break their bonds to each other. If parent-parent bonds can be broken, so can parent-child bonds.

Often there's bitterness between the parents that makes it difficult for them to discipline their teenagers. Teens can and do manipulate divided parents. They pit them against each other or live with the one who has the fewest rules and the least supervision. Teenagers are not always good judges of what they need and often choose to live with the parent who promises to buy them the new stereo or take them on vacation. The parent who insists on schoolwork and chores is often the parent they avoid.

Legal actions, particularly custody battles, tear adolescents apart. Often they end up blaming both parents for the anguish they experience and so they have no one left to trust. They discount adults and rely only on peers for comfort and companionship.

Divorce is particularly difficult for teenage girls, who are already stressed by cultural forces. When their families break apart, they have too much coming at them too fast. Girls deal with this situation in various ways. Some get depressed and hurt themselves, either with suicide attempts or more slowly with alcohol and drugs. Some withdraw and sink deep within themselves to nurse their wounds. Many react by rebelling. Here are some stories of girls and how they dealt with divorce.

MYRA (14)

Lois called for an emergency appointment after she was hit by her daughter. That afternoon in my office she spoke softly, glancing at her daughter with every sentence. Her daughter, Myra, dark-haired and muscular, was much more outspoken. She interrupted, contradicted and insulted her mother at every juncture. Myra was good at blaming, and Lois was good at accepting blame. Watching the two, I could see how things might get violent.

Until two years ago, when her parents divorced, Myra led the life of a pampered only child. Her father was a banker and her mother was an audiologist. They lived in a small community a hundred miles from our city, where Myra was the biggest duck in the puddle. Her father's grandparents had been the founders of the town. Everyone knew and respected her family.

Then Lois went to a convention in Los Angeles, and when she came home she asked for a divorce. She had had an affair at the convention, but that wasn't really the issue. The affair made her realize that the marriage wasn't working, that things were wrong way beyond fixing. She announced that she wanted to move to a city where she could build a life of her own.

I looked at this small, shy woman and was amazed at her boldness.

Lois said, "I know the affair was wrong. I've apologized to Randy and to Myra, but the divorce was right for me. I have never been happier than this last year."

Myra groaned. "Yeah, but what about me and Dad? You ruined our lives."

Lois spread her palms upward in a hopeless gesture and looked beseechingly at me. I could tell that she wanted to defend herself but felt too guilty. I asked Myra to tell me what happened after the divorce.

"At first I stayed with Dad, but that didn't work out. He spent all his time at the bank and the Legion Club."

She glared at Lois, who continued the story. "Myra wasn't getting much supervision. Her grades dropped and she skipped school. Randy couldn't control her. He had always left the discipline to me. Finally he gave up and sent her here."

Lois looked at her daughter. "I love Myra. After the separation I tried to stay close, but she was too angry. When Randy brought Myra down, I was eager to get back together but also afraid. I had my own life for the first time, a good job and friends. I didn't want everything screwed up by Myra's anger."

"Nobody wanted me." Myra tossed her black hair. "I'm pissed. I miss our big house. Now we're in a cramped apartment. I miss my boyfriend. I hate Mom's friends and the kids at school. This whole thing is an enormous fucking drag."

Lois said, "It's hard for her. She knew everyone in town and was involved with everything—music, sports and the church. The city is a big adjustment. I thought we could work things out, but recently Myra has been hitting me." She showed me a bruise on her left arm. "I don't know how to handle this."

Myra scowled. "I didn't hit you, I pushed you. You always over-react. I never hit you."

We spent the rest of that first hour working out a contract about hitting. It was agreed that if Myra hit her mother again she would be grounded for a week. Lois left feeling relieved, while Myra left angry that I had been influenced by her mother.

The next week I saw Myra alone. Like many teenagers, she was much more pleasant when her mother wasn't around. She said that she hadn't hit her mom since we talked and then quickly changed the subject to the divorce. She had hated living with her dad, who was depressed and self-absorbed. She had hated eating frozen pizzas and potpies and doing the laundry herself.

She had missed Lois, who was a good homemaker. Even though Lois had worked, she always had time for Myra. She helped her with lessons, sewed school costumes, decorated for holidays and fixed gourmet meals. She arranged parties that everyone in town loved. In short, Lois had spoiled Myra and her father.

Myra said, "After Mom left, there were nights when I sat alone in our big old house, looked at pictures of Dad, Mom and me. I cursed Mom for being selfish and breaking up our family."

As we talked, things seemed a little less simple, even to Myra. Her father was financially successful but hard to live with. He had expected Lois to take care of the house and of Myra. He drank after work and some days he came home boisterous, other days sullen. He directed most of his anger at Lois, who wasn't good at standing up for herself. Watching her mother, Myra decided that she would never take anyone's bad treatment. Still she was angry when her mother made the same decision.

Myra said, "One reason I'm mad at her now is that she was such a great mom when I was little."

"What happened after your mother announced she wanted out?"

"Dad and I worked on her. Dad told everyone about her affair. She didn't get alimony. Both sides of the family pressured her. She about had a nervous breakdown."

I said, "Your mom sounds like she can be as stubborn as you."

We discussed Myra's current social life. She had been popular in her hometown, but here she was a loner, going from a school of 225 students to one of 3,000. Even if she wanted to make friends, it would have been tough. But she didn't want to. Myra particularly missed her boyfriend, who had been her main confidant. He wrote her for a while, but by now he had another steady girlfriend.

Myra had all the ordinary vulnerabilities of early adolescents, plus the pain of losing her family. Her trust level was zero, and she was too angry and discouraged to make friends. I was amazed she talked to me, and when she left I congratulated her on her willingness to trust a new adult.

Our next session began with Myra describing a blowup with Lois. She shouted when she told me about her mother's refusal to buy her a computer.

"She says she can't afford it, but I know she could borrow the fucking money."

I asked her if she had any other feelings besides anger about the incident.

"I'm embarrassed. I know it's wrong to call her a bitch. She is a bitch, but I shouldn't call her that." She said, "I want to kill her I get so mad."

We talked about anger control. I recommended she punch a pillow the next time she felt angry. I also suggested that she jog until she had "outrun" her anger. It's hard to be angry when physically exhausted. I encouraged her to write. "Write everything you can think of. Get those feelings out of your chest and onto a piece of paper. Then you can throw the paper away."

Myra brought me her writing. At first it was pure rage—her mother was the source of all pain in her life and virtually all evil in the universe. But gradually as she wrote the anger softened. She began to write about the issues that the divorce raised for her—the loss of her life as she knew it, missing her boyfriend, her fear of a new school, her concern about being liked and the lack of trust that relationships could work.

I was pleased when the writing became more Myra-focused. She had been so obsessed with her mother that she hadn't cared for herself. Too much anger, like too much compliance, stops growth. It's impossible for blamers to take responsibility for their lives and get on with it. But now, after several months, Myra acknowledged that her mother had a right to her own life and had not been placed on the planet to meet her needs. She had expected her mother to live for her but now she could see that this wasn't realistic. It set both of them up to fail in certain ways. It kept Lois from having a life and Myra from learning she could make herself happy. Myra still had angry times, but her temper tantrums were over. Between arguments, Lois and Myra had some good times together.

As Myra's anger waned, she had more energy for her own life. She mourned her past, but then she set some goals for her future. She improved her abysmal grades. She exercised and even considered going out for track. She fought back her fears and talked to kids in her classes.

AMY (12)

Joan brought Amy in for counseling because she and Chuck were divorcing. Last year Amy had been lively, lighthearted and fun-loving. This year she was quiet, withdrawn and serious.

Joan was an articulate schoolteacher who was venomous on the subject of her husband, Chuck. He was evil incarnate, the Adolf Hitler of husbands and without a good motive to his credit. She poured out her anger while Amy shrank deeper into my couch. Amy looked like she was evaporating as her mother talked, her serious little face grew smaller, her body more childlike.

Joan explained how she and Chuck had tried counseling, but that Chuck, even though he was a therapist himself, wouldn't cooperate. She had done her best, but he sabotaged her efforts to save the family. And now that she had filed, he was doing everything he could to destroy her life and turn Amy against her.

Joan listed her concerns about Amy. She had lost five pounds since May. She wasn't communicating and was avoiding friends and activities. Joan finished by saying, "I think she's depressed by her dad's behavior."

I asked for examples of Chuck's behavior. "Do you have all day?" Joan asked. "We're fighting for custody and he keeps pressuring and bribing Amy to choose him. He puts me down constantly and he sets me up to be angry. Last week he called to change visitation three times. He disappoints Amy by not coming when he says he will."

Weakly Amy protested, "He comes when he says."

Joan continued as if she hadn't heard. "We have psychologists evaluating Amy for the custody decision, but I wanted someone to help her with the stress of the divorce."

With some reservations I asked to talk to Amy alone. In the last few months she'd talked to attorneys, judges and psychologists and her trust for adults was at an all-time low. From her point of view, I was just one more adult who was supposed to be helping but wasn't.

I asked how her summer was going and she answered so softly I had to ask her to repeat herself. She said, "It's rained a lot and I haven't been able to swim as much as I like to."

I thought she was giving careful answers to me and probably to everyone else as well. She'd learned that what she didn't say didn't get her in trouble. I talked to her about divorce, how it stresses out kids and makes them feel alone and weird. I said that I'd seen lots of kids who were sad and mad about their parents' divorce. I told her about other kids in her predicament and I put happy endings on the stories. Amy relaxed as I talked and asked me questions about the kids in the stories. But when I asked about her, she resumed her frozen face.

I said, "Most kids hate to choose which parent to live with."

"Both of them want me and I hate to hurt their feelings." Amy shook her head miserably. "Besides, some days I hate Dad and some days I hate Mom. Some days I hate them both."

I asked about living arrangements. "Mom and I still live at home for now. Dad has an apartment in the town where he works. I don't know anyone there and I can't stand his place. Mom says that she'll have to move though, especially if Dad gets me."

She sat up straight and said, "I don't want to live with either of them right now. They're both screwed up. I want to run away from home."

We talked about running away—its dangers and appeals. Amy, like most twelve-year-olds, wanted to run to family. Older kids want to go to the coast or to move in with friends. Amy dreamed of going to her grandmother's house in Minnesota. She asked for her parents' permission, but both had wanted her with them this summer.

Once she started, Amy loved to talk. She told me about starting her period at her dad's house. She had supplies at her mother's, but nothing at her dad's, and she had to ask him to go buy her pads. Later her mom got in a fight with him because he hadn't brought her home. She'd wanted to share Amy's first period. As Amy said, "She thought it should be a mother-daughter thing."

She told me that both parents tried to buy her love with presents. "If I wanted to, I could ask for a racing bike or television right now." Worst of all was how her parents talked about each other. "They both pretend they don't rag on each other, but they drop hints all the time that the other one is the craziest, meanest person they know."

Her biggest worry was starting junior high next year. If she lived with Dad, it would be a new school where she had no friends. If she lived with Mom, all the kids would know her parents got divorced. She said, "I don't know how I'll get my homework done. Mom helps me with math and Dad knows French."

She told me how ashamed she was of the divorce. She had tried unsuccessfully to keep it secret and had been embarrassed when kindly adults offered her sympathy. She avoided her friends because they might bring it up. She was sure she had the strangest parents in America.

I said, "They have lots of competition for strange, believe me." She smiled for the first time that day, and I caught a glimmer of what the pre-divorce Amy must have been like.

I ended the session by calling Joan in and suggesting that Amy go spend a few weeks with her grandmother while the adults worked things out. After she returned, we'd talk again and maybe Amy could be in a divorce group for young teens.

Joan said, "Chuck will never agree with this." I offered to call him. Chuck was immediately angry when he heard I'd seen Amy. I talked to him about releases, consent to treatment and confidentiality. Then, after he calmed down, I asked him how Amy was doing. He said, "Since the separation, she's a different kid." Of course, he had his own theory about Amy. "Confidentially," he said, "Joan is the biggest bitch on the planet."

I listened patiently while he bad-mouthed Joan. As he talked, I thought how miserable these two people had made each other and how right it was that they divorce. But unfortunately, because they had Amy, they couldn't really separate. In fact, in some ways they would need to negotiate and coordinate efforts even more now that they lived in separate households. And the same things that destroyed the marriage could keep them from adequately parenting Amy over the next few years.

I reminded myself that underneath the parents' anger was pain. No doubt they both needed guidance sorting through this failed marriage. But my job was to help Amy. I feared that unless these parents settled down, Amy was at high risk for depression and, perhaps later, delinquency. I wasn't sure these parents were capable of putting Amy's needs first and working as a team, but I had nothing to lose in trying to help them do this.

I suggested Chuck and Joan come in for some divorce counseling. I told Chuck that it's better to talk about Amy in therapy than in an attorney's office. It's cheaper and non-adversarial. Perhaps because he himself was a psychologist, he had to agree.

Chuck said he was willing, but he doubted Joan would do it. I offered to talk to her. I could see Amy's drawn face as I hung up the phone. Maybe while she was at her grandmother's I could have Chuck and Joan in for some sessions. Maybe by the time she came home and started junior high, they would have started to do what adults need to do in situations like this, which is to put their own pain aside and help their child.

JASMIN (13)

Long before I met Jasmin, I'd seen her parents in marital therapy. Joe and Georgeanne were good, likable people, but their marriage wasn't working. They had married right out of high school because Georgeanne was pregnant. Joe was an extrovert and an excitement seeker, while Georgeanne was quiet and liked routines. She seemed always to be in the shadows when Joe was around. On the other hand, Joe spent many nights at home when he would have preferred a social outing. They had compromised for years—probably they'd compromised too often and too much.

They did all the things couples do to save their marriages. They saw a therapist, tried communication exercises, read self-help books and went on dates and a second honeymoon. But the spark was gone. Without ever really arguing, they were ready to call it quits.

Now they wanted help divorcing. Both of them loved Jasmin and wanted to keep the divorce from damaging her. They weren't sure what to tell her about the divorce or how to handle living arrangements and money. I suggested that together they give Jasmin a brief but honest account of why they were divorcing. I encouraged them to make it clear that they both loved her and would keep on caring for her. Also, I recommended that they keep Jasmin's life as routine as possible. Then I asked to see Jasmin.

Jasmin was small and blonde like her mother, talkative like her father. When I first met her she'd known the news for three days. She had been stunned by their announcement. I asked how she felt when her parents told her the news. Jasmin said, "At first I thought it was a joke. Then when I caught on they were serious, I wouldn't even listen to them. I put my hands over my ears and ran out of the room."

She looked out my window. "I still think they'll get back together. This is just a phase they are going through—what do you call it? Middle-age crisis. But in the meantime, they shouldn't do this. They don't even fight. We have fun together."

I asked her if she'd told her friends yet. She nodded her head yes. "I told my best friend."

She told me, "She's trying to understand, but she can't. I got mad at her yesterday because I was jealous. She has a family and I don't.

"I haven't told any other kids, but word gets around quick. Dad moved out yesterday and there was a U-Haul truck parked in our driveway."

Jasmin had all the usual worries: Where would she live? Would she see both her parents? Would there be enough money? Would she be forced to choose?

She said, "I thought divorce was what happened to other families— you know, families where the dad drank or beat the kids. I can't believe my parents would do it. Just last week Dad brought roses home to Mom."

I recommended she attend a divorce group for teenagers and she agreed. We talked about what else she could do to deal with her feelings. Jasmin said, "The main thing that helps is my cat. I lie on my bed with Orange and listen to music. I tell her everything."

After the initial visit, I alternated sessions between Jasmin and her parents. I talked to Joe and Georgeanne about living arrangements and joint custody. They were both struggling with their own issues but remained committed to helping Jasmin through it all. Joe found an apartment in the neighborhood so that Jasmin could walk between homes and so that her friends and school were handy.

For more fractious couples, joint custody doesn't work. All the issues that sabotaged a marriage also sabotage joint custody. In worst-case scenarios, families with joint custody can get trapped in years of limbo, with parents neither together nor apart and children torn into pieces by the fighting.

But Joe and Georgeanne were low-key and rational and they could agree on basic issues. They could communicate about Jasmin without fighting. They did have some differences about rules and expectations, but that was to be expected. Jasmin could learn to behave differently in different houses. What was important was that the parents not criticize or second-guess each other.

Both felt okay about their time with Jasmin. They tried to make it as ordinary as possible. Jasmin had chores, schoolwork, orthodontist's appointments and outings with both parents. Money was tight, but money had never been a big deal to this family. They all knew how to have fun without spending a lot. Joe and Jasmin hiked and played sand volleyball. Georgeanne took Jasmin to art galleries and museums.

Like all adults, Joe and Georgeanne were needy after the divorce. Georgeanne spent six months on antidepressants. Joe got so lonely in his apartment that he thought he'd go crazy. But somehow they managed to keep their own pain from interfering too much with their parenting. Both of them were grown-ups in the truest sense of the word.

I saw Jasmin once a month for the first year. In addition, she attended a support group. The kids helped each other talk about feelings and cheered each other on through the tough times. She also had her true friend and her beloved Orange.

At our last session we talked about the year. Jasmin looked relaxed and vibrant as she talked, very different from the shaken and shocked girl of a year ago. I admired the way Joe and Georgeanne had stayed emotionally committed to Jasmin.

Jasmin liked her living arrangements. At her mom's, her bedroom was old-fashioned and filled with mementos from the past. Her bedroom at her dad's was Art Deco with built-in bookcases. She had a carrying case for Orange and took her to both homes. She said, "Wherever I go, Orange goes."

Still she nurtured a small hope that her parents would get back together. She was sad about the divorce, but no longer mad. She said, "They tried to make it work and they couldn't. I know my parents are just people and make mistakes like everyone else."

She acknowledged that both her parents seemed happier. "Mom's more outgoing now that Dad's not around. She's stronger than I thought she was."

She wrinkled up her face. "Dad's dating someone. I'm not ready for that, and I try to avoid her."

She was pleased that her parents got along fine. They both attended her events. Jasmin put it this way: "They like to get together and brag about me. They love me and that gives them a bond."

One of the things that helps saplings survive the hurricane is the root system. With divorce, the root system splits apart. Girls are oftentimes unsupported, at least temporarily. They face the strong winds without the support of a home base, and they are at risk of blowing over.

Still, divorce is not always avoidable and it's not always a mistake. Parents and girls have some control over the effects of divorce. Girls are likely to do well if they come from families in which the parents have a working relationship, in which the girl feels loved by both parents and in which the family is not economically depressed. Girls do better if they are neither manipulated nor allowed to manipulate, if they have adequate supervision and a safe environment.

Jasmin is a good example of a girl whose parents handled things well. Julia had a tougher time because of all the step-family issues and the emotional loss of her father. Amy, whose parents are bitterly feuding, had the hardest time. Myra learned that her mother is a person with a life independent of Myra's. In the years following the divorce, she became responsible for herself. Divorce, like all experiences that are properly handled, can be an opportunity for growth.

Chapter 8

WITHIN THE
HURRICANE—DEPRESSION

■

MONICA (15)

Monica was brought to my office by her kindhearted and slightly out-of-touch parents. Born when her mother was approaching menopause, Monica was an only child. Her parents were concerned about her lack of friends and her depression. Her dad thought Monica had no friends because, with her IQ of 165, she was too smart for other kids. Mom thought it was because their family was different. The parents were both professors, bookworms and political radicals. Monica hadn't been exposed to many common childhood experiences, such as television, Disneyland, camping or sports.

Her mother laughed. "We're an odd family. We talk about philosophy and science at dinner. We know more about chaos theory than we do about movie stars."

Monica said flatly, "It's my looks. I'm a pimply whale."

Monica's parents were eager to turn her over to someone younger and more knowledgeable about teens. I agreed to meet with Monica and discuss "peer relations." Monica wasn't optimistic, but she was desperate.

Most of her social experience was on computer networks. Nightly she used her computer modem to communicate with teenagers all over the country. They didn't know that she was chubby. On the modem she could use her wit and intelligence to make friends she would never have to meet face-to-face.

Under her drab, tentlike clothes and depressed demeanor, Monica had real personality. She delivered insightful comments about her situation with a wry twist. She had the social scene down. She said, "All five hundred boys want to go out with the same ten anorexic girls." She said, "I'm a good musician, but not many guys are looking for a girl that plays great Bach preludes."

"Boys get teased if they even talk to me," she moaned. Most boys treated her as if she were covered with invisible ink. A few actually harassed her. One boy called her the Killer Whale and pretended he was afraid she'd smash up against him. Her Spanish lab partner couldn't look at her without smirking.

Monica had given up on girls too. She told of sitting with all these "tiny girls who were on diets and complaining how fat they were. If they think they're fat, they must view me as an elephant." Some girls giggled about her and teased her. Most just chose prettier friends. No one was all that eager to be seen with her on Saturday nights.

Monica had more perspective on her problems than most girls her age, but unfortunately insight does not take away pain. She told me ruefully that she hated her fat body and hence, herself. She showed me her poems, which were full of despair about her large, unlovable body. She said, "Let's face it, the world isn't exactly waiting for girls like me."

She'd resisted the culture's definitions of what was valuable in girls, but she was tired. She said, "When I walk down the halls I feel like a hideous monster. I understand my parents' point that looks aren't that important in adulthood, but I'm not in adulthood."

I encouraged Monica to fight her depression by exercising regularly. Monica said that she came from "a long line of slugs." She agreed to break tradition and walk and bike. She chose these activities because she could do them alone and without wearing a swimsuit.

At first she had trouble. She told me, "I hate to sweat. Ten minutes out and I'm red in the face and sweating like a marathon runner." Once, when red-faced and panting, she biked by a tennis court and some guys pointed at her and laughed. She thought of a million excuses not to exercise, but she managed to make her goal of three times a week.

She also decided to fix herself up and bought some "semi-punk" clothes. She had her hair cut by someone who knew what they were doing and started wearing a little makeup.

She respected the fact that her parents were not big consumers of the mass culture. She said, "In some ways it's been good. I wasn't exposed to all these messages that women were sex objects and that bodies were what mattered. But in some ways it's been bad. I wasn't prepared for real life."

I asked her to elaborate. She told me, "I guess I thought we'd all sit around and discuss books we'd read. I was shocked by how superficial everyone was, how into looks."

We talked about what kinds of relationships Monica wanted. She wanted to be appreciated for her wit and her musical gifts. She wanted to be seen as a person, not a dress size, and she wanted friends who cared more about her ideas than her weight.

I suggested we start slowly. Rather than worrying about popularity, we focused on making a few new friends. Monica liked the idea, but was hesitant about the actions required to carry it out. She'd been rejected so often that she was reluctant to take more risks.

Because she was a Suzuki viola student, I used the Suzuki method as a metaphor for how we would work. Dr. Suzuki believed that any student could learn to play the most difficult classical works. All that was necessary was that the steps be small and the practice regular. Thus a small child practices holding the bow, touching the bow to the strings, curving her fingers correctly and playing a note beautifully. Eventually this child will play a Vivaldi concerto. We could do the same things with social experience. Eventually small steps would lead her to a fuller and richer social life.

Monica pushed herself—to speak in class and to smile in the halls. It was scary because sometimes she was rewarded, other times scorned. In spite of her talents and intellect, she had feelings like everyone else. Rejection stung. I encouraged her to focus on her successes instead of her failures and to view her occasional rejections as stones in the path to a healthy social life. She learned to walk around them.

Monica joined the writing and political clubs at her school. One day she announced to me that she was "tearing up the Young Democrats with her political satire." Another day she said she'd been elected secretary of the Writers' Club. "It's a job reserved for terminal geeks," she said proudly.

I encouraged her to think of boys not as dates, but as friends. Monica selected a sensitive poet from her writing club. She shyly tried a joke on him and he laughed. He began joking with her. After a few weeks he offered to let her see his poetry.

At the same time that she made some friends, she remained aware that there were many students who would never give her a chance. She said, "I can see people look me over, size me up as unattractive and look away. I am not a person to them."

Monica came in most of her sophomore year. She was a large, big-boned person who gradually became physically fit. She actually began to enjoy exercise in spite of all her predictions to the contrary.

She, like most adolescent girls who do not fit our cultural definitions of beautiful, needed a lot of support to make it through this time. Her self-esteem crumbled as she experienced taunts and rejections. Still Monica built some friendships that held. She spent time with her poet friend and a few others. She still enjoyed communicating with teenagers around the country by computer modem, but it was no longer her primary social scene. She could actually go out on Saturday nights, an experience that helped her depression enormously.

Monica had found a niche in an alien environment. She was happier, but still aware of how tough life was going to be for her. She knew that she would never be a pretty package and that many guys were intimidated by her smarts. She knew that some people were so put off by her plain appearance that they never gave her personality a chance.

She made a good adjustment to a bad situation. She didn't deny her brightness or musical talents so that she could fit in, but she developed some skills for diffusing the tension her gifts created. She used humor to diffuse some of her pain about being chubby.

Monica was lucky in that even though the culture was hostile to her development, she had many resources of her own. Her life had exposed her to ideas not explored by popular culture—she had some perspective on her experience. Her parents were by no means agents of the culture. Both were feminists who decried the narrowness of women's roles and their lack of public power. They did all they could to help her through adolescence—music lessons, a bicycle, new clothes and therapy. They encouraged Monica to be true to herself and resist the message that she got from peers. They knew she was wonderful.

Monica had a mild case of depression which has many manifestations. It makes some young women sluggish and apathetic, others angry and hate-filled. Some girls manifest their depression by starving themselves or carving on their bodies. Some withdraw and go deep within themselves, and some swallow pills. Others drink heavily or are promiscuous. Whatever the outward form of the depression, the inward form is the grieving for the lost self, the authentic girl who has disappeared with adolescence. There's been a death in the family.

There are numerous ways in which this death occurs. Some may destroy their true selves in an effort to be socially acceptable. Others strive to be fully feminine and fail. They aren't pretty enough or popular enough in just the right ways at the right times. Others make the sacrifices necessary to be fully feminine, even as they are aware of the damage they are inflicting upon themselves. They know they have sold out and blame themselves for their decision. They have chosen a safer path, but it's a path with no real glory. When they lose their subjective fix on the universe, they are adrift and helpless, their self-esteem hostage to the whims of others.

Some girls are depressed because they have lost their warm, open relationship with their parents. They have loved and been loved by people whom they now must betray to fit into peer culture. Furthermore, they are discouraged by peers from expressing sadness at the loss of family relationships—even to say they are sad is to admit weakness and dependency.

All girls experience pain at this point in their development. If that pain is blamed on themselves, on their own failures, it manifests itself as depression. If that pain is blamed on others—on parents, peers or the culture—it shows up as anger. This anger is often mislabeled rebellion or even delinquency. In fact, anger often masks a severe rejection of the self and an enormous sense of loss.

Depression is not an absolute quantity, but rather a matter of degree. If we picture depression on a continuum, at one extreme would be severe depression with some biochemical basis and disturbed family functioning. At the other end of the continuum would be ordinary adolescent misery. At the severe extreme, I think of a client whose family history was filled with depression and alcohol abuse, who had an alcoholic father and psychotically depressed mother. When she hit adolescence she had neither internal nor external resources to support her. She ended up on medication and in the hospital for several months. At the other extreme are psychologically healthy girls, such as Monica, who suffer as they catch on to the diminished roles women are offered. Most girls suffer depression somewhere between these two extremes.

Adolescence is a time when development and culture put enormous stress on girls. So many things are happening at once that it's hard to label and sort experiences into neat little boxes. And there are many casualties. For example, a girl who is suffering from a mild case of adolescent misery may try to kill herself, not because her life as a totality is so painful, but because she is impulsive, reactive and unable to put small setbacks in perspective. Some girls are suicidal because of biochemical factors, some because of trauma and others because of the confusion and difficulty of the times. Obviously they need different kinds of attention, but all are potentially dangerous to themselves and must be taken seriously.

CINDY (14)

I first heard about Cindy from her school counselor, who said she seemed to be suffering from "failure to thrive." She wasn't growing physically, socially, emotionally or intellectually. Indeed, even her baby teeth weren't falling out. She wandered about her classroom as if in a dream. Cindy had few internal or external resources. She had no perspective on herself other than what she was told by her critical parents and peers. At a time when most adolescents are involved with peer culture, she had no positive relationships with kids her age.

The counselor hadn't been able to involve Cindy's parents with the school. They worked at a truck stop and claimed to be too busy to come to staff meetings. The one time the mother had come to school, when Cindy was sick and needed to be taken home, the counselor had smelled alcohol on her breath. I asked about other resources. "There is no other family that we know of. Cindy is in a special class with two girls her age and they ignore her."

I felt discouraged before I even met the family, but I agreed to try to help. A week later Delores and Cindy sat on my couch, a study in contrasts. While Delores was heavy and energetic, Cindy was small and childlike with tiny motionless hands. She hugged an old blue car coat to her chest as we talked.

Delores said, "Joe couldn't come. It's crazy at work and he doesn't believe in this stuff anyway. And don't count on me coming in regular. I've got work myself. Cindy is the one with problems."

Delores had a litany of complaints: Cindy didn't do her homework or chores. She wouldn't talk to people or make friends. She was sullen and sulky.

I asked Cindy what she thought, and she agreed that her mom was right.

Her slow movements and apathy clearly indicated depression. I thought of those monkeys isolated from their mothers in a famous psychology experiment. I remembered their haunting pictures in textbooks: small, sad monkeys embracing their towel mothers. Cindy's posture and eyes reminded me of those monkeys.

I wanted to run from this seemingly hopeless situation, but Cindy's eyes kept me from saying no. I wanted to hug her, to take her out for a hot fudge sundae and to see if I could make her laugh.

I saw Cindy alone and gradually we got acquainted. Rarely had I known anyone with a more emotionally impoverished life. She woke up after her parents left for the truck stop, dressed, rode the bus to school and sat quietly through her school day. Some days she spoke only to her teacher and then rode the school bus home. When Cindy arrived home she fed the dog, fixed herself a frozen TV dinner or potpie and watched television till bedtime. She liked the Disney and shopping channels.

Once she was so lonely that she called the shopping channel and pretended to buy a garnet ring, but she got in trouble for that and never tried again. Usually her mom called home about eight to check on her. Then Delores and Joe hit the bars. Usually they came in long after Cindy was in bed.

At school she was in the worst category a girl could be in: She was a slow learner, shy and dressed in K Mart clothes. She had no older siblings to look out for her, no parent advocate or best friend to protect her. She was largely ignored by the other kids.

Cindy told me all this slowly over the course of several sessions. We talked about her beloved dog, Laddie. I asked about her school papers, her teacher and her time with her parents. When, during our fourth session, she left her "huggable" blue car coat in the waiting room, I took that as a sign of progress.

At my suggestion Cindy wrote down three things she was proud of each day and brought those in to share. She read me the lists: "I made my bed, did my dishes, took Laddie for a walk, remembered to turn off the lights when I went to bed, turned in my math paper." I congratulated her on every victory.

I invited the parents in for a session. Joe, a big man who smelled of gasoline and tobacco, told me that Cindy was fine just as she was. He didn't see the point of getting "her head worked on." He said, "No offense, but I personally don't believe in this shit."

Delores was only slightly more promising. She was willing to discuss Cindy, but grew uneasy when the topic was her or Joe. She didn't want to discuss her drinking or long hours away from home. But when I asked about Cindy's birth and health history, Delores' voice grew husky with emotion. She said, "I drank when I was carrying her. That was before we knew about fetal alcohol syndrome. I'm to blame for her being retarded."

I handed her some Kleenex and watched as she wiped her red eyes. I said, "What's important is the future. Will you help Cindy now?"

Delores looked at Joe, who shrugged his shoulders. She said, "I'll come once a month if you think it will help."

I wasn't sure it would help, but I wanted to try. Cindy was in desperate need of emotional nourishment. This seemed a case where a little attention might go a long way.

Cindy loved our sessions. She brought me her school papers and pictures of Laddie. Soon she was chatting happily to me. I read her children's books, gave her small gifts, told her jokes and listened to stories about her week. I helped her set small goals for herself and cheered her on whenever she met them.

I asked the counselor to take Cindy out to lunch once a month. I encouraged Cindy's teacher to get involved. She encouraged the other two girls in Cindy's class to include her in some of their activities and also arranged for a student volunteer to spend one period each day with Cindy, sometimes helping her with homework, but other times just visiting. The volunteer was a good-hearted girl who occasionally invited Cindy to her house for dinner.

We all encouraged Cindy to join an activity. She thought about it for weeks, but finally she decided on the Home Economics Club. Soon she was telling me about making chocolate cake and place mats, about taking measurements for a dress and arranging flowers.

Delores came in monthly and grudgingly admitted that Cindy was doing better. As Cindy became happier and more involved with school, Delores began to enjoy her more. She was proud of her cooking and sewing. She agreed to take Cindy to the fabric store and help her select cotton prints for her sewing projects.

Cindy's baby teeth began to fall out and she grew two inches in the first three months of therapy. She began showing some signs of puberty. Because happiness is largely a matter of contrasts, soon Cindy was happy. Her world had changed from one in which no one would listen to her to one in which a teacher, school counselor, volunteer and therapist would listen. She no longer carried her car coat with her.

When therapy stopped, Cindy gave me a pot holder with the words "God Bless Our Happy Home" embroidered on the front. I gave her a box of stationery and stamps and told her to write. She sends me carefully printed notes. Laddie is still her best friend at home. At school, her volunteer helps with her home economics projects.

The counselor has kept up regular meetings with Cindy. Periodically she calls to say that Cindy is growing physically and doing okay at school. She is more inclined to smile and talk to other kids. She laughs in the lunchroom and volunteers for school outings and projects. She says the parents haven't changed; in fact, their drinking seems worse. Recently the father was arrested for driving while intoxicated. She is considering reporting this family to child protective services.

PENELOPE (16)

Penelope was inundated with many of the blessings that Cindy had been denied. She made straight As with little effort at her private prep school. She was tall, tanned and regal in her expensive outfits and stylish shoes. She was a member of the country club clique and the school's prize-winning debate team. Penelope had been to Europe twice and on an African photo safari. Every fall her mother took her to Chicago to buy clothes, and every summer she attended the finest camps in the Rockies. Yet she was a "poor little rich girl" who came to me after an almost successful suicide attempt.

Penelope walked into my office dressed in a white tennis outfit and carrying her racket. She fanned herself and made the exaggerated motions of someone who is hot and out of breath. I asked why she was in my office.

"I took some pills and the dumb doctor at the emergency room wouldn't release me unless I had a therapy appointment."

"Your mother told me that you almost died."

Penelope dropped her mouth open in a look of mock amazement. "No way. I was sick but they released me the next day."

"Why did you do it?"

"I was upset with my parents. I want a car for my birthday. Nothing expensive, just a Mazda or a Honda Accord. They wouldn't buy me one."

She slammed her fist into the chair. "They have plenty of money. They are just saying no to teach me a lesson. I hate them."

"Tell me about your parents."

"They expect me to do chores and clean my room. That's utterly stupid. Mom sits on her fat butt all day and hires a housekeeper to do her work. So why should I have to work?"

Penelope had a common rich kid's problem—she expected to be given everything she wanted. Kids from more modest homes learn early that they can't get everything they want—their parents can't afford it. But I sensed that there was more going on than just the money, and I asked her to talk more about her parents.

She sighed. "They don't get along. Dad works all the time. He doesn't come home unless he has to—for clean clothes and a shower. Mom hates him, but she wants his money."

She ran her hands through her glossy brown hair. "Mom gets back at Dad for being gone so much. When he was away last Thanksgiving, she bought herself a diamond bracelet."

Penelope seemed to be following in her mother's footsteps. She was investing her emotions in objects, not people, and settling for merchandise instead of love. She had not learned to value relationships and was using money to keep score. With the storms of adolescence, this superficial way of processing reality wasn't adequate. Penelope needed more support and a new way of viewing her own experiences. Nice clothes and cars don't get girls through adolescence. I wanted to help Penelope find some more sustaining values.

Mother Teresa says that Americans suffer a greater poverty than the people of India. Americans suffer the poverty of loneliness. Penelope was a good example of that kind of poverty. She's caught between parents who dislike each other in a home without nourishing values. She lived her life without any real emotional connections to others and lacked many of the qualities that are necessary to any abiding happiness. Not getting what she wanted made her utterly miserable. She had no appreciation of others and she was self-centered. Penelope hadn't learned that happiness comes not from using others, but from being useful.

We ended our first session by talking about her goals. True to form, she wanted to be a corporate lawyer like her dad and make a lot of money. She wanted a Swiss chalet, closets full of designer clothes and a yacht.

Surprisingly, Penelope was willing to reschedule. I asked her, "Why are you coming back?"

She said, "You listen to what I have to say. It's sort of interesting."

I said, "Think what you would want on your epitaph and tell me next time."

Penelope arrived with an epitaph that she'd heard her dad quote. "The girl with the most toys wins in the end."

I laughed and told her I suspected that underneath she was deeper and more caring than she pretended. In fact, I even suspected that she was looking for love.

Her carefully arranged face fell and she was quiet.

I pressed on. "What are you feeling?"

"Why are you asking me these corny questions?"

"I want to understand what's important to you."

"Fame," she said. "No, I was kidding. I really meant to say getting rich. No, not that either. I don't know."

I gently told Penelope that while she had many using relationships, she didn't appear to have any caring ones. She agreed. "I'm cynical. Guys just want sex. Girls want to be seen with me. Even my parents like me because I make good grades and bring glory to the family. You're seeing me for the money. Everyone's a user."

I was humbled by my inclusion in the user category and pondered what to say next. Protest seemed useless; only time might help her see that relationships might be about something other than money.

Fortunately Penelope moved on to another topic—her parents. Her father couldn't understand why Penelope wasn't happy. He'd been poor as a kid and thought that Penelope was lucky. He couldn't believe that all her luxury wasn't enough. He expected a happy child, and instead he had a daughter who'd attempted suicide.

Like most adolescent girls, she was critical of her mother, who she felt was a chump. She told me that her mom did whatever her dad wanted because she was dependent on him for money. She said, "Mom is even lazier and more screwed-up than I am. I would never stay with a man for money."

I asked Penelope what she'd learned about relationships from watching her parents. She thought for a while. "That nobody really loves anybody. That you'd better take what you can get."

Even though she was popular, she had no close friends. Real friends require honesty, openness and even vulnerability. They also require attention and simple acts of kindness. I encouraged Penelope to work on developing one honest relationship with a person her age.

We discussed the suicide. Penelope admitted that she couldn't handle frustration. "When I don't get what I want, I go crazy. It scares me."

I agreed that Penelope needed to learn to tolerate frustration and to control her impulses. She'd had almost no practice. I borrowed an idea from psychologist John Lehnhoff and suggested that she develop the almost nonexistent "hate it but do it center" in her brain. This "hate it but do it center" is something many girls need to develop if they are to meet their own long-term goals. I use this phrase to discuss the difference between immediate versus long-term gratification of needs. Often what hurts in the short term is ultimately rewarding, while what feels good in the short term is ultimately punishing. This concept is hard for adolescents to grasp, but important for their growth into adulthood. Only when they have a "hate it but do it center" can they work in a systematic way toward goals.

For her next assignment, I suggested that she record and report her victories—defined as times she handled frustration in a mature way.

I felt good when Penelope left. I planned to do a kind of awakening therapy with her that involved building her a value system that was more nourishing than the one that had failed her. I wanted her to discover that relationships could bring joy and that the world is full of riches that have nothing to do with money. I hoped I could get her parents into some marital counseling.

But a week after our session, Penelope again tried to kill herself. Her parents had refused to buy her something she wanted and she'd swallowed pills. This time her doctor hospitalized her at an expensive private hospital. I never saw her again.

In my first ten years as a therapist, I never saw a client who mutilated herself. Now it's a frequent initial complaint of teenage girls. Girls deal with their internal pain by picking at their skin, burning themselves or cutting themselves with razors or knives. This trend is particularly disturbing because most young women who have this problem think they are the only ones. As more young women came to my office with this problem, I asked myself why this is happening now. Why are young women choosing, even inventing, this at this particular time? What cultural changes have fostered the development of this widespread problem?

Just as depression can be described as anguish turned inward, self-mutilation can be described as psychic pain turned inward in the most physical way. Girls who are in pain deal with that by harming themselves. There are obvious explanations: Girls are under more stress in the 1990s; they have less varied and effective coping strategies to deal with that stress, and they have fewer internal and external resources on which to rely.

In my experience, behaviors that arise independently and spontaneously in large numbers of people often suggest enormous cultural processes at work. Eating disorders, for example, are related to the pressure that our culture puts on women to be thin. Self-mutilation may well be a reaction to the stresses of the 1990s. Its emergence as a problem is connected to our girl-piercing culture.

Self-mutilation can be seen as a concrete interpretation of our culture's injunction to young women to carve themselves into culturally acceptable pieces. As a metaphorical statement, self-mutilation can be seen as an act of submission: "I will do what the culture tells me to do"; an act of protest: "I will go to even greater extremes than the culture asks me to"; a cry for help: "Stop me from hurting myself in the ways that the culture directs me to" or an effort to regain control: "I will hurt myself more than the culture can hurt me."

Once girls begin to cut and burn themselves, they are likely to continue. Inflicting harm on the body becomes cathartic. In the absence of better coping strategies, hurting the self becomes a way to calm down. With time, the habit of inflicting harm on the self becomes more ingrained, so the sooner young women seek help the better.

What is the treatment? Ideally, we will change our culture so that young girls have less external stress to contend with in their lives. But for now, young women must learn better coping strategies and develop more internal and external resources to cope with stress.

Therapy can teach girls to identify early that they are in pain. They need to label their internal state as painful and then *think* about how to proceed. They must learn new ways to deal with intense misery and also new ways to process pain. Their stock way has been to hurt themselves. They must learn to recognize pain and help themselves.

Fortunately this tendency to inflict harm on the body when in psychic pain is quite curable. Young women can be taught to process pain by thinking and talking, instead of punishing themselves. Most young women respond quickly to guidance about how to stop this behavior and develop more adaptive ones. They stop the self-mutilating and begin to talk about the stresses they are under.

TAMMY (17)

Tammy came in after her mother discovered her cutting her breasts. Alice had awakened around three and noticed a light on in Tammy's bedroom. She went in to check on her and found her sitting on the bed surrounded by bloody newspapers, a razor in her hand. Alice woke Brian and they drove Tammy to the hospital. The doctor stitched up the deeper cuts and made an eight o'clock appointment for the family with me.

Alice and Brian were pale with fear and anxiety. Brian could narrate the events of the night. Alice couldn't stop crying. Tammy's face was red and puffy from tears, but she was not crying. Instead, she wouldn't look at me or speak above a whisper.

In spite of the current crisis, this seemed a rather typical, traditional family. Brian was the minister of a small church and played saxophone in a jazz band on weekends. Alice was a music teacher and a stay-at-home mother. Tammy was the third of four children. The older two were in college and the youngest, a ten-year-old boy, was doing fine. There was a history of depression on Alice's side of the family, but otherwise this family was unique for its lack of previous problems.

The family took long summer vacations every year. Often on Sunday nights they played music and sang together. Alice had served as a PTA president and a Girl Scout leader. Brian was a slightly absentminded man who shut his eyes during the violent scenes in movies and fainted at his pre-wedding blood test.

Tammy, even with her puffy face, was a pretty girl with long blond hair and alabaster skin. She was dressed in a silk jacket, designer blue jeans and stylish green boots. Brian reported that she was a good student and an easy-going daughter. She made the honor roll every semester and was a twirler in the high school band. Like her parents, she loved music, sang in the church and school choirs and played flute with her school orchestra. Brian said, "She's the best musician of all the kids."

Alice added, "We're in shock about this."

I spoke to Tammy alone.

"Do you know why you do this?" I asked gently.

Eyes averted, she said, "After a fight with my boyfriend."

We talked about Martin, whom she had met her sophomore year at all-state music camp. Martin played bass for the biggest school in the state. He was everything a high school girl could desire—good-looking, athletic and popular.

Tammy said, "All the girls were after him. I was shocked that he picked me."

"What's the relationship been like?"

Tammy sighed. "We fight a lot. Martin is jealous."

"What else?"

"He does things my parents wouldn't like. He smokes pot and drinks." She paused and looked at me suspiciously.

"Are you sexually involved with him?"

She nodded miserably.

"How do you feel about that?"

"I don't know. I'm afraid of getting pregnant."

She spoke softly but rapidly. "Martin's really into sex. This New Year's Eve, he had a party and rented porno videos for all the couples to watch. The guys liked it, but us girls were really embarrassed. We didn't want to watch."

"When did you have the fight that led to your cutting yourself?"

Tammy brushed her hair off her face. "It was after the porno night. I think maybe the next weekend. We went to a party and I had a wine cooler. Martin was mad because I talked to a friend of his. He took me home early and pushed me out of the car. I fell down on our driveway and he just drove off. That's the night I was so mad I didn't know what to do."

"Try to remember exactly how you felt."

Tammy said, "I slipped into my room so Mom and Dad wouldn't see me. I thought I was going crazy. There were scissors on my dresser and the idea of cutting myself came to me. I don't even know how I did it. But later I had cuts on my arms and I felt better. I could go to sleep."

She looked at me. "Do you think I'm crazy?"

I said, "I think you are scared."

Tammy said, "After that first time, it happened again. Whenever Martin and I fought, I felt this need to cut myself. I couldn't relax until I'd done it."

"Has Martin ever hit you?"

Tammy said, "Don't tell my parents this. He doesn't mean to, but he's hot-tempered. Afterwards, he's really sorry."

I called Alice and Brian in and said that I'd like to work alone with Tammy for a while. I explained that she'd developed a bad habit, which was to hurt herself physically when she was in emotional pain. Also, I added, we needed to explore her relationship with Martin.

Alice said, "Martin seems like a great guy."

I thought to myself, This minister and his wife have no idea how complicated the world has become for their lovely flute-playing daughter. I was careful not to betray Tammy's confidence, but I said, "Parents don't always know what's going on."

GAIL (15)

Gail was very different from Tammy. She was younger and, to quote her, "trapped in the halls of a junior high." She was dressed in a way that signaled "I am different" with her head half shaved and half purple punk. She had a nose ring, eight earrings, mostly of skulls and snakes, a tattoo of a dragon on her left arm and tiny tattoos on every finger. She wore a stained T-shirt with a FREE TIBET logo, black jeans torn at the knees and heavy boots.

She was the oldest daughter in a family of artists. The mother was a dancer and the father a sculptor. Gail's family was financially poor but culturally enriched. They couldn't afford trips, new cars or nice clothes for their daughters, but they could afford cheap tickets to the symphony, used books and therapy.

Gail's parents, Stephen and Shelly, were warmhearted, quirky people who seemed baffled at being in a therapist's office. Shelly's first comment was to compliment my overflowing bookcase. She said, "I see you like Jung. So do I."

I asked why the family was in my office. Gail looked out the window. Shelly and Stephen looked at each other. Stephen said, "We hate to tell on Gail. We made her come today."

Shelly said, "We've been worried since she began junior high, but last Saturday night we discovered that she was burning herself with cigarettes. We decided we had to do something."

"Before junior high, Gail was the star of the family," Shelly continued. "She was such a joy. The school classified her as highly gifted, so she qualified for special tutors and programs at the university. Her artwork made it to the state fair."

"She had everything going for her," her father added. "She had friends and was the comedian of the school. She stayed up all night reading and then went to school the next day and did fine."

Shelly said, "She was so competent and independent. We weren't prepared for her to have trouble. We didn't see it coming."

I turned to Gail, who was reading my book titles with interest, and asked, "What happened with junior high?"

Gail spoke slowly and with great precision. "I hated being warehoused and sent from room to room at the sound of a bell. I felt like a cow in a feedlot. I got teased when I took gifted classes and bored in the regular classes. I liked art class, but I'd just get out my supplies and the bell would ring."

"How about the other kids?" I asked.

"Do you know the slogan 'Sex, drugs and rock and roll' from the sixties?" I nodded and she continued. "In the nineties that's 'Masturbation, booze and Madonna.' I don't fit into that scene."

Stephen said, "Gail changed from outgoing to a real loner. She didn't like anyone. The phone stopped ringing for her."

Gail continued, "Junior high wasn't the worst thing. I was down about the environment. I couldn't sleep at night because I was worried about oil spills and the rain forests. I couldn't forget about Somalia, either, or Bosnia. It just seemed like the world was falling apart."

I see these problems in other highly gifted girls. Often because they are so bright, adults expect them to be mature emotionally. And they aren't. They react to global tragedies with the emotional intensity of adolescents. Though bright girls are perceptive enough to see through the empty values and shallow behavior of their peers, they have the social needs of adolescents. They feel utterly alone in their suffering. They have the intellectual abilities of adults in some areas and can understand world problems, and yet they have the political power of children.

Gail made the choices of many girls like herself. She avoided mainstream kids and gradually found a few of her own kind. She discovered the smoke-filled back room of the local coffeehouse where the alternative crowd gathered to talk. She made friends with gay men, with runaways, school dropouts and unhappy intellectuals like herself. She pierced her ears and then her nose. She went with her best friend to a tattoo parlor and had her dragon professionally done. Unfortunately, this crowd had its share of problems. Many were into drugs both as painkillers and experience producers. Soon Gail was smoking pot and dropping acid.

School, meanwhile, grew even more difficult. Gail was the only girl in her class with a nose ring and tattoos. Kids giggled and pointed at her when she walked past. By the time she was in ninth grade, she'd read more on the environment than her science teachers. The easy classes made her cynical about education. Her grades dropped. She skipped school and went to the park to smoke dope.

Stephen and Shelly knew that things weren't going well and encouraged Gail to try therapy. She refused. Her best friend moved to California and Gail became a loner again. Last week they'd found her with the cigarette burns.

The next week I met with Gail alone. She wore the same boots and jeans with a T-shirt that said "Life sucks and then you die." In spite of her odd appearance she struck me as beautiful and sensitive. I thought of the Allen Ginsberg line about "the drunken taxicab of absolute reality." It had crashed into Gail in early adolescence.

I told her about reading *The Diary of Anne Frank* in my small town thirty years earlier. I said, "When I discovered the evil that people do to each other I wanted to die. I didn't really want to be part of a species that produced the Nazis."

Gail agreed with me and said she'd felt that way when she heard the public radio reports about women being raped in Bosnia. She felt that way when she read that Stalin killed even more people than Hitler, that the Khmer Rouge killed 6 million Cambodians and that the Serbs practiced ethnic cleansing. She said, "The Holocaust wasn't an isolated event. It happens all over."

I said, "What saved me was reading Whitman and Thoreau. Shortly after I read about Anne Frank, I discovered them. It was summer and I would take my Whitman and go to the woods. I would read and watch the wind in the trees. I sat on my back porch at sunset and read *Walden*. Thoreau is such a good antidote to superficial people and shallow ideas. He gives dignity to loneliness."

Gail said, "Going to the park with my friend helped me, but now he's gone."

"Tell me about burning yourself."

Gail said, "That happened automatically. I was smoking in my room and I felt helpless and angry. The next thing I knew I was burning my arm and it felt good. It felt clean. I was careful to burn only my upper arm, so I could hide the marks. Afterwards I felt calmer."

"You were turning all your rage at the world against yourself," I said. "You need a better way to express rage and to fight back."

We talked about protest marches, recycling, boycotts. All of these seemed too abstract. Gail's despair could be assuaged only by direct action. Even though she was young, I encouraged her to work at the soup kitchen for the homeless. She needed to make the world better for real people. Gail agreed to look into that. As she left, I handed her my worn copy of *Walden*.

Gail came in for many months. Mostly I encouraged her to talk and write about her pain. As we became acquainted, she talked more about her current life. One of her gay friends was HIV-positive. A girlfriend of hers had been raped. Another friend was using drugs and getting sick.

She developed an emergency plan for those times when she was tempted to burn herself. She would pull out a notebook and write, write, write every painful, angry emotion she was feeling. She needed to get those emotions out of her body and onto a piece of paper.

Some of this writing she later shared with me. She wrote about the snobby girls at her school who teased the poor students. She wrote about the backstabbing and pettiness, the scramble for the right clothes and the right friends. She wrote about the poverty her hard-working parents had faced their entire lives. She wrote about the faces in Somalia, old people freezing in the Bosnian winter, homeless people and Rodney King.

She wrote until the craving to burn herself passed. Sometimes it didn't and she asked one of her parents to hold her and comfort her until she could sleep. Sometimes she called me and I talked her down. And, of course, sometimes the craving was too strong and she gave in and hurt herself. But this happened less and less as she learned to talk and write about her problems.

It helped that Gail was enjoying her life. She liked the other volunteers and many of the clients at the soup kitchen. The homeless all had stories and the time to tell them. When she saw homeless people on the streets, she often knew their names and stopped to chat. She knew she would be fixing them soup later. Even though her contributions were small, they took the edge off her despair.

By now Gail's appearance had changed slightly. Her hair was returning and shone a lovely auburn color. The last session we invited her parents to join us.

Shelly said that Gail was laughing again and playing with her younger sisters. The phone was ringing now and she had the most interesting friends. Stephen said that he was pleased that Gail was again working on her art. The tone of her work seemed slightly more optimistic. She had rejoined the land of the living. Gail gave some credit for her changes to therapy, which she compared to spring-cleaning. "You get the dust off everything and sort through stuff. You get to throw a lot of junk away."

Chapter 9

WORSHIPING THE GODS
OF THINNESS

■

HEIDI (16)

Heidi arrived in my office after gymnastics practice. Blond and pretty, she was dressed in a shiny red-and-white warm-up suit. We talked about gymnastics, which Heidi had been involved in since she was six. At that time, she was selected to train with the university coaches. Now she trained four hours a day, six days a week. She didn't expect to make an Olympic team, but she anticipated a scholarship to a Big-8 school.

Heidi glowed when she talked about gymnastics, but I noticed her eyes were red and she had a small scar on the index finger of her right hand. (When a hand is repeatedly stuck down the throat, it can be scarred by the acids in the mouth.) I wasn't surprised when she said she was coming in for help with bulimia.

Heidi said, "I've had this problem for two years, but lately it's affecting my gymnastics. I am too weak, particularly on the vault, which requires strength. It's hard to concentrate.

"I blame my training for my eating disorder," Heidi continued. "Our coach has weekly weigh-ins where we count each others' ribs. If they are hard to count we're in trouble."

I clucked in disapproval. Heidi explained that since puberty she had had trouble keeping her weight down. After meals, she was nervous that she'd eaten too much. She counted calories; she was hungry but afraid to eat. In class she pinched the fat on her side and freaked out.

The first time she vomited was after a gymnastics meet. Coach took her and the other gymnasts to a steak house. Heidi ordered a double cheeseburger and onion rings. After she ate, she obsessed about the weigh-in the next day, so she decided, just this once, to get rid of her meal. She slipped into the restaurant bathroom and threw up.

She blushed. "It was harder than you would think. My body resisted, but I was able to do it. It was so gross that I thought, 'I'll never do that again,' but a week later I did. At first it was weekly, then twice a week. Now it's almost every day. My dentist said that acid is eating away the enamel of my teeth."

Heidi began to cry. "I feel like such a hypocrite. People look at me and see a small, healthy person. I see a person who gorges on food and is totally out of control. You wouldn't believe how much I eat. I shove food into my mouth so fast that I choke. Afterwards, my stomach feels like it will burst."

I explained that bulimia is an addiction that's hard to break. It requires enormous willpower to fight the urge to binge and purge. And unlike people with other addictions such as alcohol or cocaine, bulimic women can't avoid their drug of choice. Heidi would need to learn controlled eating. Fighting the urge to binge is just one part of the treatment. She also needed new ways to deal with her own psychic pain. Bulimia, like all addictions, is a way to run from pain. Heidi needed to learn to face her feelings. I suggested Heidi record how she felt at the time of binges. Later we would examine her writing.

I asked about her family. Heidi's father was a local pediatrician and her mother a homemaker who worked with the Junior League. She was the oldest of three children. Heidi said that she had a wonderful childhood. Her family took trips every summer—one year to the coast of Maine, another to Sanibel Island in Florida and another to Alaska.

She loved elementary school. She'd been busy with her family, church and gymnastics. She was the kind of girl other kids like—easygoing and energetic. Heidi paused. "I had the perfect life—great parents, good friends and my own bedroom with a canopy bed and a balcony. I had walls full of ribbons and trophies."

I asked, "When did it stop being perfect?"

"After my thirteenth birthday things got tough. I graduated from my neighborhood school and moved into a consolidated school. I made friends there, but I felt under more pressure. School was harder; gymnastics was harder. I gained weight when I started my periods. Coach put me on a diet."

Heidi sighed. "Social life got harder. The girls were competitive. I hated the gossiping. With boys, everything got sexual. I was friends with some of the guys in the neighborhood, but we stopped hanging out together. We didn't know how to handle stuff."

I asked how Heidi felt about her appearance and wasn't surprised to hear that she had felt ugly in junior high. "Appearance was all we talked about. I tried not to get caught up in it, but I couldn't help it. I wanted to be pretty like everyone else."

As is often the case, Heidi's bulimia began with anxiety about weight gain. She was in a high-risk category—women who make a living or have an identity based on being thin. This category includes gymnasts, dancers, actresses and models. Many acquire eating disorders as an occupational hazard. However, once bulimia is entrenched, it functions, like alcohol or other chemicals, as a stress reducer. Young women binge to relax, and afterward they feel better, temporarily.

We ended our first session with a talk about expectations. Heidi felt pressured to be attractive, athletic and popular. She was amazingly successful at meeting these expectations, but she was paying a big price. Her perfectionism was taking its toll on her physical and emotional health. She needed to strive to be ordinary and to cut herself some slack. Eventually, unless she conquered bulimia, she wouldn't be athletic, attractive or popular.

Next session Heidi came with careful notes on her bulimia. She had binges at home, in the kitchen late at night after all her work was done. Usually she went to bed and tried to sleep, but almost always she was too anxious to settle down until she had binged and purged. Then she slept, only to wake the next morning hung over and ashamed.

Heidi wrote that before bingeing she felt tired, she worried about her tests or was upset about practice or her boyfriend. We discussed ways she could deal with those feelings besides bingeing: She could talk to someone, write in a journal, listen to music or learn relaxation techniques. Heidi agreed to write in her journal before she binged. She didn't think it would stop her, but it might slow her down and maybe she would learn something about herself.

We talked about how bulimia had changed her life. She no longer liked family dinners or social occasions where food was served. It made her nervous to be around normal eaters. She could either pick at her food or binge, but she'd lost the ability to have an ordinary meal. She was afraid that Sunday dinners with her grandparents would cause her to lose control, so she avoided them. She missed her grandparents and she knew they missed her. They felt hurt by her lack of attention.

Heidi was exhausted from the time and planning that bingeing required. Sometimes she stayed up past midnight to have the kitchen to herself. Sometimes she missed outings because she knew the house would be empty and she could binge in private. She said, "My parents don't try to stop me, but I hate to do it when they are around. I don't want my little brothers to find out."

She continued, "My boyfriend knows and is real supportive, but it hurts our relationship. I won't eat out with him. Sometimes I want him to take me home so I can binge. I'll make up an excuse to end our date."

She looked at me. "I hate to say this, but I'd rather binge than make out.

"I get real moody if anything interferes with my bingeing," she continued. "I'm irritable before and depressed afterwards. It seems like I'm never happy."

I congratulated Heidi for being in therapy. "You have the discipline and capacity for hard work that will be required to fight this. You'll make it back, I can tell."

THE FOOD ADDICTION

Bulimia is the most common eating disorder in young women. It starts as a strategy to control weight, but soon it develops a life of its own. Life for bulimic young women becomes a relentless preoccupation with eating, purging and weight. Pleasure is replaced by despair, frenzy and guilt. Like all addictions, bulimia is a compulsive, self-destructive and progressive disorder. Bingeing and purging are the addictive behaviors; food is the narcotic.

Over time young women with bulimia are at risk for serious health problems: Often they have dental problems, esophageal tears, gastrointestinal problems and sometimes dangerous electrolytic imbalances that can trigger heart attacks.

They experience personality changes as they grow to love bingeing more than anything else. They become obsessed and secretive, driven for another binge and guilty about their habit. They experience a loss of control that leads to depression. Often they are irritable and withdrawn, especially with family members.

While anorexia often begins in junior high, bulimia tends to develop in later adolescence. It's called the college girl's disease because so many young women develop it in sororities and dorms. While anorexic girls are perfectionist and controlled, bulimic young women are impulsive and they experience themselves as chronically out of control. They are more vulnerable to alcoholism than their anorexic peers. Unlike anorexic girls, bulimic young women come in all shapes and sizes.

Estimates of the incidence of bulimia run as high as one-fifth of all college-age women. Bulimic young women, like their anorexic sisters, are oversocialized to the feminine role. They are the ultimate people pleasers. Most are attractive, with good social skills. Often they are the cheerleaders and homecoming queens, the straight-A students and pride of their families.

Bulimic young women have lost their true selves. In their eagerness to please, they have developed an addiction that destroys their central core. They have sold their souls in an attempt to have the perfect body. They have a long road back.

PRUDENCE (16)

Prudence and her mother came to my office one sunny winter afternoon. Mary was a plump, middle-aged lady dressed in a stylish red wool suit with a fur collar. Prudence, also plump, wore blue jeans, a faded sweatshirt and Birkenstocks.

Prudence told me that she started bingeing three years ago and now binged twice a day, sometimes three times. She described her binge episodes as a kind of craziness when she fell into a trance and inhaled whatever was around. Her preferred foods were breads, cereals and graham crackers, but she ate anything. "Once I lose control, I'll eat whatever I can find."

Mary added, "We tried locking up the food, but Prudence bashed open the pantry with a hammer. When she wants to binge, there is no stopping her."

Prudence said, "I've tried to stop, but I can't."

Mary said that Prudence never ate normally. If she wasn't bingeing, she was starving herself. She said, "She's always on a diet. She won't eat anything except when she binges."

Prudence said, "I want to lose weight, but I can't. I weigh more now than ever."

"This is all my fault." Mary sighed. "I'm always on diets."

I asked about the family. Mary worked at the telephone company, as did her husband. In fact, they met there eighteen years ago. Mary said, "I'm definitely not one of those modern women who stands up for herself. I have a hard time saying what's on my mind."

"She's the family servant," Prudence said. "She lets Dad push her around and apologizes for any mistake she makes. She needs to get a life."

I was struck, as I often am, by how closely daughters observe their mothers and by how strongly they feel about their mothers' behavior. Prudence described her father as a good provider, but quiet. Mary put it this way: "Prudence means the world to him, but he doesn't have much to say to her. He's not the type to show his feelings."

"Are there other children in the family?"

Suddenly the tone of the interview changed. Mary sighed and Prudence bit her lip. Mary said, "Prudence's older brother was killed three years ago in a car accident."

"I don't want to talk about Greg," Prudence said.

I looked at the two frozen-faced women. I suspected that the family had hardly discussed Greg's death and that most of their grieving was still ahead of them. I knew this work needed to be done, but not in this first session.

Instead we talked about Prudence's school, which was in the wealthiest part of town. The population was suburban and homogenous. Most of the girls had designer clothes, straight white teeth and beautiful hair. Hardly any girls were even chubby. Nobody even wore glasses. It was a breeding ground for eating disorders.

Prudence laughed. "When I first went there, all the girls looked alike to me. It took a while to learn to tell them apart."

She gestured toward her somewhat unconventional outfit and said, "I refuse to play the designer-clothes game. I'm not a Barbie doll. I'm embarrassed to have bulimia. It's such a preppy disease."

The next time I saw Prudence I asked to see a picture of Greg. She pulled out her billfold and showed me his senior-class picture. "Greg wasn't like most brothers. He was my best friend. He didn't mind having me around, even when his buddies were over. He gave me advice and protected me. The worst thing Greg could say was that he was disappointed in me. That would shape me up fast. He got on my case if I made Bs. He taught me to pitch and to ice-skate."

I asked, "How was he killed?"

Prudence bit her bottom lip. "He was out with friends after the state basketball tournament. I knew he would be drinking but I wasn't worried. He explained to me that the group had a designated driver. But that night their designated driver was drunk. He hit a bridge outside of town. He wasn't hurt, but Greg died instantly."

She told me about the memorial service at the high school. More than 2,000 people came. The high school choir sang, and the captain of his basketball team gave the eulogy. She told me of the church service. "Everyone in the family put something in the casket for him to take along. Mom and Dad put in his fishing pole, basketball and his yearbooks. I put in my stuffed Russian bear, Misha."

Prudence cried as she told me about their last serious talk. Greg had warned her about junior high and all the temptations she would face. He'd advised her to avoid sex and alcohol at least till high school. "I've followed his advice about sex," she said. "I really don't want to get involved anyway."

She said, "After he died, we stopped talking about him. Mom shut his bedroom door, and we acted like he was away at camp or sleeping in late. I felt our family would fall apart if I brought it up."

"The only person who could have helped us through this was Greg," she said. "He knew the right things to say."

I handed Prudence a Kleenex, and five minutes later she continued. "I was mad at God. Why couldn't He have taken an old person with Alzheimer's or a child murderer on death row? Why did he have to take the best person in the world?"

She cried more, but afterward she said, "It feels good to talk about it."

"You have lots of catching up to do," I said.

I felt pleased with that session. Prudence, like many bulimic young women, had learned to deal with feelings by bingeing and purging. I was hopeful that as she faced her biggest pain, she'd be able to face others and talk rather than binge when she was upset.

Over the next few months we talked about Greg. Prudence brought in other pictures of him and letters he had written her from basketball camps. She told me stories about their adventures together. She talked about Greg with her mother and Greg's old girlfriend. She even tried to talk to her dad, but he said firmly, "Pru, I can't do it."

One day I suggested she find something in the natural world that reminded her of her brother, something that could help her feel connected to him whenever she saw it. I'd invented this strategy myself as a way to cope with loss. When I look at the Pleiades, for example, I think of a relative I lost who had many sisters. Next session Prudence came in with her connection. Her brother reminded her of cattails because he was tall, thin, brown-haired and loved the water. When she missed him, she walked to a nearby ditch with cattails and thought of him.

In addition to talking about her brother, we attacked the bulimia. Prudence found that she actually binged less on the days she talked about her brother. She learned to deal with other pain by facing it as well—by writing in her journal or talking to someone she trusted.

I encouraged her to take better care of herself. I told her the Overeaters Anonymous slogan: HALT—Don't get too *h*ungry, *a*ngry, *l*onely or *t*ired. She learned to identify her feelings and not to label everything as hunger. She learned to rest when she was tired, tell people when she was angry, find something to do when she was bored.

Prudence liked the OA group very much. It was a relief to hear others talk so honestly about their eating disorders. She was heartened that some of the women were in recovery and doing well. She liked the support and conversations about feelings. She had a consciousness-raising notebook in which she kept track of lookist, sexist remarks. She brought in ads featuring thin women. She hated how women were portrayed as vacant-eyed sexual objects with no personality. Prudence prided herself on her independence and she grew even more outspoken in her resistance to being "bimboized."

Then she decided to fight the incredible cravings to binge. This is a necessary and critical step in recovery, but it's terribly difficult. From my clinical experience, I've learned that fighting the urge to binge is at least as hard as fighting the urge for drugs. It requires incredible self-discipline and pain tolerance. Prudence learned to call on her brother for help. She formed a picture of his face in her mind and talked to him, asking him for the strength to fight binges. When she succeeded, she thanked him.

Of course, Prudence wasn't always successful. But gradually she was able to reduce her binges to once a day. After four months in therapy she had a binge-free day. Some of her energy was returning and her skin and hair looked healthier. She reported that there were days she didn't even think about weight.

Prudence was a good talker, more sensitive to her own and others' feelings than the average teenager. Slowly she battled her addiction. She made a commitment to live an examined life. Recently she said to me, "Greg would like who I am now."

STARVATION IN THE LAND OF PLENTY

Anorexia is a problem of Western civilization, a problem for the prosperous. It is, to quote Peter Rowen, a question of "being thirsty in the rain." Anorexia is both the result of and a protest against the cultural rule that young women must be beautiful. In the beginning, a young woman strives to be thin and beautiful, but after a time, anorexia takes on a life of its own. By her behavior an anorexic girl tells the world: "Look, see how thin I am, even thinner than you wanted me to be. You can't make me eat more. I am in control of my fate, even if my fate is starving." Once entrenched, anorexia is among the most difficult disorders to treat. Of all the psychiatric illnesses, it has the highest fatality rate.

Its victims are often the brightest and best young women. In my experience, it is the good girls, the dutiful daughters and high achievers who are at the greatest risk for anorexia. Anorexia often begins in early adolescence with ordinary teenage dieting. But instead of stopping the diet, perfectionist young women continue. They become progressively obsessed with weight and increasingly rigid in their thinking about food. They see themselves in a competition to be the thinnest girl around, the fairest of the fair.

The word "anorexia" implies an absence of hunger, but in fact anorexic girls are constantly hungry. They are as obsessed with food as any starving people. They have many of the physical symptoms of starvation—their bellies are distended, their hair dull and brittle, their periods stop and they are weak and vulnerable to infections. They also have the psychological characteristics of the starving. They are depressed, irritable, pessimistic, apathetic and preoccupied with food. They dream of feasts.

Anorexic girls are great at self-denial. They are obsessed with weight, which becomes their one important and all-defining attribute. They feel confident if they are losing weight and worthless and guilty if they are not.

By the time the anorexia is full-blown, family members are terrified.

They try everything to make their daughters eat—pleading, threatening, reasoning and tricking. But they fail because the one thing in life that anorexic girls can control is their eating. No one can make them gain weight. Their thinness has become a source of pride, a badge of honor.

Anorexic young women tend to be popular with the opposite sex. They epitomize our cultural definitions of feminine: thin, passive, weak and eager to please. Oftentimes young women report that they are complimented on their appearance right up until they are admitted to hospitals for emergency feeding.

I think anorexia is a metaphor. It is a young woman's statement that she will become what the culture asks of its women, which is that they be thin and nonthreatening. Anorexia signifies that a young woman is so delicate that, like the women of China with their tiny broken feet, she needs a man to shelter and protect her from a world she cannot handle. Anorexic women signal with their bodies "I will take up only a small amount of space. I won't get in the way." They signal "I won't be intimidating or threatening." (Who is afraid of a seventy-pound adult?)

SAMANTHA (16)

Against her will Samantha was brought to my office by her German-Lutheran mother. Wilma kept her coat on and her arms folded across her ample chest as she explained that her husband wanted to come but was in the fields. The corn needed to be brought in before the predicted snow fell this weekend. Wilma reported that the family doctor had said Samantha was anorexic. She hadn't had a period in several months and her cholesterol level was 135, so low it could trigger a heart attack.

Wilma said that Samantha used to be a cheerful and peppy girl. Now she rarely smiled, and she was irritable and lethargic. Once she'd been a strong worker on the farm, now she could do only the lightest of chores. When she was home, she hardly spoke to the family and spent all her time exercising or studying in her room. Samantha was a straight A student, a cheerleader, and she was popular with her classmates, but Wilma said, "She doesn't enjoy those things like she used to. She does everything like it's one more job to complete."

As her mother talked about her health problems and behavior changes, Samantha listened without emotion. She was 5 feet 6 inches tall and weighed ninety-nine pounds. Her head clearly showed the outline of her skull, and her eyes were watery and sunken. Her light brown hair, though attractively arranged, was dull and brittle. She dressed in a blouse and heavy sweater to disguise her thinness. She had the furry arms that often come with anorexia. It's called lanugo—the soft, woolly body hair that grows to compensate for the loss of fat cells so the body can hold in heat.

I asked Samantha what she thought of her mother's description of her. She said, "She's exaggerating. I eat plenty. Just last night I had pizza and ice cream."

Wilma looked doubtful and said, "Only a spoonful of ice cream and less than one piece of pizza. You took off all the cheese first."

"I don't like cheese," Samantha said. "You know that."

Wilma said, "She plays tricks on us with food. She pretends to eat but really just rearranges things on her plate. She says she ate at school, but we'll find out from her friends that she didn't."

"Has your personality changed in the last year?" I asked.

"I am different now, I admit it. I don't have as much fun, and I get stressed out. I have trouble sleeping."

"When did you begin to lose weight?"

Samantha said, "I went on a diet." She pointed at her mom. "You encouraged me."

Wilma shook her head sorrowfully. "Yes, and I tried to lose weight with her. Only I stopped after a week of misery and Samantha never stopped."

We spent the rest of the first session talking about treatment. I told Wilma to throw the scales away. Once a month Samantha could be weighed at her doctor's office. Samantha was to keep track of her eating and exercising so that we could talk about patterns. I stressed that Samantha couldn't get well unless she decided that anorexia was her enemy and made a conscious decision to fight back. Otherwise, she'd perceive me and her family as her enemies, trying to make her do something she didn't want to do. She'd fight us and she could win.

Wilma agreed with me. "It is so painful to watch Samantha eat a dinner of lettuce and a few grapes when I know she's starving. But we've learned that we can't make her eat. We tried and it was awful. Samantha lost weight even quicker."

Samantha said she was scared to lose the scales. "I can't get fat. If I can't weigh myself I'll be too nervous to sleep."

I gave her a list of books to read and scheduled an appointment for over the lunch hour. I wanted to see Samantha alone with a sack lunch.

Samantha arrived wearing a blue sweatshirt with white kittens on the front and blue jeans that looked ironed. I pulled out my cheese sandwich and apple and suggested we eat as we talked. Samantha showed me her lunch—two crackers, celery and carrot sticks and a small bunch of grapes. She explained that she had had a big breakfast and wasn't hungry.

I asked what triggered her anorexia. "I broke up with Brad," Samantha said. "We dated all through junior high. I thought I could trust him and that we'd be together forever."

I put down my sandwich. "Why do you think he dated someone else?"

"He teased me about my thunder thighs. He wanted someone thinner."

Samantha nibbled on a carrot stick. "I was much better at dieting than Mom or my friends. I lost five pounds the first week and then three the second. Twice I fainted at school."

"How did others react to your diet?"

Samantha smiled in memory of the time. "I got lots of compliments. My friends were jealous, but I made new friends. Guys who wouldn't have considered me before asked me out."

Samantha was at risk for anorexia because of her perfectionism and enormous amount of self-discipline. She could will herself into starving, but soon anorexia was running the show. Samantha became obsessed with food and weight. The most important time was weigh-in time, first thing in the morning. If she lost weight, she felt great, but if she gained, she was distraught. Nothing else, not grades or social success, had much effect on her well-being.

She learned to love the "high" she experienced from fasting. She began running three miles a day, then five and then eight. Even though this running exhausted her and depleted her limited energy reserves, she wouldn't cut back. She devised tests for herself to prove her control over food. For example, she invited her friends over for a party and, weak with hunger, watched as they devoured lasagna and ice-cream sundaes. She baked brownies for her family and would not even sample the ones fresh from the oven. She watched other people scarf down food with their animal appetites and felt superior. Samantha did what many girls with anorexia do: She reduced her complicated life to one simple issue—weight.

Samantha reminded me of a brainwashing victim. She had her own rigid ways of thinking about herself and the universe and was impervious to the influence of others. She thought people who wanted her to eat were jealous of her thinness. Like most anorexics, she didn't want to fight her anorexia. She had brainwashed herself into thinking that anorexia was her friend. She was in my office because her parents and doctors wanted her to fight. We were her enemy, not the anorexia. She lied, distorted and hid her eating to protect herself from those who wanted to help her.

Therapy must be a kind of reverse brainwashing. I attacked the anorexia, but not Samantha. As she finished her meager lunch, I asked her questions that I learned to ask from psychologist David Epston. "If anorexia is your friend, why is he making you so tired and weak? Why is he encouraging you to do something that has made your periods stop and your hair fall out?"

These questions surprised her and were not easy to dismiss. She said, "I don't know what you mean."

I asked her to take home questions to think about, to write about. "We will continue to explore the lies that anorexia has told you, the lies that are costing you your life." I also told her I would work with her only if she agreed to stop her long-distance runs for now. I explained that these runs might trigger a heart attack. She resented my limits, but agreed.

Work with Samantha proceeded laboriously. I assigned her consciousness-raising work. She was to look at models and movie stars and ask, Who picked this thin, passive type as our standard of beauty? I asked her to think about women she really respected. Were they weight- and appearance-conscious?

With Samantha, as with most anorexic women, the biggest step was realizing that anorexia was not her friend but her enemy, even her potential executioner. After that, she resisted its claims on her soul. One day Samantha came in and said that she realized that anorexia had lied to her. She said, "He promised I would be happy when I was thin, and I'm miserable. He promised I would accomplish great things and I'm too tired to even do what I used to do. He promised I'd be healthy if I ran, and instead my bones ache from the pressure of my body. He promised me friends, and everyone is mad at me. Anorexia has stolen all the fun out of my life." That day I felt Samantha would recover.

COMPULSIVE EATERS

In this culture we are all socialized to love food. Rich, sweet foods are connected to love, nurturance and warmth. We associate grandmothers and parties with cookies and cakes, not carrot sticks. Emotional nourishment is linked with physical nourishment. Many of our words for those we love are food words, such as sweetie, sugar and honey.

In addition to the emotional power of food, it has a chemical power that's addictive as well. We all have experienced that sedating effect after Thanksgiving dinner. We feel sleepy and mildly euphoric. Sugar has particular power, and many women use sugary foods as a way to calm themselves and medicate away pain and anxiety.

In my experience, certain populations of women are most at risk for compulsive overeating. These are the women who are caretakers, whose life work is nurturing others. Nurses, for example, are notorious for having goodies in their nursing stations and eating when they are overworked and tired. Many develop into compulsive eaters.

Young women who eat compulsively have learned to use food as a drug that medicates away their emotional pain. This is harmful because they do not learn to deal with emotional pain and because they become obese, which sets them up for much more pain and rejection. It's virtually impossible in America to be heavy and feel good about oneself. A vicious cycle has begun.

Compulsive overeaters are often young women with a history of dieting. They diet and feel miserable, then they eat and feel better, but meanwhile their dieting makes their metabolism grow more and more sluggish. Over time weight loss becomes associated with control, and weight gain with out-of-control behavior. They become more obsessed with calories and weight. Soon it's not just their eating but their lives that are out of control.

Writer Susie Orbach distinguished between "stomach hungry," which is genuine physical hunger, and "mouth hungry," which is a hunger for something other than food—for attention, rest, stimulation, comfort or love. Compulsive eaters are mouth-hungry eaters. All feelings are labeled as hunger. Eating becomes the way to deal with feelings. Compulsive eaters eat when they are tired, anxious, angry, lonely, bored, hurt or confused.

Treatment for compulsive eating is similar to the treatment for bulimia. Young women need to identify their real needs and not label all need as hunger. If they are restless, they need stimulation; if they are tired, they need rest; if they are angry, they need to change or escape the situation that angers them. Of course, compulsive eaters need to learn controlled eating. Often they can benefit from a support group such as Overeaters Anonymous.

It's difficult to be a healthy eater in this country. Unhealthful food is everywhere, and we are encouraged to consume without thinking of the consequences. Support groups help women stay focused on long-term goals, not immediate gratification. They also give women a new way to deal with painful experiences: They can talk about them.

Violet was living on the streets when we first met, but soon after she moved into a shelter for homeless young women. She had a more difficult life than many compulsive eaters, but she shared essentially the same issues. Compulsive eating, unlike anorexia, is not primarily a problem of the middle class, but an equal-opportunity problem. Violet associated food with love and nurturance. Like many compulsive eaters, she was a good-natured, hard-working people pleaser. Violet was good at caring for others, but when she needed care, no one was around. Food was her pain medicine.

VIOLET (18)

I met Violet when I worked at our local homeless center. During the day homeless people and transients came there to shower, use the phones, pick up mail, escape the weather and play cards. As a volunteer, my job was to make coffee and put out trays of day-old donuts and rolls. I was to enforce the rules—no swearing, no alcohol, no obscenities and no weapons.

When I wasn't busy, I played cards and gave advice about local jobs and services. Most of our customers were men, but increasingly in the last few years women and families have come to the center. Cigarette smoke fills the room with a blue haze by midmorning. I'm struck by how many of the homeless are hooked on caffeine, sugar, cigarettes and alcohol.

I noticed Violet right away because she was an unusual age for a shelter visitor. She looked about eighteen, maybe even younger. She was chubby and dressed in jeans, a T-shirt and plastic thongs. Like most of the people at the center, she had bad teeth. When I first saw her she was playing cards at a table of regulars. She laughed easily and was popular and accepted by the group. They joked with her, offered her smokes and advice on survival in our town.

Later, when the men hit the streets, I visited with Violet. She had just run from what she said would be her last foster-care placement. She'd had six and that was plenty. She'd also lived on the reservation with her mother, who was sick and alcoholic, and she'd lived in an institution for difficult kids with no place else to go. She was ready to be on her own and said, "I'd rather live on the streets than have anyone tell me what to do."

I worried aloud that she might get raped being on her own, and she looked at me strangely. "Do you think that hasn't happened to me before?"

Before she left that day she pulled out a picture of her mother's home on the reservation. It was a trailer surrounded by squalor—old tires and car engines, even a toilet. But Violet looked longingly at it. "I miss my own place, but Mom's just too hard to live with."

Violet came in for several months. Like many of our local homeless, she sold her blood and "volunteered" for drug studies at a pharmaceutical company. She wove leather armbands that she sold on the streets. Violet made enough money to buy herself and her friends food. She bought presents for children whenever they turned up at the center. Soon I was busy answering the question "Where's Violet?"

In fact, Violet had lots of friends. She wasn't a complainer and had a way of laughing about troubles that made them seem less serious. She was big on hugging others when they were down and had nicknames for everyone.

One morning she showed me all the scars on her arms and leg—from a knife fight with her mother's ex-boyfriend, from her mother when she was drunk, from a foster father who believed in physical discipline. Another day she said, "You're a shrink. I wonder what I should do about this tendency I have to eat everything that isn't nailed down."

She told me how she always associated food with comfort. Her fondest memories were of her childhood visits to her grandmother's. There she'd had a calm, clean place to play and rest. She said her grandmother was a good cook and always had oatmeal cookies and angel food cake for her to enjoy. "Mom never had food around, only booze. Grandma's place had good food."

She lit a cigarette. "I had lots of bad homes. Food was the one thing I could count on. No matter how wrecked I was, eating helped me feel better. But there was never enough food. That's what worries me now. I can't get enough. I eat until my stomach hurts, and then I'll keep on eating."

I said, "It sounds like you've got things pretty well figured out."

She smiled. "I know what's wrong, but how do I fix it?"

Eating filled a deep need that Violet didn't know how to fill in other ways. I knew she could learn healthy ways to take care of herself. Because she was such a good worker, I was sure she could work her way into a decent job and a more stable life. I started to tell her this, but Violet waved her hands. "Whoa. Don't get too deep on me."

I apologized. "We shrinks have a tendency to do that." Then someone asked me to make some more coffee.

I bought Violet a copy of Orbach's book *Fat Is a Feminist Issue* and told her about a free support group near the center. She didn't like to hang out with people with money (it made her self-conscious), but she did read the book.

One day she told me that she thought her eating was related to her fears about sex. She said, "I figure that if I'm fat enough maybe guys will leave me alone. It's a kind of armor, soft armor, but it works pretty well."

Another day I said, "Everyone counts on you to cheer them up." She was pleased by my observation. I continued. "I wouldn't want you to change, except maybe to follow some of that sensible advice that you give other people."

She looked at me. "Like what?"

I answered, "Like getting off the street. I'll help you when you're ready."

I wish I could say that Violet's story had a happy ending, but after a few months she left for California to pick fruit with a man she met at the center. She sent me a postcard from the Central Valley. It said: "The weather's great and there's work. But I miss my shrink. I'll be back. Don't worry."

Violet comes from an extreme situation, but in terms of dynamics, she's similar to most compulsive eaters. She learned to associate love with food and to use food to comfort and nurture herself. She's good at caring for others, but relatively poor at meeting her own needs. She's good at burying her pain.

Her sexual fears are quite typical of compulsive eaters. Many date the start of their compulsive eating to an incident involving sexual abuse. Others are fearful of men or their own sexual appetites and see their weight as a form of protection. Many have had the experience of being pursued by men when they lose weight. Often they gain to avoid the choices and dangers that pursuit causes in their lives.

If I could have seen Violet in therapy, I would have encouraged her to examine her feelings carefully at the times when she felt tempted to gorge. No doubt she had pain from her past life, with its foster homes and institutions. She had abandonment issues and physical and sexual abuse issues to deal with. She learned that while people let her down, food was an ever-faithful friend.

I would have taught her to respect rather than run from her feelings. I would have encouraged exercise as a way to fight depression, manage stress and feel better about her body. I would have taught her to set limits with others and even to ask for help. I would have encouraged her to stay in our town and work her way through problems. We could have found money for her to go back to school or get some technical training so that she'd be employable. I would have found her a good dentist.

Beauty is the defining characteristic for American women. It's the necessary and often sufficient condition for social success. It is important for women of all ages, but the pressure to be beautiful is most intense in early adolescence. Girls worry about their clothes, makeup, skin and hair. But most of all they worry about their weight. Peers place an enormous value on thinness.

This emphasis on appearance was present when I was a girl. Our high school had a "gauntlet" that we girls walked through every morning. It consisted of all the boys lined up by their cars along the sidewalk that led into the front doors. We walked past them to catcalls and remarks about our breasts and legs. I wore a girdle made of thick rubber to flatten my stomach on days I dressed in straight skirts.

But appearance is even more important today. Three things account for the increased pressure to be thin in the 1990s. We have moved from communities of primary relationships in which people know each other to cities full of secondary relationships. In a community of primary relationships, appearance is only one of many dimensions that define people. Everyone knows everyone else in different ways over time. In a city of strangers, appearance is the only dimension available for the rapid assessment of others. Thus it becomes incredibly important in defining value.

Secondly, the omnipresent media consistently portrays desirable women as thin. Thirdly, even as real women grow heavier, models and beautiful women are portrayed as thinner. In the last two decades we have developed a national cult of thinness. What is considered beautiful has become slimmer and slimmer. For example, in 1950 the White Rock mineral water girl was 5 feet 4 inches tall and weighed 140 pounds. Today she is 5 feet 10 inches and weighs 110 pounds.

Girls compare their own bodies to our cultural ideals and find them wanting. Dieting and dissatisfaction with bodies have become normal reactions to puberty. Girls developed eating disorders when our culture developed a standard of beauty that they couldn't obtain by being healthy. When unnatural thinness became attractive, girls did unnatural things to be thin.

In all the years I've been a therapist, I've yet to meet one girl who likes her body. Girls as skinny as chopsticks complain that their thighs are flabby or their stomachs puff out. And not only do girls dislike their bodies, they often loathe their fat. They have been culturally conditioned to hate their bodies, which are after all themselves. When I speak to classes, I ask any woman in the audience who feels good about her body to come up afterward. I want to hear about her success experience. I have yet to have a woman come up.

Unfortunately girls are not irrational to worry about their bodies. Looks do matter. Girls who are chubby or plain miss much of the American dream. The social desirability research in psychology documents our prejudices against the unattractive, particularly the obese, who are the social lepers of our culture. A recent study found that 11 percent of Americans would abort a fetus if they were told it had a tendency to obesity. By age five, children select pictures of thin people when asked to identify good-looking others. Elementary school children have more negative attitudes toward the obese than toward bullies, the handicapped or children of different races. Teachers underestimate the intelligence of the obese and overestimate the intelligence of the slender. Obese students are less likely to be granted scholarships.

Girls are terrified of being fat, as well they should be. Being fat means being left out, scorned and vilified. Girls hear the remarks made about heavy girls in the halls of their schools. No one feels thin enough. Because of guilt and shame about their bodies, young women are constantly on the defensive. Young women with eating disorders are not all that different from their peers. It's a matter of degree. Almost all adolescent girls feel fat, worry about their weight, diet and feel guilty when they eat. In fact, the girls with eating disorders are often the girls who have bought the cultural messages about women and attractiveness hook, line and scales. To conform they are willing to make themselves sick.

Particularly in the 1980s and 1990s, there's been an explosion of girls with eating disorders. When I speak at high schools, girls surround me with confessions about their eating disorders. When I speak at colleges, I ask if any of the students have friends with eating disorders. Everyone's hand goes up. Studies report that on any given day in America, half our teenage girls are dieting and that one in five young women has an eating disorder. Eating disorders are not currently the media-featured problem they were in the 1980s, but incidence rates are not going down. Eight million women have eating disorders in America.

Chapter 10

DRUGS AND ALCOHOL— IF OPHELIA WERE ALIVE TODAY

■

TRACY (13)

As her mother talked, Tracy, who sat as far away from her mother as was possible in my small office, opened her mouth in mock disbelief. Wendy ignored Tracy's histrionics as she explained that Tracy had skipped school, cheated on tests and yelled at her teachers. Recently she had been expelled because the principal found a bottle of schnapps in her book bag.

"We can't believe this is happening to our daughter," Wendy said. "Maybe it's her liberal school. We don't know what to do."

Tracy said, "You can stay out of my life."

"We took Tracy to our minister, but he said she needed professional help. He thinks she might be an alcoholic."

Tracy tossed her head in disdain. "I just hate our family, that's all."

"We can't control her," Wendy continued. "She slips out at night. We've found cigarettes in her dresser. She's so moody and irritable that we don't know what to say to her. We're worried about her future."

"That's your problem, Mom," Tracy said. "You're always talking about my future and you don't care about my happiness now."

Wendy protested weakly and Tracy said, "Bug off. Why can't you be like normal parents and let me do what I want?"

I handed Tracy money to go next door and buy lemonades. After she left, the room seemed calmer and quieter. Wendy told me that she and her husband both came from homes with alcoholics. They were determined to have a different kind of family than the ones they remembered. They attended a fundamentalist church and said daily prayers and grace at every meal. They searched the children's rooms once a month and monitored their phone calls and mail. Bedtimes were at nine and rigidly enforced. They allowed Tracy to listen to only Christian rock and roll. Television was carefully supervised.

Wendy and Ned had studied many books on Christian parenting. They believed in "spare the rod and spoil the child." But they had stopped spanking Tracy when she was ten and, since then, they hadn't known how to control her. "Ned thinks we should still spank her," she confided. "But I think she's too old for that."

I agreed wholeheartedly.

Wendy said, "All I learned about parenting from my own mother was what not to do." She talked some about her life as a child. Her own mother was unmarried and alcoholic. Wendy remembered being hungry as a child and picking her clothes from church charity baskets. The other kids in town were not allowed to play at her family's trailer. Wendy and her sisters grew like weeds, unsupervised and out of control. "Most of the time Mom couldn't have cared less what I was doing, but when she did notice, I was in deep trouble," Wendy continued. "She called me every name in the book. Once she hit me with a two-by-four. Another time she scalded my head when she washed my hair."

She paused. "With the help of God, I've forgiven her, but I've promised myself I'll never be like her." I congratulated her on giving her daughter many things she hadn't had—sober parents, love and consistent messages about her behavior.

Wendy asked, "So why does Tracy resent me? I only want what's best for her."

"What are you most worried about?"

"I'm afraid she'll be an alcoholic."

Because of the family histories of alcoholism, Tracy was at risk. But I thought that right now the drinking was only part of a larger issue, which was how this family could protect their daughter and allow her to grow. Tracy was furious at the intrusion and controls. Wendy and Ned showed their love by discipline and surveillance, ways unlikely to win the affection of any teenager. Their parenting policies weren't flexible and made few allowances for growth and autonomy. Clearly Tracy was testing the limits of the system.

Tracy walked in with our lemonades and I asked Wendy to leave us alone.

Tracy tried hard to act sullen and hard-core, but she was young and not very good at it yet. Within about two minutes I had her smiling. But when I asked her what she wanted to talk about, she turned gloomy. "I hate my mother. She's always in my face. She wants to control my life. She listens in on my calls and reads my diary."

I asked about her dad. She told me that he preferred her brother, whom he took fishing and hunting. However, she didn't mind their outings because when her father was around, he was mad at her. She said, "Both of them drive me crazy. They are the nosiest parents in the world. Can't you just tell them to get off my case?"

I empathized with her need for more privacy and independence and promised that in family therapy we would talk about her rights as a teenager. But I also felt it was important that Tracy hear that I respected her mother. I said, "It sounds like your mom has tried to give you many things she didn't have as a girl."

"I'm sick of hearing Mom's sob stories. Grandma isn't that bad." She sighed. "I'd rather live with her than my parents. At least she doesn't watch me like a hawk and read my mail."

We talked about alcohol and drugs. Tracy drank only with her friends, usually on weekends. She liked the kids who drank—they were wild and fun, not "uptight goody-goodies" like the girls her mom preferred. When she was drunk, she laughed more and wasn't so self-conscious with boys. She knew several kids who drank more than she did. She tried marijuana, but it made her paranoid. When she was on a diet, she took caffeine and amphetamines.

We talked about her fights at school. "Something inside me just tells me to be bad. Afterwards, I'm sorry, but nobody believes me." Tracy continued, "I want to explode sometimes. Drinking calms me down."

I wondered about all this anger. It could be a reaction to her parents' efforts to control her life and their unrealistic rules for a girl her age. Or it could be related to something else. Once Tracy trusted me, I would ask more about it.

I called Wendy back in and recommended family therapy. I told Wendy that I didn't think Tracy was an alcoholic. Her use of alcohol was pretty typical of kids her age. But because of both her genetic background and her anger at the family, Tracy was at risk of developing alcohol problems.

I thought that Tracy might settle down if Wendy and Ned changed their parenting style. They were relying on rules to keep Tracy safe. But rules, in the absence of loving relationships, inspire rebellion in adolescents. Relationships are what hold girls' lives in place.

Wendy and Ned had reacted to their families of origin by rigidly structuring their own children's lives. This was catching up with them. Tracy wasn't just rebelling against their overly strict rules, but also against their perfectly reasonable ones. These parents were so eager to protect Tracy that they gave her no personal space. I would encourage them to stop reading Tracy's diary and listening to her calls, and I would negotiate for a later bedtime.

Most likely Tracy had concerns that she wasn't discussing with her parents. Maybe if she talked about her life she would have less need for self-prescribed anxiety medication. Right now Tracy saw alcohol as a way to meet some of her very understandable needs—to feel comfortable with boys and to relax and laugh. I wanted to educate her on responsible drinking and the signs of problem drinking.

Tracy was at risk of developing the identity of a delinquent. She desperately needed something to feel proud of besides her ability to get in trouble. I wanted to help Tracy channel all her rebellious energy into activities that thrilled her but wouldn't get her hurt. Maybe she would like acting—that's pretty scary—or fencing.

Over the last few decades many more teenagers have been using alcohol and drugs. Teenagers use chemicals for a variety of reasons: biological predispositions, psychological problems, social pressure and familial factors. Some of the reasons have to do with complicated psychological processes, and other reasons are as simple as availability. Often the community determines the chemical most likely to be used. A girl who lives in the New Haven ghetto surrounded by drug users is more likely to become a drug addict than a girl growing up in a small Nebraska community.

Alcohol is the drug of choice of most teens. It's cheap, powerful and sold everywhere. But drugs are much more available than most parents suspect. Most kids have been offered drugs by the time they are in seventh grade. By eighth grade, most kids know kids on drugs.

Even my rural state has problems. The interstate that dissects our state is a national conduit for drugs, and the small communities along I-80 have drug problems. Teenagers from towns like Alvo (population 144) and Aurora (population 3,717) come to my office with drug habits that once could be found only in cities. As one of these girls put it, "The drug business at my school is major."

I want to emphasize that not all drug and alcohol use is pathological. Healthy, reasonably well-adjusted teenagers use drugs and alcohol. Some experimentation is normal. Drinking at parties is widespread and not necessarily a sign of anything except a desire to fit in and do what others do. It's important not to label all drug and alcohol use in teenagers as addiction. The labeling process can do harm. Rather, kids and adults need guidelines for what is normal experimentation and what is self-destructive use.

Research on adolescents shows three basic motives for chemical use. The first is for expanded awareness, or the desire to increase sensitivity and insight. The second is for thrill seeking and new experiences with peers; and the third is for the drug effect—that is, to get high. All of these reasons have in common the desire to achieve an altered state of consciousness. Of course, thrill seeking can be dangerous. Using chemicals for effect can also lead to dependency.

Chemical use as a coping strategy is tremendously appealing to teenage girls, who are often confused, depressed and anxious. Alcohol and marijuana are popular because they offer teenage girls a quick, foolproof way to feel good. Caffeine and amphetamines help girls avoid hunger and eat less. (Losing weight is probably the most common goal of girls this age.) Plus, chemical use often enhances status with friends.

How do we know when alcohol or drug use is a problem? Heredity cannot be overemphasized. Thirty percent of the children of alcoholic parents become alcoholic. Girls from families with serious problems are certainly more at risk than girls who come from healthier families. But I don't want to overstate this. Teenage girls from well-adjusted families sometimes develop serious problems with chemicals. Peers play a role. In general, kids whose friends are heavy users are more likely to use, while kids whose friends abstain are more likely to abstain.

Certain patterns, such as drinking to escape reality or drinking to get wasted, are more dangerous than others. I worry about girls who drink more than their friends or who drink regularly. Drinking alone or being secretive about drugs and alcohol are bad patterns. But each case must be evaluated separately. Often drug and alcohol use are symptoms of other problems.

Particularly with teenage girls, it's important to try to understand the context in which chemical use occurs. So much is happening at this time. Often heavy chemical use is a red flag that points to other issues, such as despair, social anxiety, problems with friends or family, pressure to achieve, negative sexual experiences or difficulty finding a positive identity. The stories in this chapter attempt to show how chemical use is tangled up with all other aspects of adolescent girls' experiences. The girls use alcohol or drugs for different reasons, and the response to their use must be tailored to each unique situation.

Rita (16)

Rita looked as if she'd stepped out of an MTV video. Her brown hair was decorated with feathers and beads, and she was dressed in a skin-tight satiny dress. But Rita's personality didn't match her flamboyant clothing. She was soft-spoken, almost shy, and eager to be liked. In a tentative way, she told me that she had just been arrested for drunken driving. This embarrassed and scared her. Her dad was an alcoholic and the last thing she wanted was to follow in his footsteps.

Rita said, "I'm here because I want to get fixed while I'm young. I don't want to live a screwed-up life like my parents."

Rita was the oldest of three children. Her dad was a salesman at a discount furniture store and her mother was a homemaker. Things had been bad for as long as Rita could remember. Her mother had arthritis and couldn't work. Her dad was a womanizer and a compulsive gambler who worked long hours, then hit the bars or keno parlors. He wasn't around home often, but when he was it was chaos and misery.

"I was hit a lot myself." She showed me a scar above her left eye where she'd been hit by a beer bottle. "But that wasn't the worst of it. Dad said horrible things when he was drunk, like 'You'll never get a man, you're too ugly,' or 'too big of a bitch,' or 'too much of a slut.'"

She shuddered. "I stayed out of Dad's way. I lay awake and listened to him yell at Mom. Sometimes he hit her."

She pushed her long hair back from her face. "When I was fourteen I told Dad that if he ever touched Mom again I would kill him. He knew I meant it too. He hasn't hit her since then."

As we talked, it became clear that Rita had way too much responsibility for a sixteen-year-old. Like many parental children, she took better care of others than she did of herself. She worked too many hours at the rock-and-roll radio station. She comforted her mother, and on the days her father couldn't make it out of bed, Rita called his boss with an excuse. She helped her brothers with their homework while ignoring her own.

Rita had a boyfriend, Terry, who at nineteen was an alcoholic and a gambler. He worked part-time at a bar/keno parlor. He had met Rita at a street dance and been immediately attracted to her. That night he danced with her and invited her to a barbecue at his place on Sunday. Rita brought a cake and did all the cooking.

She said, "He's nicer than Dad. I know he's got problems, but he never gets mad at me." She paused, embarrassed. "I know dating Terry is dumb, so don't tell me."

I decided to save the topic for another day. Like many daughters of alcoholics, Rita was choosing men like her father. Love was connected to anger, violence, unpredictability and shame. She dated Terry in the hope that this time the story might have a happy ending. She dated him because the familiar was comfortable, even if it was the familiar chaos of a relationship with an alcoholic.

Even though Rita considered herself an adult, she really wasn't. She hadn't developed any identity except that of helper. She hadn't thought through issues like her own sexuality or career plans. She had no personal goals or sense of direction. She had bad judgment about relationships, and she was uneasy socially and failing in school.

Like most girls who have been emotionally or physically abused by their fathers, Rita had internalized many of the messages that he sent. She didn't think that a decent guy would like her or that she was worthy of a loving relationship. She saw her value to men in primarily sexual terms. As is true of many women with abusive fathers, Rita was patient, tolerant and good-hearted, all qualities that helped her survive in the home of an alcoholic. She was competent and responsible, but under the surface Rita believed her value was in serving others.

I wanted to help her develop a sense of herself independent of this family. She needed guidance in even imagining good relationships. She was unsure what a healthy male would be like. Men were like boys to her; they needed patience, care and humoring. Women were either like her mother—weak and ineffectual—or like herself, required to take on the weight of the world and handle it without complaint.

Rita had a genetic tendency toward alcohol abuse; she had observed the misuse of alcohol, and she was under a great deal of stress and unsure of herself. Alcohol was her way to deal with pain. I recommended she stop drinking and find a support group.

Rita was ready for change. She had a difficult background to overcome and limited support. She was young and overburdened, but she had energy, honesty and openness. I was hopeful that Rita would avoid a "screwed-up life like [her] parents." At the end of our session I asked Rita when she would like to come back. She tossed her lovely hair and said, "Tomorrow."

CASEY (18)

Casey came in with her parents after her father discovered diet pills in her purse. This alone might not have alarmed him, but the pills fit with other evidence that Casey had been using drugs. So he called for an evaluation of her chemical use.

Casey sat between her parents. She was a gawky young woman in white shorts who seemed much younger than her eighteen years. Her legs were red and covered with goose bumps from the cold outside. Her mother pointed to them and said, "You should have worn slacks." Casey flushed. "I thought it was warmer than it is."

I asked how she felt about coming and she responded with a glib "okay." Her father contradicted her with a shake of his head. "We had to force her to come." He outlined Casey's problems. She was messy, dishonest, irresponsible with money and immature socially. She had come home drunk several times in the last month.

I asked Casey what she thought about her dad's remarks. She was cheerful and agreeable. "I do drink quite a bit."

We talked some about the history of the family. Casey was the second child. Her older sister had died as a baby two years before Casey was born. Losing a baby made Casey's parents protective and indulgent, "worrywarts," as Casey called them. Her parents worried about her health, her relationships, her schoolwork and her tendency to chubbiness. She'd seen many doctors, had tutors and been sent to special camps for the chubby and socially awkward. Her parents had worked to cushion Casey from the slings and arrows of ordinary life, and now they had a daughter who had no confidence or experience in meeting challenges.

We talked about Casey's upcoming high school graduation, her summer plans and her new part-time job as a waitress. Her parents were happy she had a job, but worried that she wouldn't show up for work or that the stress might be too much.

I thought that Casey was being killed by too much kindness and concern. Her parents were "inflicting help" on her. I wanted them to back off and let her take care of herself. Certainly she would make mistakes, but she would have a chance to learn from them and grow. Right now, except for her size, Casey wasn't growing much at all. I decided to see Casey alone. Meanwhile I predicted she would do fine at her waitressing job.

At our first individual session, Casey plopped down on the couch and groaned, "I got drunk again last night. I'm scheduled to wash dishes and mow the lawn until I die of old age."

I decided to save alcohol questions for later and asked what concerns she had about herself. Her face reddened and she was quiet. "I'm fat," she said. "That's why I took the pills. I want a boyfriend."

She told me about her first date her sophomore year. Stan picked her up for a movie, but instead of driving downtown, he opened a beer and headed toward the country. A more experienced or confident girl would have told him to take her home, but Casey was paralyzed. She had no idea what to do. She plastered herself to her door and stared out the window. Stan stopped by a state lake and opened another beer. He turned up the radio and pulled Casey toward him. She was terrified and stiff and Stan tried to warm her up with kisses and joking, but she stayed unyielding. She was afraid he might rape her, and this could well have happened had not another car of lovers pulled up. He swore and called her a lesbian. Then, much to her relief, he started the motor and drove her home.

After that Casey wondered if she was a lesbian. She knew very little about sex and was afraid to tell her parents what had happened. She was afraid to talk to other girls because they might think she was naive. Casey determined that the next guy who asked her out would realize she was sophisticated and a 100 percent heterosexual. When Sam asked her out, she got loaded and offered to have sex with him before he even asked. After Sam, there were others. Always she got drunk and then "did it." Finally she quit dating. She knew she wasn't handling things well and she was afraid of getting AIDS.

Alcohol was a way of deadening her anxiety so that she could have sex, and also of killing her guilt feelings afterward. If Casey learned to deal with her sexuality, she would have less need to drink. As we talked, it was clear that Casey had allowed guys to define her relationships with them. She felt so badly about her appearance that she was grateful that anyone wanted her. She was so eager to please that she never considered whether her needs were being met. As an assignment, I asked her to think about what kind of men she liked. What qualities would they have? What would be their interests? How would they treat her?

The next time Casey came in with a list. She pulled it out of her pocket and smoothed it on her knee. She read aloud, "I like guys who are handsome, athletic, caring and good listeners." She paused. "I know this is asking too much, but I like guys who enjoy what I enjoy—horseback riding and basketball."

"Do you know any guys who have these qualities?"

Casey thought for a while. "I know three guys like that, but they wouldn't ask me out."

"It's the nineties," I said. "Women can ask out men."

Casey giggled at my suggestion, but wanted to talk about how exactly she might do it. I encouraged her to plan something low-key, to pay her own way and to avoid alcohol and sex. She looked at me incredulously. "What kind of a date will that be?" But when I started to answer, she waved it away. "I was joking. I'll give it a try."

Next time I saw Casey she had good news. She liked her job. Her room was still a mess, but she had managed to put thirty dollars in her savings account. Best of all, she had asked a guy on a date and he had accepted. She told me, "We went to the basketball game. I drove my parents' car and met him at the auditorium. Afterwards he took me out for a frozen yogurt and we talked."

Casey was amazed that she had the power to make an evening go her way. She was surprised and pleased that a man could value her for other reasons besides her sexuality. Furthermore, this guy asked her for another date, something that rarely happened with her previous dates.

We rehearsed saying no to sexual advances. Casey wrote a little speech to give when necessary. "I'm someone who likes to start slow and get acquainted before I get too physical. So let's go out a few times and become closer friends. Later we can talk about whether we want a physical relationship."

Over time Casey learned to check and recheck: "Is this person meeting my criteria for a good date?" If he wasn't, she learned to say good-bye gracefully but firmly. She decided she did not want to have sex with anyone till they had known each other for several months and had talked about what sex would mean to both of them. They didn't need to be engaged, but they needed to trust each other.

As she gained confidence, she spent less time with her family. She fought less with her parents as she developed more of a life for herself. Even though Casey was more confident socially, she still had the habit of drinking. She had learned to rely on alcohol to relax. I recommended a group called Women for Sobriety. Casey liked the atmosphere there. She had two serious slips in the first months of therapy, both of them triggered by anxiety about dating. But as she grew more independent and took more responsibility for her life with her parents and peers, she became more prudent in her consumption of chemicals.

DANIELLE (16)

Because Danielle's parents were blind, I offered to drive to their home for a family therapy session. Danielle had been to my office earlier to discuss her recent arrest for being a minor in possession of alcohol. She was alarmed and guilty about the arrest. She hated to worry her parents, whom she loved and respected.

Danielle's family lived downtown in a small pink clapboard house. Danielle, a tall, sturdy girl with red-gold hair, met me at the door. Today she was dressed in jeans and a Mexican-style blouse. She showed me into the small living room where her parents, Martin and Antoinette, waited on the couch. Martin was a studio musician and a piano tuner. Antoinette ran a small telephone answering service. In the early evening calls were infrequent; nevertheless, the phone rang just as we sat down.

The cat, Bon-Bon, sat on Antoinette's lap. The room was dusty and cluttered with tapes, CDs and records. Harpsichord music was playing on the first-rate stereo system. Danielle poured strong tea for all of us.

Watching Danielle make introductions and serve tea, I was struck by how close this family was. Many things seemed understood—who would answer the door and be hostess, how to hand over the cups of steaming tea, who needed the sugar and cream, how phone interruptions would be handled and who would talk first.

It was Danielle. "Thanks for coming. I told my parents about our talk."

Martin sipped his tea. "Danielle has always been a good daughter. We don't want you to think otherwise. It's highly unusual for her to be in trouble."

Antoinette said, "She takes care of us and keeps things lively around here. She makes us laugh." She stroked Bon-Bon thoughtfully as she talked. "Danielle has been quieter this year. We've had trouble keeping track of her. There have been nights she came in late and wouldn't tell us where she'd been."

"She's been moodier," Martin added. "But still, she's not a rebellious girl. We're proud of her."

I was amused by how difficult it was for these parents to speak harshly of their daughter. I assured them that I too thought Danielle was marvelous. However, Danielle jumped in to argue with us. "I haven't been a perfect daughter. I've lied to you and let you down."

Martin said, "We weren't prepared. The first time we smelled alcohol on Danielle's breath we were too shocked to respond."

"I got away with more than most kids because they couldn't check on me." Danielle continued, "I'm the one who drives in the family. I told them I was going one place and went another. If they called and caught me lying, I'd tell a bigger lie."

Martin said, "Yes. Our car supposedly had ten flat tires this year. I checked with a friend and he told me this wasn't likely."

"Why did you start drinking?"

Danielle shrugged. "I always felt different from other kids. Everyone told me how much my folks depended on me, how important I was to them. In junior high I got sick of that. I wanted to be normal. All the normal kids were getting in trouble, and I thought, Why can't I?"

I watched the parents' faces as Danielle talked. Their faces were less guarded than those of sighted people. They had spent less time on impression management. Their faces showed curiosity, concern, pride and fear.

Danielle continued, "I know this sounds lame, but I like to get high. I like the experience of being relaxed and happy. I like marijuana too. It was wrong to be loaded and driving; I won't do that again. But otherwise I don't want to change. My parents want me to go into treatment, but it would wipe out their life savings. I won't let them spend their money that way."

Antoinette asked me, "What should we do to help Danielle?"

Martin looked hopefully in my direction. "Please reason with her. Her health is the most important thing to us."

I thought Danielle used chemicals in an experimental and recreational way. I saw no reason to doubt her explanation that she wanted to be a normal kid. I suspected that she pressured herself to be an ideal daughter to these two loving parents. Perhaps I could help her lower her expectations of herself and also learn to relax in healthier ways.

I said that Danielle was already on her way to being more responsible about her alcohol use. She'd admitted she had a problem and talked about it with her family in an honest, open way. She'd promised not to drive and drink again. I agreed with the parents that her health was the most important thing, but I wasn't sure that Danielle needed a treatment center. We could try therapy first.

Danielle picked Bon-Bon off her mother's lap. "I'll try therapy, but I want to pay for it myself."

"No, no," her parents said in unison. "We want to help you." Martin came over and gave her a hug. So did Antoinette. I thought as I watched this family with their cat and their music that they were fortunate people.

KELLI (15)

Dressed in green polyester pants and a yellow golf shirt, Kevin looked provincial in spite of his international work as an agronomist. Roberta, who was a public health nurse, was sweet-faced and matronly. She began, "We found pot in Kelli's bedroom."

"We have known Kelli was on something for months now," Kevin said. "She and her boyfriend, Brendan, act too goofy sometimes."

I asked about alcohol, and Roberta said, "Kelli wouldn't touch the stuff. She's a vegetarian and hates alcohol and tobacco. She's attracted to the drugs of the sixties. She's a hippie at heart."

Kelli was the youngest of three daughters. Her older sisters were smart, successful and attractive. Carolyn had been a straight-A student and a Miss Nebraska finalist who was married to an attorney and pregnant with her first child. Christina was in her senior year at Grinnell, where she'd been a student leader. Soon she'd be on her way to medical school.

Roberta said that they were an ordinary family who liked church, Big Red football and community socials. Their first two daughters were easy to raise. "We mainly stayed out of their way. Other kids flocked around them. They never needed rules or curfews. We actually told Christina not to study so hard.

"Kelli is so different," she said. "We've been at a loss what to do with her. She likes different food, movies, music and people. She's attracted to strangeness. All the things that worked with the others seem to be wrong for her."

"The older girls were self-motivated while Kelli doesn't care about success," Kevin said. "She's hard to punish because she doesn't want money, television or new clothes. Once we tried to ground her from her boyfriend and she threatened to kill herself. She would have too."

"We're sure she's having sex," Roberta added. "Brendan and she are inseparable. He's a nice enough boy, but we know they do drugs together. Her sisters never drank or took drugs."

"It sounds like the older girls are a hard act to follow," I said.

Kelli was desperately seeking her own niche, different from her sisters. Since they had the glorious and successful niches, Kelli was left with the black-sheep niche.

"One of the problems with your earlier success is that it makes it hard to do things differently. It was easy to parent Christina and Carolyn. But for Kelli, you may need a consultant."

"Kelli thinks we love her sisters more than her, but it's not true," Roberta said. "We're just mainstream people and Kelli is harder for us to understand."

The next week I met with Kelli, who was tall and thin with long brown hair. She could have been a beauty queen if she tried, but clearly she wasn't trying. She wore an orange shirt, torn jeans and combat boots with thick olive socks. She was polite but distant. I had the feeling she was enduring this session, so I talked about the sixties for a while.

Kelli said, "I wish I'd been alive back then. I have nothing in common with the kids of today."

"What do you like to do?"

"Hang out with Brendan. We feel the same way about things. He likes me just the way I am."

She looked at me suspiciously. "Did my mom tell you we were having sex?"

I nodded.

"It's no big deal," Kelli said. "We love each other and I'm on the pill."

I asked her what a "big deal" was from her point of view.

She tossed back her hair and said, "My parents. They just aren't like me. They like to play bridge and do crossword puzzles. They watch John Wayne movies and listen to Conway Twitty albums. I feel like the hospital made a mistake and sent me to the wrong home. My sisters were perfect for my parents. They are middle-class success stories. I'm not going to be."

I asked how she felt as she talked. "It hurts. They try to love me as much as my sisters, but they can't. My parents love it when we achieve—that's what makes us worth something. They don't know what to love about me."

"What do you want?"

"Enlightenment—what the Buddhists call 'Nirvana.' "

I said, "That's pretty ambitious."

"Brendan and I read about Buddhism. When we have the money we're going to the Naropa Institute in Boulder."

We spent the rest of the session talking about Buddhism. Kelli knew a surprising amount for a fifteen-year-old. She was animated on this subject, and at the end of our time she seemed reluctant to go.

The next session Kelli wore those same boots, jeans and socks, but this time with a rose-colored T-shirt. She brought me some drawings she'd made of the Buddha, the tree of his enlightenment and the elephant god. She said, "I hate alcohol and cigarettes. They destroy consciousness."

"How about other drugs?"

"We take mushrooms now and then and acid." She paused. "Some of the best moments of my life were on acid."

She liked the way LSD changes reality—the way music sounds different, colors are more vivid and oranges taste better. She had a battered old copy of Timothy Leary's *Road Maps to the Mind.* But she said, "I prefer a natural high."

We discussed nonchemical ways to alter consciousness. I told her about psychological research on "flow experiences." We talked about how meditating and also the creative process can alter consciousness. Kelli asked if she could bring Brendan in to meet me and I agreed.

I met again with Roberta and Kevin and agreed with them that Kelli was different from her sisters. They would need different ways to approach her. For example, maybe they could take her and Brendan to visit the Naropa Institute or help them enroll in a course on Buddhism. Kelli needed to define herself in new ways, not as different from her sisters, not as a drug user, but as a sensitive, idealistic and philosophical person.

––––––––

When I talk to teenagers about chemical use, I try to remember that curiosity and exploration are normal at this age. Healthy teenagers experiment, and it's not sensible to label every teenager who uses chemicals as an addict. Except in extreme cases, it's better to deal with the problems that inspire chemical use and the problems that chemical use causes. I avoid labels.

Relationships are powerful agents for change. I work at connecting and at helping parents connect with teenage girls who are abusing drugs or alcohol. I also try to find something to substitute for the chemicals—a new habit that's more positive and a new identity that's less self-destructive. And I include friends in the process. I acknowledge bonds and encourage teens to help each other.

Research shows that girls are less likely to be heavy drinkers if they are introduced to moderate drinking in their homes. Teenage girls who drink only when they are with peers are more at risk for problems. Probably it's a good idea to offer girls a small glass of wine at special dinners or on holidays. That keeps drinking from being viewed as rebellious behavior.

Heavy chemical use in teenagers can be a signal that families need to make changes. Often chemical abuse is a cry for help. Sometimes teenagers may simply need more attention. Ordinary families may need help dealing with the stresses of adolescence. Or they may need lessons in how to communicate, relax, appreciate each other or have fun. Other times parents may have their own addictions to conquer, or the family may have secrets to unravel. Heavy alcohol or drug use may indicate self-hate or despair about unsolved family problems.

It's good that schools now have early and fairly extensive education about chemical use and abuse. Everyone should learn the signs of problem drinking and drug use. For example, the National Council on Alcoholism recommends the 1, 2, 4 rule. That is, don't have more than one drink an hour, two drinks a day or four drinks a week total, and you'll be safe from developing problem drinking. Most girls are shocked when I share this rule. They say, "Everyone I know drinks more than that."

Teenagers are eager to help family members and friends with chemical abuse problems and they can be given guidance in this. Peer counseling and support for moderate use is highly effective. Everyone should know where to go for help and, regardless of income, have access to that help.

Finally our culture needs to change. For many adolescents, smoking and drinking stand for rebellion and maturity. The media contributes to this illusion, linking sophistication with self-destructive, unrestrained behavior, not prudent, thoughtful behavior. The characters with self-control are often portrayed as boring geeks.

Corporate America encourages girls to consume products such as Cokes and designer jeans, and chemicals such as alcohol and nicotine, to sedate their natural and understandable pain. As the cigarette companies have discovered, adolescent girls are perfect targets for anyone peddling sophistication. In fact, adolescent girls are the only population group whose smoking has increased over the last twenty years.

Advertising teaches that pain can be handled by buying and consuming products. There's big money to be made in creating wants and then encouraging consumers that these wants are needs, even rights. We are taught to go for it. We're encouraged that if it feels right, it is right. And we're told, "Don't worry, spend money."

The junk values of our mass culture socialize girls to expect happiness and regard pain as unusual. Advertising suggests that if they aren't happy, something is wrong. Pain is presented as something that can and should be avoided by consuming the right things. It's treated as an anomaly, not an intrinsic and inescapable part of being human. Contrast this worldview with Thoreau's line: "The mass of men lead lives of quiet desperation." Or with Buddha's statement: "Life is suffering."

America in the 1990s places enormous emphasis on the gratification of every need. It hasn't always been so. When Robert E. Lee was asked the best message to teach the young, he replied, "Deny thyself." Freud wrote that happiness was the experience of loving and working. He believed that the gratification of all wants was impossible and would be dangerous to individuals and society as a whole.

As a society we have developed a "feel good" mentality. We need to rethink our values and to break the link between negative feelings and chemical use. Ideally, we would offer our children new definitions of adulthood besides being old enough to consume harmful chemicals, have sex and spend money. We would teach them new ways to relax, to enjoy life and to cope with stress. We have a responsibility to teach our children to find pleasure in the right things.

SEX AND
VIOLENCE

■

CHRISTY (14)

During our shifts at the homeless shelter, Christy and I talked about her life. Her mom was a state worker and her father an engineer. They were strict but loving, child-centered parents. They were also devout Catholics who taught Christy that sex was for marriage. They lived in a ritzy neighborhood, and Christy was a member of an elite track club. As a child, she'd won many races. She was in the gifted program and attended summer camps for gifted kids. Because she was ahead of her classmates, she skipped third grade. But this meant that when she hit junior high she was immature socially and physically.

"I was nervous about school," Christy said. "I wanted to prove I was as cool as the other kids. I wanted a boyfriend to take me to the parties that the popular girls got invited to. I knocked myself out to get into that crowd."

I asked how she did that.

"I realized right away that being smart was trouble. I felt like I was 'severely gifted.' I got teased a lot, called a brain and a nerd. I learned to hide the books I was reading and pretend to watch television. This one guy in my math class threatened to beat me up if I kept breaking the curve. I made Bs and Cs. My parents were mad at me, but I ignored them. I knew what I needed to do to get by."

Christy joined her school's cross-country team. Some of the boys in the elite group invited her to parties. She had a gang of friends who were the jocks and the preps at the school. By the end of seventh grade, she even had a boyfriend.

"He was great, really sweet. We kissed and held hands but nothing else. We talked on the phone about twenty hours a week. Our parents wouldn't let us go out."

Her first boyfriend moved after the seventh grade. But soon many other boys were asking her out. She liked Adam, who was older and more experienced than her first boyfriend. She said, "I remember this one party. We were drinking margaritas and playing this question game. Someone asked about sex. Have you ever gone all the way, or had sex in a car, or had oral sex, or sex with two people at once—stuff like that. If the answer was yes, we had to drink our margaritas."

"I was the only one who never took a drink and I felt so embarrassed." Christy paused.

Christy explained that she liked Adam and wanted to make out, maybe "go to second base," but stop before they had intercourse. She was curious about sex and eager to try things, but she didn't want to lose her reputation or break her parents' rules. She said that making out worked for a while, but then she and Adam started fighting all the time because he wanted to have sex and she didn't. Finally she broke it off.

Several other guys asked her out right away. She accepted a few offers, but all the dates ended as wrestling matches. Some of her friends became sexually active during this time and they encouraged her to follow their example. But she said, "They want me to have sex so they won't feel guilty. I won't help them out that way."

"I wanted to date but not have sex," Christy said. "It's hard to be popular without a boyfriend, but I didn't care. I wanted to wait at least until I got my braces off. Maybe it was all that Catholic guilt."

She said, "Now mostly I go on group dates. I always make sure I pay my own way so I don't owe a guy anything. I'm careful not to get too close. I hide my looks and my intelligence. I've learned that being too smart or too pretty can get me in trouble. I want to be ordinary, to fit in."

After class one day a group of coeds stood around my desk. I'd just given a lecture on sexuality in the 1990s and they had observations to share. Ginger said, "Your ideas about healthy sexuality are interesting, but they won't work in the real world. No one talks about sex like you suggest. It would be too embarrassing."

Jane added, "Everyone is so mixed up that they just get drunk and do it. They try not to think about it the next day."

"I'm scared to go on dates," Suzanne said. "I'm afraid of getting raped, of getting AIDS."

Marianne said, "I'm lucky that I have a steady boyfriend. We've been together since our freshman year. He's not perfect, but it's better than dating."

In unison they all said, "Anything's better than dating."

Girls face two major sexual issues in America in the 1990s: One is an old issue of coming to terms with their own sexuality, defining a sexual self, making sexual choices and learning to enjoy sex. The other issue concerns the dangers girls face of being sexually assaulted. By late adolescence, most girls today either have been traumatized or know girls who have. They are fearful of males even as they are trying to develop intimate relations with them. Of course, these two issues connect at some level and make the development of healthy female sexuality extraordinarily complicated in the 1990s. The first section of this chapter will deal with the old issues of emerging sexuality, and the second section will discuss sexual trauma and its effects on young girls.

America doesn't have clearly defined and universally accepted rules about sexuality. We live in a pluralistic culture with contradictory sexual paradigms. We hear diverse messages from our families, our churches, our schools and the media, and each of us must integrate these messages and arrive at some value system that makes sense to us.

Paradigms collide within each of us as we make decisions about our own sexuality. For example, Louise, a dignified widow, came in to discuss how she should behave sexually. She enjoyed dating, but her friends had warned her that men liked sex by the third date. Louise had been dating one man for several months and felt like a prude for refusing to have sex. She was afraid she'd lose him, and yet her values were that sex comes with marriage.

Paradigms collide between people. There are no clear agreements about the right ways to be sexual, so each couple must negotiate an agreement for themselves. At best, communication in this area tends to be awkward and fragmented. At worst, no one even tries. The real crash-and-burn misunderstandings come when people with radically different ideas date without discussing their paradigms. For example, two people go on a date and one of them believes sex is recreation while the other believes sex is the expression of a loving relationship. The next morning they awake with rather different expectations about their future together.

Or, a couple in therapy reported that their sex life had stopped. He was a consumer of pornography and a sexual adventurer. She was a social worker who counseled rape victims daily. He wanted sex to be frequent, experimental and recreational. After her long days as a therapist, she couldn't tolerate many of his ideas about sex.

Our culture is deeply split about sexuality. We raise our daughters to value themselves as whole people, and the media reduces them to bodies. We are taught by movies and television that sophisticated people are free and spontaneous while we are being warned that casual sex can kill us. We're trapped by double binds and impossible expectations.

A recent study of teenagers in Rhode Island documents the confusion. Teens were asked to respond to questions about circumstances under which a man "has the right to have sexual intercourse with a woman without her consent." Eighty percent said the man had the right to use force if the couple were married, and 70 percent if the couple planned to marry. Sixty-one percent said that force was justified if the couple had had prior sexual relations. More than half felt that force was justified if the woman had led the man on. Thirty percent said it was justified if he knew that she had had sex with other men, or if he was so sexually stimulated he couldn't control himself, or if the woman was drunk. More than half the students thought that "if a woman dresses seductively and walks alone at night, she is asking to be raped." Clearly at least 80 percent of these teenagers didn't know that a man never has a right to force sex.

Our cultural models for ideal female sexuality reflect our ambivalence about women and sex. Men are encouraged to be sexy and sexual all the time. Women are to be angels sometimes, sexual animals others, ladies by day and whores by night. Marilyn Monroe understood and exploited this split. She was an innocent waif and a wildcat, a child and a sultry sexpot. Understandably, girls are confused about exactly how and when they are to be sexy.

Girls receive two kinds of sex education in their schools: one in the classroom and the other in the halls. Classroom education tends to be about anatomy, procreation and birth. Students watch films on sperm and eggs or the miracle of life. (Even these classes are controversial, with some parents thinking that all sex education should come from parents.) Some schools offer information about sex, birth control and STDs, but most schools' efforts are woefully inadequate. Most do not help students with what they need most—a sense of meaning regarding their sexuality, ways to make sense of all the messages, and guidelines on decent behavior in sexual relationships.

In the halls of junior highs, girls are pressured to be sexual regardless of the quality of relationships. Losing virginity is considered a rite of passage into maturity. Girls may be encouraged to have sex with boys they hardly know. Many girls desperate for approval succumb to this pressure. But unfortunately the double standard still exists. The same girls who are pressured to have sex on Saturday night are called sluts on Monday morning. The boys who coaxed them into sex at the parties avoid them in the halls at school.

At the Red and Black Cafe, where local teens dance to grunge bands, the graffiti on the walls of the rest room speaks to the confusion. One line reads: "Everyone should make love to everyone." Just beside that line another girl had written: "That's how you die of AIDS."

Adolescent girls approach their first sexual experience with a complicated set of feelings. Sex seems confusing, dangerous, exciting, embarrassing and full of promise. Girls are aware of their own sexual urges and are eager to explore them. They are interested in the opposite sex and eager to be liked by boys. Sex is associated with freedom, adulthood and sophistication. The movies make sexual encounters look exciting and fun.

But girls are scared of many things. They are worried that they will be judged harshly for their bodies and lack of experience. They are worried about getting caught by their parents or going to hell. They fear pregnancy and STDs. They worry about getting a bad reputation, rejection and pleasing their partners. They have seen sex associated with female degradation and humiliation, and they have heard ugly words describing sex, words that have more to do with aggression than love. So they are fearful of being emotionally and physically hurt. For the most part, girls keep their anxiety to themselves. It's not sophisticated to be fearful.

Today more adolescent girls are sexually active earlier and with more partners. More than half of all young women ages fifteen to nineteen have had sex, nearly double the rates of 1970. Five times as many fifteen-year-olds are sexually active in 1990 as in 1970. Twice as many sexually active girls had multiple partners in 1990.

My own belief is that junior-high girls are not ready for sexual experiences beyond kissing and hand holding. Girls this age are too young to understand and handle all the implications of what they are doing. Their planning and processing skills are not adequate to allow them to make decisions about intercourse. They are too vulnerable to peer pressure. They tend to have love, sex and popularity all mixed up. And when they are sexual, they tend to get into trouble quite rapidly. They aren't emotionally or intellectually ready to handle the responsibilities that arise. The decision to have sex should be a North Star decision, that is, one that's in keeping with a sense of oneself, one's values and long-term goals.

By high school, some girls may be mature enough to be sexually active, but my experience is that the more mature and healthy girls avoid sex. Because of my work, I see the unhappiness of early sexual intimacy—the sadness and anger at rejection, the pain over bad reputations, the pregnancies, the health problems and the cynicism of girls who have had every conceivable sexual experience except a good one. I'm prepared to acknowledge exceptions, but most early sexual activity in our culture tends to be harmful to girls.

I want to make a distinction here between intercourse and other sexual experiences. It's healthy for girls to enjoy their own developing sexual responsiveness and to want to explore their sexuality. It's possible to be sexual and be a virgin. But one of the difficulties that girls have in the 1990s is that there's no established or easy way to stop a sexual encounter. Thus some girls avoid dating and touching because they do not know how or when to draw a line, to say stop. Ironically, the sexual license of the 1990s inhibits some girls from having the appropriate sexual experiences they want and need. They avoid intimacy because they have no control over what happens once they begin to explore.

As a graduate student in the 1970s, my first clinical work was to teach a sex-education class for delinquent teenage girls at a state institution. The girls were between thirteen and sixteen. All were sexually active. Two had been pregnant, one had been gang-raped, one had been involved in prostitution and another was known as the blow-job queen of the institution.

As we sat around the table for our first group, I was struck by how young these girls were, how unsophisticated and utterly ignorant they were about sex. They swore like longshoremen, but they knew little about their own bodies, contraception or pregnancy. One girl announced that "you can't get pregnant without oral sex cuz that's when the sperm goes into your belly." Another girl, who had been pregnant, said earnestly, "I really never had sex." Sex education had been the movies and television. Sex education had been their lessons on the streets.

The lack of physical information was bad enough. Worse was that these girls didn't have any guidelines for making decisions about sex. They were barely aware of what they were doing and afterward often "forgot" that they had had sex. They didn't know they had the right to make conscious decisions about sex. They didn't know how to say no.

I developed a sexual decision-making course. We role-played seduction scenes. I role-played the seducer with lots of animated tips from them. They were their embarrassed and inept selves—they giggled, looked down, barely whispered their objections and were easily cowed by small amounts of pressure. With lots of practice, they learned to deliver a loud, firm no. If the guy persisted, they learned to shout, push, punch and escape.

Then we talked about making decisions to be sexual. I explained that a girl's first sexual experience is important. It's a template for later experience. If she's fortunate, her first experience is with someone she loves and who loves her, and sex occurs in the context of an emotionally committed relationship. If she's fortunate, the lovemaking is gentle, passionate and deepens the caring between the two participants.

Almost none of the girls in that group were so fortunate. Their experiences had been confused, hurried and impersonal. Intercourse happened to them. Most of them had been coerced into sexual encounters. None had had sex as the result of a conscious choice to share love in a relationship.

I helped them do imagery work. Until they could picture a good experience, I doubted that they could have one. So I told them to have fantasies of good dates with respectful guys who were interested in where they wanted to go and what they wanted to do. The date should last all evening and include compliments, talk and fun. At first they found this impossible. They didn't think dates like that occurred, but gradually they could conceive of a decent date.

These girls desperately wanted acceptance and would do anything, including have sex with virtual strangers, to win approval. I taught them to develop their own list of criteria. At first the lists were heartbreaking. One girl said, "The guy should spend money on me—you know, take me to McDonald's or someplace." Another said, "The guy should say he likes me."

We started where they were. Any criterion was a step in the direction of assuming responsibility for making conscious choices about sex. They learned that they could decide who was a worthy sexual partner. After a few weeks some of the girls developed slightly tougher criteria.

All girls need help making sense of the sexual chaos that surrounds them. As opposed to what they learn from the media, they need to be told that most of what happens in relationships is not sexual. Relationships primarily mean working together, talking, laughing, arguing, having mutual friends and enjoying outings. Girls need to be encouraged to be the sexual subjects of their own lives, not the objects of others'. They need help separating affection from sex.

Girls want to be sexy but respected. They want to be cool and sophisticated, yet not jaded and promiscuous. They want to be spontaneous, yet not die of AIDS. Lizzie and Angela are examples of girls with typical problems with sexuality in high school. Lizzie is a good student; Angela is a dropout. Lizzie comes from a strong family and Angela from a broken home. Lizzie was popular and well adjusted, mature for her age; Angela was immature and impulsive, with few close relationships. Both girls were casualties of our cultural chaos.

LIZZIE (17)

Lizzie was referred by her school counselor because she wanted to transfer to a different school. Lizzie drove to my office for an after-school appointment. She was a willowy senior dressed in a plaid skirt and fashionable sweater. She was friendly and polite, but cautious about therapy. Early in the session she said, "I think I'm a healthy person mentally. I'm not sure I should be here. All my problems are in the real world, not in my head."

I asked what those real-world problems were. "My friends," she said. "Or rather the people I thought were my friends. At this point, most of them aren't talking to me."

She told me her story. Lizzie was from a working-class neighborhood. As a girl, she fished with her father and bowled with her uncle

Leon. She had a loving grandmother nearby who taught her to cook. Her parents worked in a tire factory along with most of the parents of her friends. The children had attended the same schools, played on the same soccer and baseball teams and hung out in the same parks and cafés. Lizzie had been well liked by both the girls and the boys. She was a good athlete in elementary school, and in junior high and high school she was a cheerleader.

Her sophomore year she started dating Paul. She had known him since kindergarten, but they began dating after a church hayrack ride. For over a year it was a wonderful relationship. He was a handsome football player. All of Lizzie's friends told her how much they envied her. Lizzie's parents liked Paul, and his parents liked her. Their junior year they were homecoming prince and princess. Everyone was sure that their senior year they would be king and queen.

The summer of Lizzie's junior year she worked all summer at a camp in the Rockies. It was great. The kids were fun, the scenery was breathtaking, and she liked one of the counselors. At first she and Myron were just friends. They took walks in the mountains and canoed on the clear lake under the cold stars.

Myron was from Chicago and on his way to Northwestern in the fall. He was everything that Paul was not—worldly, sophisticated and new. Lizzie resisted falling for him, but he was around every day and, as she said, "It's easy to fall in love in the mountains."

One night after talking for hours under a blanket on the shore of a mountain lake, they began kissing. Myron took off her shirt and then her slacks. He was eager for sex and Lizzie, while not quite so eager, was eager to please Myron. They became lovers that night.

The summer sped by. Lizzie answered Paul's weekly letters carefully. She told Paul that she missed him but was too busy to call or write long letters. She never mentioned Myron.

In late August she said good-bye to Myron. He invited her to come visit Chicago, but he didn't believe in long-distance relationships and warned her that he would date other girls. Lizzie was hurt about this, but told herself that, after all, they weren't engaged.

When she returned home, Paul asked, "Did you sleep with anyone?"

Lizzie looked stunned but didn't deny it. Paul interpreted that as an admission of guilt and he began to sob. They talked far into the night. Paul was hurt and upset, but communicative. He left saying he wanted to be friends.

The first few weeks of school were fine. Her friends were happy to see her and she was busy with cheerleading and the yearbook. She had some classes with Paul and his friends, which at first were comfortable, then awkward, then unbearable. Paul quit speaking to her. When she walked down the hall, Paul's friends called her names—slut or bitch—names she was surprised they would use, especially with her.

Lizzie tried to talk to Paul but he refused. His friends grew more belligerent and even warned her to leave him alone. She tried to wait it out, but time didn't seem to help. In fact, more friends chose sides over time. Most of the boys and several of the girls whom she'd known all her life quit speaking to her.

In October she was not invited to the party for the cheerleaders and athletes. She resigned from the cheerleaders. She considered talking to her parents, but knew that they would be most upset that she had had sex. So she went to the school counselor's office.

Telling me about all this, Lizzie was sad and angry. She knew this wasn't fair. She knew she had a right to decide who she would date. She resented being called a slut.

At first we managed the crisis. I encouraged her to cry, shout and do whatever helped her express all her feelings. We talked about immediate practical problems: Who could she sit with at lunch? (There were a few friends who had remained steadfast.) What should she do when guys called her names in the halls? (She decided to look them in the eye and say, "I hope you never have to go through something like this.") How could she spend her Saturday nights? (She decided to work at a shelter for abused women. That would help her feel less sorry for herself.) She decided to stay at her school. She didn't want to give Paul's friends the power to drive her out of her school in her senior year.

We talked about basic issues. I asked her, "What kind of people do you really want for friends? What do you have to give other people? What really makes you happy? What makes you feel proud of yourself? How do you set priorities and make good decisions about your time? How do you have a life that truly reflects your values?"

Meanwhile Myron no longer answered her letters. He wrote three times after they parted, but each letter was shorter. Lizzie admitted that the relationship was more important to her than it was to him. Having sex had also set her up to feel more pain when they separated. She felt some guilt about her decision. A part of her believed the boys who were hissing in the halls that she was a slut. Suddenly sex seemed fraught with peril.

Lizzie developed her own policies about sex, policies that were mature and thoughtful for a high school student. She decided to wait until she was in a long-term relationship with someone who cared for her at least as much as she cared for him. She wanted to discuss how sex would affect the relationship, and she wanted protection from pregnancy and STDs. She also decided that she would make her decisions to be sexual in the cold, clear light of day, not in the heat of passion on a date.

For now, Lizzie developed ways to treat herself after the long tough days at school—walks in Wilderness Park, good library books and trips to the coffeehouse with a friend. She reminded herself that there was life after high school. Lizzie begin looking into college.

Gradually things calmed down. Paul started dating another girl, and he and his friends lost interest in punishing Lizzie. Lizzie was not as popular as she had been her junior year, but popularity mattered less to her. She stayed close to two of her girlfriends since childhood and made some new friends at the shelter.

When she stopped therapy she was dating a college student. They made out, but stopped short of intercourse. Lizzie had decided to wait for a while. She wasn't ready to handle the pain that followed losing a lover.

Lizzie was a strong, well-adjusted young woman, but like all teenagers, she was caught between competing values when it came to sex. Her parents expected her to be a virgin when she married. Her boyfriend over the summer encouraged her to have sex, even though the relationship would be short-term. Her high school friends were outraged, not that she had had sex, but that she had had it with someone they didn't know. Lizzie learned some lessons from her experiences. She learned to take care of herself and withstand disapproval. She learned to think about her relationship choices and to take responsibility for sexual decisions.

ANGELA (16)

I first met Angela when she was four months pregnant by Todd, her boyfriend of several months. She bounded into my office wearing a black leather skirt and a low-cut T-shirt that had SKID ROW printed on the front. In a matter of moments, Angela was spilling out her life story.

Her dad had had an affair when Angela was in eighth grade. Her mom left for Arizona with her younger brother and she seldom heard from them. Angela lived with her dad, his new partner Marie and her three young children.

Angela complained that she seldom saw her dad alone and that the kids were "spoiled and hyper" and stole her stuff. She had no privacy and her dad and Marie expected her to baby-sit so that they could go out on weekends.

I asked her about school and she wrinkled her nose. "I had to go to the learning center till I turned sixteen, but I hated it there. As soon as I had my birthday I dropped out."

"What did you hate?"

Angela sighed elaborately and stretched her white arms above her spiky red hair. "It was boring. I hated all the junk we had to take. The girls were snobs."

"Tell me about your parents."

She sighed. "Mom's ultra-religious. When I told her I was pregnant she started to pray. Then she disowned me. She likes my brother best. He's too young to have sinned all that much."

She leaned back into the couch. "I get on better with Dad. He's more low-key. He's mad, but he still loves me. He wants me to live with him and Marie till the baby is born."

"What about after the baby is born?"

Angela said, "I want to live with Todd, but if I can't do that, I'll move into subsidized housing. I'm already signed up."

"Is Todd the baby's father?" I asked.

She giggled like the young girl she was. "Todd's great. He's so cute."

"How long have you gone with him?"

She held up her hand. "Five months. That's the longest I've stayed with anyone."

"Will he help you with the baby?"

"He wants to, but he's got two kids already," Angela answered. "He has to pay both of their mothers child support and he has a car payment. He promised to go to the hospital with me. He's happy I'm pregnant."

I asked Angela for more details about her life after her parents' divorce and listened as she told me her story in a matter-of-fact, even chatty, way. I felt overwhelmed by so many problems facing someone who failed eighth-grade math. At the end of our session I asked her, "If you weren't pregnant, what would your goals be?"

Angela grinned and said, "I'd want to be an MTV star."

Our time was up. I handed Angela an appointment card. She chided me gently, "You didn't ask about the names."

I smiled at her.

"Alexandra or Alex, what do you think?" she asked.

"I think they are beautiful names."

After Angela left, I thought about her. Her perkiness in the face of her enormous problems was both endearing and unnerving. I liked her naiveté, optimism and energy. I hoped she had enough to pull her through the next few months.

The next session we talked about Angela's social life. Since the divorce, she escaped to a video arcade that was a hangout for the lost and troubled kids in the north part of town. Nearby there were drug busts, shootings and several rapes. Angela couldn't have picked a worse place. Her third night there, Noah offered to take her for a drive in his truck. They drove to the country and he encouraged her to have sex.

Angela described the experience to me. "I thought Noah was cute, but I wasn't ready for sex. I hadn't really thought about it, but Noah came on strong and it happened. I didn't enjoy it much. I thought, What's the big deal?"

After Noah, she had a new boyfriend every few weeks. She'd be attracted to someone, go out with him, not on a date really, but cruising or to his apartment. Sometimes she had sex with guys who didn't even know her last name and vice versa. Angela always hoped this guy would become her boyfriend. Usually though, early into the relationship, they broke up. Angela would be heartbroken for a few days and then meet another "cool guy." She had crushes just the way junior-high girls always do. The difference between her and girls twenty years ago is that she had sex with all her crushes.

Todd was a regular at the video arcade. He was tall and blond with a James Dean style. Girls fell for him. Angela noticed him her first week, but he often brought his little daughter with him and Angela assumed he had a regular girlfriend.

Five months ago, after she broke up with yet one more crush, Todd approached her in the concession area and offered to buy her a Coke. Angela said, "He was so sweet. I told him I'd been dumped and he was sympathetic. He wasn't hustling me or anything, he just wanted to talk."

The next night Angela wore her best outfit to the arcade. Todd came over to talk to her again. After an hour he suggested they go to his place where they could have more privacy. Angela agreed and that night they had sex. Two weeks later she missed her period.

We ended that appointment with Angela promising to see a doctor for a checkup. I said I'd be happy to meet Todd if he could come with Angela.

Angela came to her next appointment in black tights with a white sweatshirt, her first maternity outfit. She carried a copy of *All About Babies* and told me immediately that she was depressed. Todd wouldn't come. He didn't "believe in shrinks."

She sighed and ran her hands through her hair. "I went to Birthright this week to try to get money. They made me watch their sucko film about fetuses. I've been to welfare about ADC and it's so complicated. There's piles of forms to fill out and you have to prove everything. The lady who interviewed me was a bitch. Plus, I'm trying to quit smoking."

"Have you been to a doctor yet?"

"We can't find a doctor who takes Medicaid. This week has sucked." Angela sighed. "Todd's being such a jerk. I've hardly seen him. He says he's busy at work, but he's been at Holly's house. She's the mother of his little girl."

Angela told me that Marie's kids had chicken pox. Her dad was bitching about money. Todd's car needed a hundred dollars in repairs and that made him crabby. She'd been throwing up in the morning.

I asked how she felt about having a baby, and for the first time that morning she smiled. "I'm happy about that. I'm glad I'll have someone to love."

We spent the hour talking about her pregnancy. Angela had a project that she was interested in—being a mother. She loved looking at baby clothes at Goodwill and talking about pregnancy with her friends. She no longer felt so inferior to girls who stayed in school. She had something they didn't have. I'm glad we had a happy session because the next time Angela came in Todd had broken up with her.

Angela's eyes and nose were red from crying when she told me the news. But by then she was mostly mad. "How could he be such a jerk? He promised me that he'd stay with me.

"He called me last night and said that he was moving in with Holly." She wobbled her head sarcastically. "They need him."

She continued. "I hate men. All the guys I've dated have turned out to be assholes."

At the end of our session she reported some good news. "I found a doctor and I haven't had a smoke in six days."

We talked about relationships in later sessions. Angela realized that after her folks' divorce she'd been looking for love. She fell for any guy who told her she was pretty. Because she gave herself so impulsively and easily, she was hurt frequently. She grew to expect rejection and a part of her wasn't surprised when Todd left her.

"If you take a little time, maybe you could find someone who would stick around and make you happy," I said. "Could we at least set some criteria for what needs to happen before you have sex with a guy?"

"Like what?"

"You need to decide for yourself."

Angela looked skeptical.

I continued, "It takes some time to know if someone is honest and caring. Jerks can fake things for a while. How long do you think you would need to be with someone before you knew the true person?"

Angela thought awhile before she said, "Probably at least a month."

"That's one criterion. Do you have any others?"

"That he have a job and a car. That he be fun."

"Let's write these down," I said.

I saw Angela through most of her pregnancy. We talked some about her long-term goals. We discussed the perils of looking outside oneself for salvation. I suggested that being a mother wasn't a sufficient goal. She needed to find a way to support herself and the baby, and she needed to establish relationships with people of both sexes that lasted.

Angela called me from the hospital to tell me that Alex had been born. He weighed just under six pounds and had naturally blond hair like Todd's. Marie had been her birth coach. She sounded proud and happy. She said, "If you come up to visit, bring me some chocolate. I'm starving in here."

I last saw Angela a few months ago. I was shopping at a discount grocery and she strolled by with baby Alex. She looked her old self—a happy smile, apple-red hair and black eyeliner. She handed me Alex, who was a chubby baby with spiked hair. He was dressed in a black Leatherette jacket. I held him and he cooed. I cooed. I could tell by his good health and smiles that he was well cared for. As he wiggled in my arms, Angela told me about her current situation. She had a new boyfriend now, Carey, who actually met her criteria for a relationship. He worked as a TV repairman, owned a Jeep and liked babies.

Angela was working on her GED. Her mother had never seen Alex and rarely called Angela, but Angela talked to Marie about her problems. She, Carey and Alex ate Sunday dinner with her father and Marie.

She laughed as Alex held his hands out to her and she took him back quickly. "Isn't he great?" she said as she chucked him under the chin.

I pushed my cart down the aisle, happy that I had seen her and that things were going better than I would have predicted.

SEXUAL VIOLENCE

On Sunday mornings I wake early. Everyone in my family sleeps in and I like the time alone to read our local paper. One Sunday these were the headline stories: THE NIGHTMARE BEGAN WITH GOOD-BYE was about Candi Harms, a first-year university student. Candi lived in an apartment with her parents a mile from her boyfriend's place. Between 11:40, when her boyfriend walked her to her car, and midnight, when she was due home, something happened. Her abandoned car, with her keys and purse still in it, was found in a remote area north of town.

There was an article on Kenyatta Bush, an A student and a homecoming-queen candidate. Kenyatta disappeared from her high school one morning. Her backpack and books were found beside her car. Her body was found in a ditch the day of the school's homecoming.

Another headline announced that domestic violence was at an all-time high. One out of two women will be battered at some time in her life. In 1991, more than one million women reported being the victims of violent crimes at the hands of husbands or lovers; four thousand women were killed. Police estimated that more than six million assaults actually took place. In America, a woman is a victim of domestic violence every eighteen seconds.

On an inside page of the Sunday paper, a new fashion line was on display. The photo showed skimpily clad models wearing high heels at a New York show. On their tight, short outfits, over their breasts and buttocks, were painted bull's-eyes. The caption of the fashion photo read: "Walking targets."

These stories about women and girls were being told in every paper in America. They have a chilling effect on all young women. Many report their fears of being home alone, driving and going to swimming pools or theaters. Their confidence in their ability to navigate their world is eroded. They speak to the heart of the question, What is our environment like for girls?

I recently saw a bumper sticker on a young man's car that read: "If I don't get laid soon somebody's gonna get hurt." He is not alone in his philosophy. On any given day in America, 480 women and children will be forcibly raped, 5,760 women will be assaulted by a male intimate partner and four women and three children will be murdered by a family member.

The newer the study, the worse the figures. Rape is the "tragedy of youth" because 32 percent of all rapes occur when the victim is between the ages of eleven and seventeen. More than 15 percent of all college women have been raped since they turned eighteen. There is ominous evidence that the incidence of rape is increasing over time—the younger the age category of respondents, the higher the incidence of reported rape.

Statistics gloss over thousands of sad stories. This year one of my students missed class many times because she was being beaten by her boyfriend. Another group of students presented a panel discussion that included the results of a questionnaire about abuse in our classroom. None of the men but more than half the women students reported having been abused in a relationship. The last three times I've spoken at a high school class, a girl has approached me afterward to tell me she's been raped.

Classes on self-defense are filled with women and girls who recently have been victimized. I ask in my college classes what men do to protect themselves, and they say that they do nothing. I ask about women and we fill a blackboard with the ways women are careful. Fear changes behavior in a thousand ways—where and when young women can go places, who they talk to and where they walk, study and live.

I have seen so many victims of sexual assaults, some recent, still bruised and in shock, others struggling to come to terms with assaults that occurred years before when they were children. The youngest girls I worked with were two sisters, three and five, who had been brutally assaulted by a stepfather. My oldest client was a woman in her seventies who told about a rape that occurred when she was a teenager. Fifty years later, she still had nightmares. Some days I leave work thinking that every woman in America has been or will be sexually assaulted.

Long after the physical trauma of assault, victims must contend with emotional wounds. A number of factors influence the severity of the trauma that comes from sexual violence. Generally the trauma is more severe if the victim is young, if the assaults occur with frequency and over a long period of time, if the assailant is related to the victim and if the assault is violent. The most damaging assaults are violent ones by a family member.

Other factors that are important include the reactions of the victims. The sooner girls tell someone what happened and seek help, the better. The more support they have from family and others, the better. Finally, girls vary in their own resiliency and ability to handle stress. Some are capable of a quicker, more complete recovery than others. All victims of sexual assault are helped by posttraumatic stress work, either with family, friends or therapists.

ELLIE (15)

The first appointment with Ellie and her parents was painful for everyone. Ellie sank into my big chair and curled up like a small child. Her dark eyes were filled with tears. Her dad, Dick, was so overwhelmed he could barely talk. Ronette, who was small and dark-haired like her daughter, did most of the talking. She began our session by saying, "I'm so shattered by this that I can barely speak."

Dick was a welder and Ronette ran a hair salon in their home. They were hard workers who put their daughters first. Dick had an American flag flying in their yard and flag decals on all the vehicles. He'd been wounded in Vietnam and was president of his local VFW.

Ronette liked the country music at the VFW and was proud that she and Dick were good dancers. They'd taken dance lessons at the local community college. She was a good-hearted, hard-working woman who had run into few problems she couldn't solve. Both cared deeply about Ellie, who was the oldest of their three daughters.

Ronette took deep breaths and gave me an outline of events. "Ellie acted up some in eighth grade. She argued about everything—her chores, the telephone and her studies—but we weren't really worried about her. We knew kids acted that way. Her grades were pretty good, mostly Bs. She was on the swim team. We liked her friends."

Ronette sighed. "What worried us most was her disobedience. She skipped school several times and she slipped out at night with her friends. We were afraid she'd get hurt."

Ellie began sobbing as her mother talked, and Dick curled and uncurled his fists like a boxer ready for a fight. Ronette's face was tear-stained and tense, but she continued. "This last month she's driven us crazy. She's been insulting to us and mouthy at school. Yesterday she was called into the counselor's office because she pushed a kid in the hall. That's just not Ellie. Her grades dropped and she quit going out with her friends. We knew something had to have happened but we couldn't figure what."

Dick said, "We asked her what was wrong and she wouldn't tell us."

"Thank God Ellie told her counselor," Ronette said. "Things were going downhill fast."

I asked, "I know this is difficult, but what exactly happened?"

We all looked at Ellie, who buried her face in the chair.

Dick said, "We don't know many details. It's too hard to talk about."

Ronette said in a dull voice, "Ellie sneaked out to a bowling alley. She thought her friends would be there but they weren't. When she walked across the parking lot to come home, four boys pulled her into their car and raped her."

"I wish we'd known," Ronette said. "Ellie's not telling hurt us almost as much as the rape. We thought she trusted us more than this. We thought we had a good family."

I said, "It's common for girls to keep these things secret. It doesn't mean that you don't have a good family." I asked everyone how they were feeling as we talked.

Ronette said, "I can't believe this happened to Ellie. I feel guilty that I somehow didn't prevent this."

Ellie spoke, "I want to die."

Dick said, "I'd like to kill those guys."

"What should we do now?" Ronette asked. "None of us can sleep. We can't eat. Dick has missed the last four days of work."

The whole family was in shock and would need treatment. No doubt the younger girls were also in great pain. I planned to do some family work, but first I wanted to see Ellie alone.

I saw her for our next session. She looked a little better—her dark hair was out of her face and her eyes were dry. We visited a few minutes about school and her last swim meet. Then I brought up the rape.

She hugged a couch pillow to her chest and grew silent. Her fingernails and the tips of her fingers were badly bitten. She wasn't ready to talk, so I read her stories about other kids who had been hurt and how they came to terms with it.

I talked about the nature of trauma. "When you cut your finger, it bleeds; you may not like blood, it's scary and messy, but fingers that are cut are supposed to bleed. That's healthy. If they don't bleed, something is wrong. What happened to you is horrible and you are going to feel a lot of pain. You won't like it, it's messy and scary, but it's part of healing. Burying the feelings will hurt more in the long run."

Ellie stared at me from behind the pillow; her dark eyes were filled with pain. I explained that certain things happen with trauma. She might have nightmares and trouble with sleep. She might be afraid to go out and afraid to be home alone. She might feel crazy and like she will never recover. She might feel it was her fault and that she should have been smarter and prevented what happened.

Ellie nodded in agreement and said softly, "I keep seeing those guys over and over."

I sat with her as she cried.

The next four sessions were similar to our second session. I read to Ellie or told her stories about other girls I had known who made it through experiences like hers. Ellie's fingers stayed red and bitten. She didn't want to leave the house without one of her parents. She had no interest in doing anything with her friends.

Then in our sixth session Ellie came in and said, "Today I'm going to tell you what happened." She paused. "You get better if you talk about it, right?"

I nodded. Ellie said, "I want to get better."

She picked up the couch pillow and told me the story. She had planned at school to slip out and meet her friend for a Coke, but her friend's dad stayed up late that night and she was afraid to leave or even to call. So when Ellie arrived at the bowling alley, her friend wasn't there.

She said, "I waited for an hour. I wasn't feeling all that great; I had a headache and these high school boys kept staring at me. I wasn't scared of them, but I was embarrassed being there all by myself."

Her voice grew huskier. "I left the bowling alley about twelve. I noticed those guys were leaving, but I wasn't that scared. They pulled up beside me and offered me a ride. I didn't know them so I said no. They circled the lot and returned. Then they stopped the car and two of them got out and pulled me in."

Her voice was dead now. "There were four of them. I couldn't see their faces very well in the dark car. Two of them held me down in the backseat and they drove into the alley behind the bowling alley. I started to cry and one of them said, "Let's not do this." But his friends called him a weenie and he shut up. I don't think he raped me though. Only three guys raped me."

Ellie stopped and looked out the window. Her eyes were dry but filled with pain. She caught her breath and continued. "The driver raped me first. His buddies pulled down my jeans and he jumped on top of me. He didn't kiss me or anything."

Her voice broke, but then she continued. "I never had sex before and I felt like I was being split open. When he finished he encouraged the others to do it too. The two in the backseat took turns. I threw up. Later they used my shirt to clean up the puke."

Ellie was shaking now as if she were chilled. Her voice was flat and dead. "All the time they did this, they were laughing and joking. The driver said I must have wanted it or I wouldn't have been out alone. They didn't threaten to hurt me or anything. They just wouldn't let me go. They treated me like an animal, like I didn't have feelings.

"Afterwards, they dumped me out of the car and threw my shirt after me. I put it on so I wouldn't be topless and walked home. I was crying so hard I thought I might have a stroke or something, but I didn't go in the house till I stopped sobbing. I slipped in my window and lay in bed till morning. Then I took a bath and rinsed out the shirt."

Ellie looked at me. "I was amazed that the next morning my parents didn't notice anything. At breakfast they talked about my little sister's dental appointment."

Over the next few months I heard that story many times. At first Ellie told it without much emotion, but gradually she connected her words and her feelings and she sobbed as she told the story.

I asked her to write, but not send, letters to the guys who raped her, letters that allowed her to express all her anger. She scrawled letters beginning, "I hate you for what you've done to my life. You've ruined everything for me and my family. We'll never be normal again."

Dick bought her a punching bag and hung it in the basement. Nightly she went down and punched it. At first she had trouble connecting with her anger as she punched, but I encouraged her to keep trying. I told her to visualize the boys, the car, the rape as she hit. Once she did this, she hit with a frenzy and yelled about the rape. Afterward she collapsed in a puddle on the floor, but she felt calmer. All that anger was out of her and in the bag.

Meanwhile, the court case against the boys worked its way through the system. This re-traumatized Ellie in some ways. The police came by her house with further questions, and she had to tell her story at a deposition. The newspaper carried articles. Her name wasn't mentioned, but seeing the stories always caused her pain. The trial loomed in her future as a public exposure of her shame.

Dick and Ronette came in monthly to talk about their reactions to the rape. "For a while," Dick said, "our lives had no meaning." Both of them were afraid to let their daughters out of the house. Neither could bear to read news of rape or violence against women. Dick had revenge fantasies that interfered with his work. He woke at night covered with sweat, the way he had during the war in Vietnam. Sometimes Ronette cried when she was working on her customers. She would wrap a towel around the person's head and run out of the room.

Later the younger sisters joined our group and talked about how Ellie's experience affected their lives. The middle sister swore she would never go out alone at night or hang out with boys her family didn't approve of. The younger sister wanted revenge. Since the rape, she'd had trouble in school for acting up. Everyone agreed their family was different now. Other families talked about money, school and ordinary activities. They were obsessed with the rape. They felt a distance, an estrangement that victims often feel. They, like Ellie, needed a place where they could talk and cry.

Gradually Ellie recovered. Her fingers healed and her nails grew longer. She regained her enthusiasm for the swim team and school. She went out with her friends. She and her sisters signed up for a self-defense class. She said, "I want them to know how to defend themselves."

We talked about the implications of the rape for her future. Ellie said that she felt vulnerable. Now that she'd been raped she knew that it could happen to her. She would always be more cautious and more anxious than her friends. For right now she was not interested in boys. She wanted to stay away from sex for a long time. She said flatly, "I've lost all my curiosity."

One-fourth of all women are raped. Ellie was relatively lucky in that she was not severely injured, didn't contract an STD or get pregnant. She was also lucky that her parents were so concerned for her and so loyal. She received extended therapy. Even so, Ellie is a different girl than before the rape. She's more cautious and more dependent on her family. Just when she was beginning to explore the world, her wings were clipped. She's tiptoeing, not flying, through her adolescence.

Another common experience for girls is some kind of sexual assault by a friend or acquaintance. These are especially damaging because they erode girls' trust in the world around them and make all relationships potentially dangerous. Because the assailant is someone the victim knows, often the case is more difficult to handle afterward. The victim often feels responsible and is less likely to report it. And if she does report it, there's more likelihood the assailant will argue that the sexual experience was consensual.

One of my students was walking across the athletic field one night after orchestra practice when a football player she knew from her study hall threw her down on the grass and began to kiss her. She screamed and kicked and managed to escape. She never reported the incident, but she no longer walks alone to her car after school.

A client was raped while on a field trip with her biology class. A student who came into her tent to borrow a butterfly net held her down, choked her and raped her. The next morning she pretended it never happened. She denied the experience until a year later when she went camping with her family. She crawled into their tent and stopped breathing as memories flooded her. She told her mother what had happened and her parents reported the crime. The boy involved claimed consensual sex. After a year it was hard to prove otherwise and my client dropped the case. She came to therapy because she wanted to be able to camp without having breathing attacks. She wanted to be able to trust guys again.

A client doing volunteer work over the summer at a refugee center in Colorado was cornered and assaulted by the minister in charge of the project. She didn't report it because she was sure that no one would think the minister capable of such an assault.

Another student told of being a Little Sister at a fraternity. She'd been naive and gone to the Saturday night "testosterone party." One of the guys that she liked pulled her into a bedroom and tried to assault her. Fortunately she had taken a self-defense class at the YWCA and managed to escape. She never returned to the fraternity. She gets nauseous whenever she thinks about that afternoon. When she told me about the incident she asked, "Is that how men treat their little sisters?"

Anna Lisa lived in one of the safest neighborhoods in town. Her mother was a teacher. Her dad was a coach who helped with Anna

Lisa's Little League team. She was a white-haired eleven-year-old who always had a wad of bubble gum in her mouth. Her legs were bruised from sports injuries, and her arms were as thin and hard as rifles. Anna Lisa seemed a little younger than her age. Her favorite topic was horses. Anna Lisa read horse books, attended horseback riding camps and collected model horses. She was obsessed with owning her own horse. She wanted a white horse, which she planned to name Gardenia.

Anna Lisa came in because she had been sexually assaulted twice the previous summer. In July she was home with her older brother and his friend while her parents were out shopping. Her brother biked to the mall to rent a video and left Kyle to baby-sit. Kyle molested her in the twenty minutes her brother was gone. Anna Lisa didn't tell her parents about Kyle because she was afraid she'd get her brother in trouble.

A month later she went across the street to play with a friend whose father was an insurance executive. He answered the door and invited Anna Lisa in. She smelled beer on his breath, but that didn't alarm her. She figured her friend was around somewhere. The father locked the door and put his hand down her shirt. She pulled away and ran toward the back door. He chased her around their living room calling her a "pretty little girl" and a "sweetie pie." Fortunately, at that moment, her friend's mother drove up.

Red-faced and flustered, he swore as he pushed Anna Lisa into the backyard and told her to go home. He said that he was only teasing and tried to hand her some money. This time, thank goodness, Anna Lisa couldn't keep a secret. She ran home sobbing and told her mother what had happened and about Kyle as well. Her mother called the police and set up our appointment.

TERRA (15)

Terra was referred by her school counselor, who had been worried about her for some time. Terra had been failing classes and looking depressed. Then last week she'd come to school with a black eye. The counselor asked her about child abuse, but it turned out that the black eye wasn't from her mother but from her boyfriend, who had "accidentally hit her."

Today she sat quietly in my office, a small girl with dark hair and eyes. Only her fluttering hands betrayed her nervousness.

Terra said, "I don't need to be here. Mom and my counselor are making a big deal out of nothing."

"A black eye is nothing?"

Terra said, "Court would never have hit me if he hadn't been drinking. He apologized and bought me a rose. It's over. It won't happen again."

I asked about Court. Terra described him as seventeen, a high school dropout who worked at a body shop weekdays and customized vans on weekends. She said he'd had a tough life. His dad was an alcoholic and his mother ran around with other men. Court took care of his younger brothers when he was little. Even now he slipped them money.

They had been dating for a year and Terra wanted to marry him, but she admitted there were problems in the relationship. Court was jealous and controlling. He expected her to be either at school or at home waiting for him. He got mad if she even talked to other guys, and he didn't like her to do things with her girlfriends.

I asked about school and Terra flung her arms up in despair. "I hate school. I'm killing time there until it's legal to quit."

Terra told me that her mom had quit school at sixteen to marry and she'd done just fine. Well, not with her marriage, which had ended in divorce when Terra was two, but with her money. She cleaned houses for a living and earned more money than lots of women with high school degrees.

I asked about depression and Terra denied any problems. She said, "I'd be okay if people would leave me alone."

I asked about her family history. She talked about her parents' divorce and her father's remarriage and move to another state. She never saw him and heard from him only on her birthday and Christmas. For a long time he'd sent no child support, but now he did. Terra said, "Mom and I have plenty of money."

In spite of her arguments with her mom over school and Court, Terra described her mother in positive terms. She said, "Mom's a hard worker and she'd do anything for me."

I asked about other family and she said, "I used to stay with my grandparents, but I don't anymore. When I was little my step-grandfather did nasty things to me. I told Mom when I was seven and she stopped it. He's in jail now."

Terra looked even smaller and younger than when she came in. She yawned dramatically and said, "I've had enough for one day. I don't like to talk about this."

I asked if I could talk to her mother and she agreed. She said, "Let her tell you the details. I forget."

Mona came in the next week. She was a small, wiry woman who looked a lot like Terra. But in contrast to Terra, she was energetic and talkative. Mona said, "I'm worried about Terra. Not so much her schoolwork—I did fine without school—but I don't like Court. He's bad news."

I asked about Terra's earlier abuse. She sighed. "Now, Irwin wasn't my dad. He married Mom after Dad died, but Terra always knew him as Gramps. He was a big cuddly guy who wore overalls and kept candy in his pockets for kids. I thought he was great and he seemed to love Terra."

She paused. "I worked a lot of hours in those days. I was getting my cleaning business started. Irwin and Mom watched Terra for me. When Terra was about five, she stopped wanting to go over there, but I didn't think much of it. Maybe she missed her neighborhood friends. Then when she was seven she refused to go. She grabbed my legs and howled when I tried to leave her. That's when we had a talk and Terra told me what was going on."

"What was going on?"

"Terra said Irwin was making her watch movies with him and he was having sex with her. Later she told the police about other things— oral sex, being tied up. It was awful."

"So you did get the law involved?"

"Yes, and Mom filed for divorce right away. *Thank God* we both believed Terra from the beginning."

Her voice caught in her throat, but she continued. "Terra was a mess. She hadn't sucked her thumb since she was two and she started that up again. She wouldn't let me out of her sight. I could hardly get her to school. She cried when I left her in the morning. The lawyers decided she couldn't testify, and they used her counselor's testimony instead. But that was enough to lock up Irwin. May he rot in hell."

I asked about the counseling, and Mona said it was good for Terra. Really, Terra hadn't had any trouble until adolescence. Then she seemed to fall apart again. As Mona put it, "She's attracted to every skunk in the county."

I said that Terra's reactions were common for victims of incest.

Adolescent issues often trigger earlier traumas. I warned that it might take a while to get things squared away. I also said that a sexual assault by a family member is an injury to the soul of the family. Everyone is wounded. Mona would need help forgiving herself for not protecting Terra and dealing with her own anger. I suspected all the other family members would as well. We would need to sit down together and discuss how this incident affected everyone. Also we would discuss how family members could help Terra heal.

Mona said, "Take all the time you want. Terra's welfare is all that's important."

When Terra returned I brought up the abuse. She wrinkled her nose and said, "Do we have to talk about that? It's over. I'm fine now."

I said, "Do you see any connection between the abuse with Irwin and your relationship with Court?"

"Like what?"

"He hurts you, wants you for himself and tries to control your behavior." Terra's eyes widened, but she said nothing.

Terra reminded me of many young women who were abused as children. Often they must rework the abuse when they are teenagers. They're all mixed up about love, sex, punishment and affection. They need to erase memories of bad relationships and build ideas about good ones. Otherwise they are at risk of finding boyfriends like the person who abused them.

Many issues arise with dating. For example, girls who have been assaulted often learn to block out the experience of being sexual. When they want to be emotionally present, they may find that impossible. Sexual touch may trigger a dissociative reaction. With therapy, this is something that can be changed.

Terra asked if I'd known other girls with her problems.

"Not exactly like you, but I've known lots of girls who were incest victims and had trouble in adolescence."

She asked, "How many of them did you cure?"

I sighed. "I hope I have helped quite a few. I don't blame you for doubting, though. It's hard to trust people after what you've been through."

Terra said, "You've got that right."

————

Rape is a personal problem that cries out for a political solution. The solution to our cultural problems of sexual violence lies not only in the treatment of individual victims and offenders, but also in changing our culture. Young men need to be socialized in such a way that rape is as unthinkable to them as cannibalism. Sex is currently associated with violence, power, domination and status. The incidence of rape is increasing because our culture's destructive messages about sexuality are increasing.

Rape hurts us all, not just the victims. Rape keeps all women in a state of fear about all men. We must constantly be vigilant. One day last winter I was cross-country skiing along a jogging trail. A tall man dressed in a ski mask and a black jogging suit ran toward me. It was dusk in a busy residential neighborhood, but his size and shape frightened me. As he approached, he said my name and I realized it was my own husband.

Men are fearful for their women friends and family and aware that women are afraid of them. A male student complained that he hated rape. He said, "When I walk across campus after dark, I can see women tense up. I want to reassure them I'm not a rapist." Another said, "I haven't dated a girl yet who trusts men. Every girl I've cared for has been hurt by some guy. They are afraid to get close. It's so much work to prove I'm not a jerk."

But mostly rape damages young women. They become posttraumatic stress victims. They experience all the symptoms—depression, anger, fear, recurrent dreams and flashbacks. The initial reaction is usually shock, denial and dissociation. Later comes anger and self-blame for not being more careful or fighting back. Young women who are raped are more fearful. Their invisible shield of invulnerability has been shattered. Forty-one percent of rape victims expect to be raped again; 30 percent contemplate suicide; 31 percent go into therapy; 22 percent take self-defense courses and 82 percent say that they are permanently changed.

Our daughters need time and protected places in which to grow and develop socially, emotionally, intellectually and physically. They need quiet time, talking time, reading time and laughing time. They need safe places where they can go to learn about themselves and others. They need places where they can take risks and make mistakes without fearing for their lives. They need to be valued for their personhood, not their bodies.

Today girls are surrounded by sexual violence. We have emergency treatment for sexual casualties—therapists, hospitals, rape crisis centers and support groups. But we also need a preventive program. We need to work together to build a sexual culture that is sensible, decent and joyful.

Chapter 12

THEN
AND NOW

■

Cassie reminded me of myself as a girl. She even looked like me, with long brown hair, blue eyes and a gawky, flat-chested body. Like me, she loved to walk in the woods and cried when she read poetry. She wanted to visit the Holocaust Museum and join the Peace Corps. She preferred books to clothes and didn't care a fig for money. Like me, she was the oldest daughter of a doctor. She loved both her parents even though they were now divorcing and had little energy to care for her. At school she was shy and studious. Kids with problems could talk to her.

But Cassie also wasn't like me. I was fifteen in 1963, she was fifteen in 1993. When I was fifteen, I'd never been kissed. She was in therapy because she'd been sexually assaulted. Her hands folded in her lap, she whispered the story.

She'd been invited to a party by a girl in her algebra class whose parents were out of town. The girl was supposed to stay with a friend, but she had worked out a way to be home. The kids could use her parents' hot tub and stereo system.

Cassie didn't get invited to many parties, so she accepted the invitation. She planned to leave if things got out of control. She told her mother the truth about her plans, except she didn't mention that the parents were gone. Because her mother had been to her lawyer's that day, she was preoccupied by the divorce proceedings and didn't ask for more details.

The party was okay at first—lots of loud music and sick jokes but Cassie was glad to be at a party. A guy from her lunch period asked her to dance. A cheerleader she barely knew asked her to go to the movies that weekend. But by eleven she wanted to go home. The house was packed with crashers and everyone was drinking. Some kids were throwing up, others were having sex or getting rowdy. One boy had knocked a lamp off a desk and another had kicked a hole through a wall.

Cassie slipped away to the upstairs bedroom for her coat. She didn't notice that a guy followed her into the room. He knew her name and asked for a kiss. She shook her head no and searched for her coat in the pile on the bed. He crept up behind her and put his hands under her shirt. She told him to quit and tried to push him away. Then things happened very fast. He grabbed her and called her a bitch. She struggled to break free, but he pinned her down and covered her mouth. She tried to fight but was not strong or aggressive enough. He was muscular and too drunk to feel pain when she flailed at him. Nobody downstairs heard anything over the music. In ten minutes it was over.

Cassie called her mother and asked her to come get her. She shivered outside until her mother arrived. Cassie told her what had happened and they cried together. They called her father and the police, then drove to a nearby hospital. Cassie was examined and she met with a crisis counselor.

Two weeks later Cassie was in my office, in part because of the rape and in part because of the flak she'd taken at school. The guy who sexually assaulted her had been suspended from the track team pending his trial. His friends were furious at her for getting him in trouble. Other kids thought she led him on, that she had asked for it by being at that party.

Cassie awakened me to an essential truth: In 1993, girls' experiences are different from those of myself and my friends in the 1960s. When I tried to understand them based on my own experience, I failed. There was some common ground, enough to delude me that it was all common ground, but there was much new, uncharted territory. To work with girls in the 1990s I had to understand a new world. I had to let go of my ideas and look at the girls before me with fresh eyes. I had to learn from them before I could help.

During my adolescence, I lived in a town of 400 people where my mother practiced medicine and my father sold seed corn and raised hogs. I spent my days riding my bike, swimming, reading, playing piano and drinking limeades at the drugstore with my friends. I raised all kinds of animals—baby coyotes that we bought from bounty hunters, turtles we picked up on the highway, birds washed from trees in heavy spring rains, mice pulled from their nests by dogs, and snakes and rabbits we caught in the fields on the edge of town.

I knew the names of all the people and most of the cats and dogs. Everyone "doctored" with my mother and bought corn from my father. All the children played at the same places—the swimming pool, the school yard, the swing across Beaver Creek and the fairgrounds. Everyone knew who was related to whom. When people met, the first thing they did was establish a connection. People on the street said hello to someone with whom they had a rich and complicated lifelong relationship. My pottery teacher, Mrs. Van Cleave, was the grandmother of my good friend Patti and the mother of our next-door neighbor. She was my mom's patient, and her husband went fishing with my dad. Her son was the football coach and his children were in my Methodist youth group.

I had eleven aunts and uncles and thirty cousins who showed up for long visits. The women cooked and watched babies, the men played horseshoes and fished. We all played cards in the evening. My grandfather recited limericks and demonstrated card tricks. Conversation was the main entertainment. We cousins would compare stories about our towns and families. The older cousins would impress the younger ones with their worldly wisdom. Children sat and listened as grown-ups told stories and talked politics. My fondest memory is of falling asleep to laughter and talk in the next room.

The word "media" was not in our language. I saw television for the first time when I was six, and I hid behind the couch because the cowboys' guns scared me. I was eight before we had a black-and-white television on which we watched one grainy station that showed a test pattern much of the day.

As a young teenager I watched "The Mickey Mouse Club," "American Bandstand" and "The Ed Sullivan Show." I wasn't allowed to watch "Perry Mason" or "Gunsmoke" because my parents thought these shows were too violent. We had one movie theater with a new movie every other week. The owner of the theater was a family man who selected our town's movies carefully. His wife sold us salty popcorn, Tootsie Rolls and Cokes. Kids went to the movies on Saturday afternoons and spent most of their time spying on other kids or giggling with their friends.

I loved *Tammy, Seven Brides for Seven Brothers, The Chartroose Caboose* and *South Pacific.* I scanned these movies for information about sex. Rock Hudson, Doris Day, Debbie Reynolds and Frank Sinatra fought and flirted until the end of the movie, when they kissed against backdrops of sunsets to the sounds of swelling violins. This was the era of biblical epics. In *The Story of Ruth,* a demure young Ruth lies down on Boaz' pallet for the night and the camera zooms to the stars. I asked myself, What were they doing on that pallet?

Forty-five RPM records were big in the late fifties. I listened to mushy songs by the Everly Brothers, Roy Orbison and Elvis. My favorite song was Elvis' "Surrender," a song whose lyrics gave me goose bumps and filled me with longing for something I couldn't name. My parents forbade me to listen to Bobby Darin's hit "Multiplication" because it was too suggestive. I learned to twist, a dance that was considered daring.

As Garrison Keillor said, "Nobody gets rich in a small town because everybody's watching." Money and conspicuous consumption were downplayed in my community. Some people were wealthier than others, but it was bad taste to flaunt a high income. We all shopped at the Theobald's grocery and the Rexall and ordered our clothes from Sears and JCPenney catalogs. The banker ordered a new Oldsmobile every year, and my family drove to Mexico at Christmas. A rancher's widow with asthma had the only home air-conditioning unit. The only places to spend money foolishly were the Dairy King and the pool hall.

Particularly children were outside the money economy. Most of our pleasures were free. Most of us had the same toys—Schwinn bikes, Hula-Hoops, basketballs, Monopoly games and dolls or toy soldiers. We could buy Sugar Babies or licorice at the pool, and makeup, comics and *Mad* magazines at the drugstore.

After school I worked for my mother at her clinic. I sterilized syringes and rubber gloves and counted pills. The money I earned went into a college account. By junior high, gifts went into my hope chest—good china, luggage, a dictionary and tatted pillowcases.

Elsewhere mass marketing had begun. Women were encouraged to fix up their homes and dress themselves and their children smartly. Via commercials and advertisements, they were fed a distorted image of themselves and their place in society. This image was less focused on their sexuality and more on their femininity. But because of our distance from a city, mass marketing barely touched our town.

Our town was a dry town and our state had "blue laws," which kept liquor from being advertised, sold on Sundays or served in restaurants. Even our pool hall served nothing stronger than root beer. My father brought tequila back from Mexico and would open a bottle and share it with other men on a Saturday night. Teenage boys had a difficult time finding alcohol. Once my cousin Roy drove fifty miles, convinced a stranger to buy him a six-pack, returned home and hid the six-pack in a culvert.

The Surgeon General had yet to issue his report on smoking, and cigarettes were everywhere, but marijuana and other drugs were unheard of in my town. My father told me that during World War Two a soldier had offered him a marijuana cigarette. He said, "I turned him down and it's a good thing. If I'd said yes, I probably wouldn't be alive today."

At Methodist Youth Fellowship we saw films about the deterioration of people who drank or used marijuana. Women in particular were portrayed as degraded and destroyed by contact with chemicals. After these films we signed pledges that we would never drink or smoke. I didn't break mine until I was in college.

As Tolstoy knew so well, in all times and places there have been happy and unhappy families. In the fifties, the unhappiness was mostly private. Divorce was uncommon and regarded as shameful. I had no friends whose parents were divorced. All kinds of pain were kept secret. Physical and sexual abuse occurred but were not reported. Children and women who lived in abusive families suffered silently. For those whose lives were going badly, there was nowhere to turn. My friend Sue's father hanged himself in his basement. She missed a week of school, and when she returned we treated her as if nothing had happened. The first time Sue and I spoke of her father's death was at our twenty-fifth-year class reunion.

There was cruelty. The town drunk was shamed rather than helped. Retarded and handicapped people were teased. The Green River Ordinance, which kept undesirables—meaning strangers—out of town, was enforced.

I was a sheltered child in a sheltered community. Most of the mothers were homemakers who served brownies and milk to their children after school. Many of them may have been miserable and unfulfilled with their lives of service to men, children and community. But, as a child, I didn't notice.

Most of the fathers owned stores downtown and walked home for lunch. Baby-sitters were a rarity. Everyone went to the same chili feeds and county fairs. Adults were around to keep an eye on things. Once I picked some lilacs from an old lady's bush. She called my parents before I could make it home with my bouquet.

Teenagers fought less with their parents, mostly because there was less to fight about—designer clothes and R-rated movies didn't exist. There was consensus about proper behavior. Grown-ups agreed about rules and enforced them. Teenagers weren't exposed to an alternative value system and they rebelled in milder ways—with ducktails, tight skirts and rock and roll. Adults joked about how much trouble teenagers were, but most parents felt proud of their children. They didn't have the strained faces and the anxious conversations that parents of teenagers have in the 1990s.

Men had most of the public power. The governor, the state senators, the congressmen, the mayor and city council members were men, and men ran the stores downtown. My mother was the first "lady doctor" in our town and she suffered some because of this. She wasn't considered quite as feminine and ladylike as the other women, and she wasn't considered quite as good a doctor as the male doctor in the next town.

In the fifties women were forced to surrender the independence they'd won during World War Two and return home so as not to threaten men. Women's work was separate and unequal. Many women had no access to money or transportation. Their husbands controlled the bank accounts and cars. Women's contributions, such as sewing, tending the sick and cooking church dinners, were undervalued. At its centennial, our town published its history of the last hundred years. In the seventy-five-page book, women are not mentioned.

Language was unself-consciously noninclusive—leaders were "he," hurricanes and secretaries "she," humanity was mankind. Men made history, wrote books, won wars, conducted symphonies and created eternal works of art. The books we read in school were written by men and about men. They were shared with us by women teachers who didn't comment on their own exclusion.

Schools and churches enforced male power. Men were principals, superintendents and ministers; women were teachers. We studied the Bible story of Lot's wife, who was turned into a pillar of salt because she disobeyed God's orders. When my female cousins married, they vowed obedience to their husbands.

Kent, Sam and I were the top students. The teachers praised them for being brilliant and creative, while I was praised for being a hard worker. Kent and Sam were encouraged to go to out-of-state schools to study law or medicine, while I was encouraged to study at the state university to be a teacher.

There was a pervasive, low-key misogyny. Mothers-in-law, women drivers and ugly women were sources of derisive humor. Men needed to "wear the pants in the family." Uppity women were quickly chastened and so were their husbands for allowing themselves to be "henpecked" or "led around by the apron strings." Women's talk was regarded as inferior to the important talk of men.

Femininity training was strong. We were taught that if we couldn't say anything nice about someone, don't say anything. (I remember being delighted when Alice Roosevelt Longworth was quoted as saying, "If you can't say anything good about someone, sit right here by me.") We were admonished that "it's not smart to be smart," and that we should "let boys chase us till we catch them."

By junior high the all-girl activities were different from the all-boy activities. Boys played sports while we walked around the gym with books on our heads so that we would have good posture. Boy Scouts camped and fished while Girl Scouts sold cookies and learned to sew, bake and care for children.

I read the Cherry Ames student nurse books. In every book Cherry would meet a new young doctor and have an innocent romance in a glorious setting. Thank goodness I also read Nancy Drew and the Dana sisters' mysteries. Those amateur sleuths were competent and confident, brave and adventurous. They gave me role models that were lively and active. They had boyfriends, but they were always ditching them to go solve a robbery.

The prettiest girls were the most popular. I read *Teen* magazine with its fashion and beauty tips, and I rolled up my hair at night and combed it out in the morning. I still can feel the pressure of those big spiky rollers on my scalp. I did bust-building and tummy-flattening exercises.

Boys preferred dating girls whom they could best in every way. Achievement in girls was valued as long as it didn't interfere with social attractiveness. Too much education or ambition was considered unfeminine. When I received the Bausch & Lomb science award at a school assembly, I almost expired of embarrassment.

Sexuality was seen as a powerful force regulated by God Himself. There were rules and euphemisms for everything. "Don't touch your privates except to wash." "Don't kiss a boy on your first date." "Never let a guy go all the way or he won't respect you in the morning."

Sex was probably my most confusing problem. I read Pat Boone's *Twixt Twelve and Twenty,* which didn't clarify anything. I wasn't sure how many orifices women had. I knew that something girls did with boys led to babies, but I was unable to picture just what that was. I misunderstood dirty jokes and had no idea that songs were filled with sexual innuendo. Well into junior high, I thought that the word "adultery" meant trying to act like an adult.

One of my girlfriends had an older cousin who hid romance magazines under her bed. One day when she was away at a twirling competition, we sneaked up to her room to read them. Beautiful young women were overwhelmed by lust and overpowered by handsome heroes. The details were vague. The couple fell into bed and the woman's blouse was unbuttoned. Her heart would flutter and she would turn pale. The author described a storm outside or petals falling from flowers in a nearby vase. We left the house still uneducated about what really happened. Years later, when I finally heard what the sex act entailed, I was alarmed.

I was easily embarrassed. Tony, the town hoodlum, was my particular curse. Tony wore tight jeans and a black leather jacket and oozed sexual evil. In study hall he sketched a naked woman, scribbled my name on her and passed her around the room. Another time he told me to hold out my hand, and when I did, he dropped a screw into it and shouted, "You owe me a screw."

There was a scary side of sexuality. One friend's dad told her, "Don't get pregnant, but if you do, come to me and I'll load up my gun." A second cousin had to marry because she was pregnant. She whispered to me that her boyfriend had blackmailed her into having sex. She was a homecoming queen candidate and he said he'd go to homecoming with her only if she gave in. He claimed that he was suffering from "blue balls," a painful and unhealthy condition that only sex would remedy.

Lois and Carol taught me my most important lessons. Lois was a pudgy, self-effacing fourteen-year-old whose greatest accomplishment was eight years of perfect attendance at our Sunday school. One Sunday morning she wasn't there, and when I remarked on that fact, the teacher changed the subject. For a time no one would tell me what had happened to Lois. Eventually, however, I was so anxious that Mother told me the story. Lois was pregnant from having sex with a middle-aged man who worked at her father's grocery store. They had married and were living in a trailer south of town. She was expelled from school and would not be coming to church anymore, at least not until after the baby was born. I never saw her again.

Carol was a wiry, freckled farm girl from a big family. She boarded with our neighbors to attend high school in town. In the evenings, after she had the chores done, Carol came over to play with me. One night we were standing in our front yard when a carload of boys came by and asked her to go for a ride. She hesitated, then agreed. A month later Carol was sent back pregnant to her farm. I worried about her because she'd told me her father used belts and coat hangers on the children. My father told me to learn from Carol's mistake and avoid riding with boys. I took him literally and it was years before I felt comfortable riding in cars with any boys except my cousins.

In my town the rules for boys were clear. They were supposed to like sex and go for it whenever they could. They could expect sex with loose girls, but not with good girls, at least not until they'd dated them a long time. The biggest problem for boys was getting the experience they needed to prove they were men.

The rules for girls were more complicated. We were told that sex would ruin our lives and our reputations. We were encouraged to be sexy, but not sexual. Great scorn was reserved for "cockteasers" and "cold fish." It was tough to find the right balance between seductive and prim.

The rules for both sexes pitted them against their Saturday-night dates. Guys tried to get what they could and girls tried to stop them. That made for a lot of sweaty wrestling matches and ruined prom nights. The biggest danger from rule breaking was pregnancy. This was before birth control pills and legal abortion. Syphilis and gonorrhea were the most common sexually transmitted diseases, and both were treatable with the new miracle drug, penicillin.

Sexual openness and tolerance were not community values. Pregnant teachers had to leave school as soon as they "showed." I had no girlfriends who admitted being sexually active. There was community-wide denial about incest and rape, which undoubtedly occurred in my small town as they did all over America. The official story was kept G-rated.

There was a great deal of hypocrisy. A wealthy man in my town was known for being a pincher. We girls called him "the lobster" among ourselves and knew to avoid him. But because his family was prominent, no one ever told him to stop his behavior.

I didn't know that pornography existed until I was a senior in high school. My parents took me to Kansas City and we stayed near the Time to Read bookstore. It was two bookstores in one: on the left, classics, best-sellers and newspapers from all over the world, and on the right, an eye-popping display of pornography.

In my town male homosexuals were mercilessly scorned. The one known homosexual was the crippled son of a Brethren minister. He made the enormous mistake of asking another boy for a kiss, and forever after he lived a nightmarish life of isolation and teasing. Female homosexuality was never acknowledged.

Outsiders—such as socialists, Native Americans or blacks—were ostracized in small communities. Our town took great pride in having no black or Native American citizens. Restaurant signs that read "We have the right to refuse service to anyone" were used to exclude nonwhites.

Adults told racist jokes and held racist beliefs about ethnic groups they had never even met. My father warned me never to dance with or talk to "Negroes" when I went to college or people would think I was low-class. Terms like "jewing people down" and "Indian giver" were part of the language.

Once scorned, a person was out for years. One classmate who broke into a building in the eighth grade was ostracized for years by all the "good" families. We were forbidden to associate with him. He was killed in a car wreck the week after graduation. Only then did I realize how awful his high school years must have been.

The town newspaper was full of stories about who attended whose birthday party or fiftieth wedding anniversary. Crime was garbage cans and privies being overturned on Halloween. No one locked their doors. Our town sheriff mostly looked for lost pets and speeders. I could go anywhere before or after dark without my parents' worrying. My most traumatic experience was reading *The Diary of Anne Frank* and realizing that somewhere people could be incredibly evil.

As I recall my childhood, I'm cautioned by Mark Twain's line, "The older I get, the more clearly I remember things that never happened." Remembering is more like taking a Rorschach test than calling up a computer file. It's highly selective and revealing of one's deep character. Of course, others had different experiences, but I recall small-town life as slower, safer and less sexualized. Everyone did know everyone. Sometimes that made the world seem safe and secure and sometimes that made the world seem small and oppressive.

Cassie attends a high school with 2,300 students. She doesn't know her teachers' children or her neighbors' cousins. When she meets people she doesn't try to establish their place in a complicated kinship network. When she shops for jeans, she doesn't expect the clerk to ask after her family.

Cassie sees her extended family infrequently, particularly since her parents' divorce. They are scattered all over the map. Most of the adults in her neighborhood work. In the evening people no longer sit on their front porches. Instead they prefer the privacy of backyard patios, which keep their doings invisible. Air-conditioning contributes to each family's isolation. On hot summer days and nights people go inside to stay cool. Cassie knows the Cosby family and the people from "Northern Exposure" better than she knows anyone on her block.

Cassie fights with her parents in a more aggressive way than the teens of my youth. She yells, swears, accuses and threatens to run away. Her parents tolerate this open anger much more readily than earlier generations would have. I'm confused about whether I was more repressed as a child or just happier. Sometimes I think all this expression of emotion is good, and sometimes, particularly when I see beleaguered mothers, I wonder if we have made progress.

Cassie is much more politically aware of the world than I was. By the time she was ten she'd been in a protest march in Washington, D.C. She's demonstrated against the death penalty and the Rodney King trial. She writes letters to her congressmen and to the newspapers. She writes letters for Amnesty International to stop torture all over the world. She is part of a larger world than I was and takes her role as an active participant seriously.

Cassie and her friends all tried smoking cigarettes in junior high. Like most teenagers today, Cassie was offered drugs in junior high. She can name more kinds of illegal drugs than the average junkie from the fifties. She knows about local drug-related killings and crack rings. Marijuana, which my father saw once in his lifetime, wafts through the air at her rock concerts and midnight movies.

Alcohol is omnipresent—in bowling alleys, gas stations, grocery stores, skating rinks and Laundromats. Alcohol advertising is rampant, and drinking is associated with wealth, travel, romance and fun. At sixteen, Cassie has friends who have been through treatment for drugs or alcohol. The schools attempt alcohol and drug education, but they are no match for the peer pressure to consume. Cassie knows some Just Say No leaders who get drunk every weekend. By eighth grade, kids who aren't drinking are labeled geeks and left out of the popular scene.

Spending money is a pastime. Cassie wants expensive items—a computer, a racing bike and trips to Costa Rica with her Spanish class and to the ski slopes of Colorado. She takes violin and voice lessons from university professors and attends special camps for musicians.

Cassie's been surrounded by media since birth. Her family owns a VCR, a stereo system, two color televisions and six radios. Cassie wakes to a radio, plays the car stereo on the way to school, sees videos at school and returns home to a choice of stereo, radio, television or videocassettes. She can choose between forty channels twenty-four hours a day. She plays music while she studies and communicates via computer modem with hackers all over the country in her spare time.

Cassie and her friends have been inundated with advertising since birth and are sophisticated about brand names and commercials. While most of her friends can't identify our state flower, the goldenrod, in a ditch along the highway, they can shout out the brand of a can of soda from a hundred yards away. They can sing commercial jingles endlessly.

Cassie's been exposed to years of sophisticated advertising in which she's heard that happiness comes from consuming the right products. She can catch the small lies and knows that adults tell lies to make money. We do not consider that a sin—we call it marketing. But I'm not sure that she catches the big lie, which is that consumer goods are essential to happiness.

Cassie has more access to books than I had. I was limited to a town library the size of a Quick Stop and a weekly bookmobile. She has a six-branch public library system, a school library as big as a gymnasium and three university libraries. But she reads much less than I did. Particularly the classics that I loved, *Jane Eyre, Moby Dick,* and *Return of the Native* bore her with their loopy, ornamental prose. She has more choices about how to spend her time, and like most teens raised in a media-saturated culture, Cassie does not often choose to read books.

There are more magazines for girls now, but they are relatively unchanged in the thirty years since I bought my copies of *Teen.* The content for girls is makeup, acne products, fashion, thinness and attracting boys. Some of the headlines could be the same: TRUE COLORS

QUIZ, GET THE LOOK THAT GETS BOYS, TEN COMMANDMENTS OF HAIR, THE BEST PLACES TO MEET AVAILABLE MEN and TEN WAYS TO TRIM DOWN. Some headlines are updated to pay lip service to the themes of the 1990s: TWO MODELS CHILL OUT AT OXFORD UNIVERSITY IN SEASON'S GREATEST GRAY CLOTHES or ECO-INSPIRED LOOKS FOR FALL. A few reflect the greater stress that the 1990s offer the young: REV UP YOUR LOOKS WHEN STRESS HAS YOU DOWN, THE STD OF THE MONTH, GENITAL WARTS and SHOULD I GET TESTED FOR AIDS? Some would never have appeared in the 1950s: WHEN YOU'RE HIGHLY SEXED, IS ONE PARTNER ENOUGH? and ADVICE ON ORGASMS.

Cassie listens to music by The Dead Milkmen, 10,000 Maniacs, Nirvana and They Might Be Giants. She dances to Madonna's song "Erotica," with its sadomasochistic lyrics. The rock-and-roll lyrics by 2 Live Crew that make Tipper Gore cringe don't upset her. Sexist lyrics and the marketing of products with young women's naked bodies are part of the wallpaper of her life.

Cassie's favorite movies are *The Crying Game, Harold and Maude* and *My Own Private Idaho.* None of these movies would have made it past the theater owner of my hometown.

Our culture has changed from one in which it was hard to get information about sexuality to one in which it's impossible to escape information about sexuality. Inhibition has quit the scene. In the 1950s a married couple on TV had to be shown sleeping in twin beds because a double bed was too suggestive. Now anything—incest, menstruation, crotch itch or vaginal odors—can be discussed on TV. Television shows invite couples to sell their most private moments for a dishwasher.

The plot for romance movies is different. In the fifties people met, argued, fell in love, then kissed. By the seventies, people met, argued, fell in love and then had sex. In the nineties people meet, have sex, argue and then, maybe, fall in love. Hollywood lovers don't discuss birth control, past sexual encounters or how a sexual experience will affect the involved parties; they just do it. The Hollywood model of sexual behavior couldn't be more harmful and misleading if it were trying to be.

Cassie has seen *Playboys* and *Penthouses* on the racks at local drugstores and Quick Stops. Our city has adult XXX-rated movie theaters and adult bookstores. She's watched the adult channels in hotel rooms while bouncing on "magic fingers" beds. Advertisements that disturb me with their sexual content don't bother her. When I told her that I first heard the word "orgasm" when I was twenty, she looked at me with disbelief.

Cassie's world is more tolerant and open about sex. Her friends produced a campy play entitled *Vampire Lesbians of Sodom*. For a joke she displays Kiss of Mint condoms in her room. She's a member of her school's branch of Flag—Friends of Lesbians and Gays—which she joined after one of her male friends "came out" to her. She's nonjudgmental about sexual orientation and outspoken in her defense of gay rights. Her world is a kinder, gentler place for girls who have babies. One-fifth of all babies today are born to single mothers. Some of her schoolmates bring their babies to school.

In some ways Cassie is more informed about sex than I was. She's read books on puberty and sexuality and watched films at school. She's seen explicit movies and listened to hours of explicit music. But Cassie still hasn't heard answers to the questions she's most interested in. She hasn't had much help sorting out when to have sex, how to say no or what a good sexual experience would entail.

Cassie is as tongue-tied with boys she likes as I was, and she is even more confused about proper behavior. The values she learned at home and at church are at odds with the values broadcast by the media. She's been raised to love and value herself in a society where an enormous pornography industry reduces women to body parts. She's been taught by movies and television that sophisticated people are sexually free and spontaneous, and at the same time she's been warned that casual sex can kill. And she's been raped.

Cassie knows girls who had sex with boys they hardly knew. She knows a girl whose reason for having sex was "to get it over with." Another classmate had sex because her two best girlfriends had had sex and she didn't want to feel left out. More touching and sexual harassment happens in the halls of her school than did in the halls of mine. Girls are referred to as bitches, whores and sluts.

Cassie has been desensitized to violence. She's watched television specials on incest and sexual assaults and seen thousands of murders on the screen. She's seen *Fatal Attraction* and *Halloween II*. Since Jeffrey Dahmer, she knows what necrophilia is. She wasn't traumatized by *The Diary of Anne Frank*.

Cassie can't walk alone after dark. Her family locks doors and bicycles. She carries Mace in her purse and a whistle on her car keys. She doesn't speak to men she doesn't know. When she is late, her parents are immediately alarmed. Of course there were girls who were traumatized in the fifties, and there are girls who lead protected lives in the 1990s, but the proportions have changed significantly. We feel it in our bones.

I am not claiming that our childhoods are representative of the childhoods of all other females in America. In some ways Cassie and I have both had unusual childhoods. I grew up in a rural, isolated area with much less exposure to television than the average child of the times. My mother was a doctor instead of a homemaker. Compared to other girls, Cassie lives in a city that is safer than most and has a family with more money. Even with the rape, Cassie's situation is by no means a worst-case scenario. She lives in a middle-class environment, not an inner city. Her parents aren't psychotic, abusive or drug-addicted.

Also, I am not claiming that I lived in the good old days and that Cassie lives in the wicked present. I don't want to glorify or to "Donna Reedify" the fifties, which were not a golden age. They were the years of Joe McCarthy and Jim Crow. How things looked was more important than how things really were. There was a great deal of sexual, religious and racial intolerance. Many families had shameful secrets, and if revealed, they led to public disgrace rather than community help.

I left my town as soon as I could, and as an adult, I have been much happier in a larger, less structured environment. Many of my friends come from small towns, and particularly the smart women among them have horror stories of not fitting in.

What I am claiming is that our stories have something to say about the way the world has stayed the same and the way it has changed for adolescent girls. We had in common that our bodies changed and those changes caused us anxiety. With puberty, we both struggled to relate to girls and boys in new ways. We struggled to be attractive and to understand our own sexual urges. We were awkward around boys and hurt by girls. As we struggled to grow up and define ourselves as adults, we both distanced ourselves from our parents and felt some loneliness as a result. As we searched for our identities, we grew confused and sad. Both of us had times when we were moody, secretive, inarticulate and introspective.

But while some of our experiences are similar, many are radically different. Cassie's community is a global one, mine was a small town. Her parents were divorcing, mine stayed together. She lives in a society more stratified by money and more driven by addictions. She's been exposed to more television, movies and music. She lives in a more sexualized world.

Things that shocked us in the 1950s make us yawn now. The world has changed from one in which people blushed at the term "chicken breast" to one in which a movie such as *Pretty Woman* is not embarrassing. We've gone from a world with no locks on the doors to one of bolt locks and handguns. The issues that I struggled with as a college student—when I should have sex, should I drink, smoke or hang out with bad company—now must be considered in early adolescence.

Neither the 1950s nor the 1990s offered us environments that totally met our needs. My childhood was structured and safe, but the costs of that security were limited tolerance of diversity, rigid rules about proper behavior and lack of privacy. As one man from a small town said, "I don't need to worry about running my own business because there are so many other people who are minding it for me." Although my community provided many surrogate parents and clear rules about right and wrong, this structure was often used to enforce rigid social and class codes and to keep people in their place.

Cassie lives in a town that's less rigid about roles and more supportive of autonomy, but she has little protected space. Cassie is freer in some ways than I was. She has more options. But ironically, in some ways, she's less free. She cannot move freely in the halls of her school because of security precautions. Everyone she meets is not part of a community of connected people. She can't walk alone looking at the Milky Way on a summer night.

The ideal community would somehow be able to combine the sense of belonging that small towns offer with the freedom to be oneself that small towns sometimes inhibit. Utopia for teenage girls would be a place in which they are safe and free, able to grow and develop in an atmosphere of tolerance and diversity and protected by adults who have their best interest at heart.

Chapter 13

WHAT I'VE LEARNED
FROM LISTENING

■

Fourteen-year-old Brandi was marched into my office by her mother, a tired-looking factory worker from a nearby town who insisted she come for at least one session. While Brandi rolled her eyes and grunted, her mother explained that Brandi had been sexually assaulted by an alcoholic neighbor.

Brandi interrupted her mother to say that the assault was "no big deal." She said that other things bothered her a lot more than the stupid neighbor. She complained of her mother's nagging about chores and her father's strict curfews on school nights. She said her biggest problem was that her parents treated her like a little kid and she was sick of it.

I suggested that it might help to talk about the assault. She said, "Maybe some girls, but I'm not the type who spills my guts to just anyone."

To my surprise Brandi rescheduled after that first session. The next time she came alone with her stuffed panda. She curled up on my couch and told me the real story.

Shana sat on the couch between her two psychologist parents. She was dressed in jeans and a *Jurassic Park* T-shirt and looked much younger than her thirteen years. Her father, a big bearlike man in a tweed jacket, explained that Shana wouldn't go to school. At first she played

sick, but later she just wouldn't go. They couldn't understand why—
her grades were good, she had friends and, as far as they knew, nothing
traumatic had happened.

Shana's mother, a tall, confident woman whose research in addictions I had followed, wondered about depression. Her father had killed
himself and one of her brothers had been diagnosed with bipolar
depression. She noticed that Shana stayed up nights, slept all day and
had no appetite.

I asked Shana why she wasn't going to school.

She thought for a moment and said, "I feel like I'll suffocate or stop
breathing if I go in that building."

Jana sipped a blue Slurpee as she told me about her problems at home.

"I hate my mother. She's such a witch. Sometimes I think if I have
to live with her the next four years till I graduate from high school I'll
go crazy."

I asked what her mother did that made her so crazy.

"She tries to control my life. She makes me clean my room and go
to church on Sunday. She forces me to eat meals."

Pausing, Jana looked slightly chagrined. "It doesn't sound that bad
when I tell you. But trust me, if you lived with my mother, you'd want
to puke."

My undergraduate work in anthropology has always played a role in
my work with people. I was taught to understand people within the
context of their culture. I learned to ask, "What is the culture expecting
of them? What is their script?" In graduate school in psychology, my
training was psychodynamic. On internship I was introduced to sys-
tems theory.

I've learned from many great teachers and from my own experience.
Human beings can do three things—think, feel and behave—and I try
to make an impact in all three areas. I would call myself a relationship-
oriented cognitive behaviorist. I'm influenced by the humanistic psychologists and also by social learning theorists.

I believe that talking to a listener with an accepting, empathic and
nonjudgmental stance is healing. When I first meet a client I search for
things about her that I can respect and ways in which I can empathize
with her situation. I think it's impossible to help unless I can find these

things. I don't believe that analysis of the past is always necessary. I like ordinary language. In general I don't like victim talk, self-pity or blaming. I think psychotherapy should empower people, help them be more in control of their lives and enhance their relationships with others.

I try to be what psychologist Don Meichenbaum calls "a purveyor of hope." I'm pragmatic, relativistic and collaborative. I don't like negative labels, diagnoses or the medical model. I am drawn to therapists who view families in more positive ways. I like the work of Jay Haley, Harriet Lerner, Claudia Bepko and Jo-Ann Krestan. I respect Michael White and David Epston, who believe that clients come to therapists with "problem-saturated stories." It's the therapist's job to help clients tell more powerful and optimistic stories about themselves. White and Epston stress that the client isn't the problem, the problem is the problem, and they prefer what they call "solution talk" to "problem talk."

They believe that many families are in trouble because they tell problem-saturated stories about themselves. They warn that often mental-health professionals contribute to these stories by asking questions about failure and conflict and ignoring areas in which the family is strong and healthy. White and Epston empower families by helping them tell new stories about their own functioning. I like their ideas because they take the pathology and shame out of therapy. Working as they do generates options, optimism, trust and collaboration.

My general goals for all clients are to increase their authenticity, openness to experience, competence, flexible thinking and realistic appraisal of their environment. I want to help clients see things in new ways and develop richer, more rewarding relationships. Psychotherapy is one of many processes by which people can examine their lives intelligently. It's a way to have a consultant on solving human problems. It can be good for everyone; it helps people steer, not drift, through life. Examined lives are indeed more worth living. The ideal life is calm, fun and responsible. Like Freud, I believe in the value of love and work.

Working with adolescent girls and their parents pushed me to reexamine my training about families. Much of the writing in our field views families as a primary source of pathology and pain. The language of psychology reflects this bias—words about distance are positive (independence, individuation and autonomy), whereas words about closeness are negative (dependency and enmeshment). Indeed, psychologists are so prone to pathologize families that one definition of a normal family is "a family that has not yet been evaluated by a psychologist."

Years ago Miranda and her parents came to my office. Three months earlier she had been diagnosed as bulimic and referred to a treatment center eight hours away from her hometown. While Miranda was in this program, her parents secured a second mortgage on their home to pay for her treatment. They called her daily and drove to the faraway center every weekend for family therapy. After three months and $120,000, Miranda still had her eating disorder and her parents had been diagnosed as co-dependent.

My first question to Miranda was, "What did you learn in your stay at the hospital?"

She answered proudly, "That I come from a dysfunctional family."

I thought of her parents—Dad was a physical therapist and Mom a librarian in a small community. They weren't alcoholics or abusive. They took family vacations every summer and put money into a college fund. They played board games, read Miranda bedtime stories and attended her school programs. And now, with Miranda in trouble, they had incurred enormous debts to pay for her treatment. For all their efforts and money, they had been labeled pathological.

Miranda, like almost all teens, was quick to agree with this label. It's easy to convince teenagers that their parents don't understand them and that their families are dysfunctional. Since the beginning of time, teenagers have felt their parents were uniquely unreasonable. When a professional corroborates their opinions, they feel vindicated, at least for the moment.

But in the long term, it hurts most teens to undercut their parents. My goal with Miranda was to restore some balance to her concept of her family. When I suggested that her parents deserved some credit for the efforts they'd made to help her, Miranda seemed confused at first, then visibly relieved.

Psychology's negative view of families began with Freud. He believed that character was fully formed within the family in early childhood. Because of the pathology of the parents, he felt that the character structure of most children was flawed. The goal of analysis was to save the client from the damage done by the family. It is a common view today. Many popular psychology books suggest that if the reader isn't happy, it's because of a dysfunctional family. These books ignore the crime rate, the poverty and the sleazy values of the mass culture and our drug- and alcohol-fueled life-styles.

Of course the problems of a dysfunctional culture are reflected in the lives of each family. Many men who grow up in a misogynistic culture abuse their wives and daughters. Many mothers offer their daughters passive, diminished models of femaleness. Some parents are cultural agents who are desperate for their daughters to be popular. But when so many families have trouble, it's important to look at the cultural context. Rather than blame each family for the unhappiness of its daughters, we need to examine what it is in our culture that destroys the happiness of so many teenage girls.

Psychology has much to answer for in its treatment of families. We have offered parents conflicting and ever-changing advice. We have issued dire warnings of the harm they will do if they make mistakes in parenting, and we have assured them that they are inadequate to the task. Our tendency to blame parents, especially mothers, for their children's problems has paralyzed many parents. They are so afraid of traumatizing their children that they cannot set clear and firm limits. They are so afraid of being dysfunctional that they stop functioning.

My work with adolescent girls helped me see families in a different light. Most of the parents I see clearly love their daughters and want what is best for them. They are their daughters' shelter from the storm and their most valuable resource in times of need. I respect their willingness to seek help when they are in over their heads. I'm honored that they allow me, temporarily, to be part of their lives.

Good therapists work to shore up family bonds and to give hope to flagging families. We work to promote harmony and good humor and to increase tolerance and understanding between family members. Rather than searching for pathological labels, we encourage the development of those qualities that John DeFrain found in all healthy families: appreciation and affection, commitment, positive communication, time together, spiritual well-being and the ability to cope with stress and crises.

Therapists can be most helpful when we support parental efforts to keep adolescents safe and at the same time adolescents' needs to grow and move into the larger world. We can help by teaching teenagers that they can individuate from their parents without separating from them.

We can help girls discover positive ways to be independent. We can help by discussing the effects of mass culture on families. We need to politicize, not pathologize, families.

We need to change society if we are to produce healthy young women. But I can't single-handedly change the culture, and neither can the families I see. I try to help families understand some of their daughters' behavior as a reaction to a misogynistic culture and its manifestations at home, with friends, in school and in the larger community. We work together to assess the impact of the culture on the life of each family and to develop plans for damage control. It's emergency rescue work.

Of course each family has its own history, its own unique problems and blind spots. And each family has its own unique strengths and coping mechanisms. I try to strengthen families and to give the daughters power and permission to be who they truly are.

Daughters can learn to recognize the forces that shape them and make conscious choices about what they will and won't endure. They need "awakening therapy," which is my term for consciousness-raising. This therapy helps girls become whole adults in a culture that encourages them to become forever the object of another's gaze. It means teaching a new form of self-defense.

Even with these general ideas about therapy, I found adolescent girls to be difficult. It is harder to establish relationships with them, and they are more likely to quit therapy without notice. Mistakes with them seem more serious. They are much less forgiving than adult clients. Their surface behaviors are often designed to hide their deep-structure needs so that it is hard to find the real issues. Even accurate empathy is difficult. Their experiences are not like mine now, or even like mine when I was their age. When I try to connect based on common experience, I often fail.

Here's how the work actually goes: On the first visit, girls radiate confusion and a lack of confidence. They move uneasily in their bodies. They flash me a kaleidoscope of emotions—fear, indifference, sadness, smugness, resignation and hope. They signal despair about their sexuality and loathing of their appearance. They are braced for rejection and ridicule. Questions about me form and re-form in their eyes: Do they dare discuss bad grades, bingeing, alcohol, sex, cutting themselves or suicidal thoughts? Will I be angry? Rejecting? Unable to understand? Or, worst of all, will I smugly supply answers? They look longingly at the door and smile at me in a way that says "I want you to like me, but don't expect me to admit it."

With girls this age, relationships are everything. No work can be done in the absence of mutual affection and regard. The first step in developing a relationship is helping the girl develop trust—for me, for the therapeutic relationship and for herself.

Girls have dozens of ways to test the therapist. The best way to pass these tests is to listen. Sincere, total, nonjudgmental listening happens all too rarely in any of our lifetimes. I ask open-ended questions. How do you feel about that? What do you think? What is important to you about this experience? What did you learn from this experience? Can you talk more about this?

I resist the urge to offer advice or too much sympathy. I help with sorting—what can and can't the girl control? What opinions are hers, what opinions are others'? What is most important in a story? What is a small move in the right direction?

The most important question for every client is "Who are you?" I am not as interested in an answer as I am in teaching a process that the girl can use for the rest of her life. The process involves looking within to find a true core of self, acknowledging unique gifts, accepting all feelings, not just the socially acceptable ones, and making deep and firm decisions about values and meaning. The process includes knowing the difference between thinking and feeling, between immediate gratification and long-term goals, and between her own voice and the voices of others. The process includes discovering the personal impact of our cultural rules for women. It includes discussion about breaking those rules and formulating new, healthy guidelines for the self. The process teaches girls to chart a course based on the dictates of their true selves. The process is nonlinear, arduous and discouraging. It is also joyful, creative and full of surprises.

I often use the North Star as a metaphor. I tell clients, "You are in a boat that is being tossed around by the winds of the world. The voices of your parents, your teachers, your friends and the media can blow you east, then west, then back again. To stay on course you must follow your own North Star, your sense of who you truly are. Only by orienting north can you chart a course and maintain it, only by orienting north can you keep from being blown all over the sea.

"True freedom has more to do with following the North Star than with going whichever way the wind blows. Sometimes it seems like freedom is blowing with the winds of the day, but that kind of freedom is really an illusion. It turns your boat in circles. Freedom is sailing toward your dreams."

Even in the Midwest, where we have no large lakes, many girls have sailed. And particularly in the Midwest, girls love images of the sea. They like the images of stars, sky, roaring waters and themselves in a small, beautiful boat. But most girls also feel uncertain how to apply this metaphor to their own lives. They ask plaintively, "How do I know who I really am or what I truly want?"

I encourage girls to find a quiet place and ask themselves the following questions:

How do I feel right now?
What do I think?
What are my values?
How would I describe myself to myself?
How do I see myself in the future?
What kind of work do I like?
What kind of leisure do I like?
When do I feel most myself?
How have I changed since I entered puberty?
What kinds of people do I respect?
How am I similar to and different from my mother?
How am I similar to and different from my father?
What goals do I have for myself as a person?
What are my strengths and weaknesses?
What would I be proud of on my deathbed?

I encourage girls to keep diaries and to write poetry and autobiographies. Girls this age love to write. Their journals are places where they can be honest and whole. In their writing, they can clarify, conceptualize and evaluate their experiences. Writing their thoughts and feelings strengthens their sense of self. Their journals are a place where their point of view on the universe matters.

We talk about the disappointments of early adolescence—the betrayals by friends, the discovery that one is not beautiful by cultural standards, the feeling that one's smartness is a liability, the pressure to be popular instead of honest and feminine instead of whole.

I encourage girls to search within themselves for their deepest values and beliefs. Once they have discovered their own true selves, I encourage them to trust that self as the source of meaning and direction in their lives. That sense of self becomes their North Star that helps them stay on course. I encourage them to stay focused and goal-oriented, to steer toward their own self-defined sense of who they are.

Maturity involves being honest and true to oneself, making decisions based on a conscious internal process, assuming responsibility for one's decisions, having healthy relationships with others and developing one's own true gifts. It involves thinking about one's environment and deciding what one will and won't accept.

I encourage girls to observe our culture with the eyes of an anthropologist in a strange new society. What customs and rituals do they observe? What kinds of women and men are respected in this culture? What body shapes are considered ideal? How are the sex roles assigned? What are sanctions for breaking rules? It's only after they understand the rules that they can intelligently resist them.

I teach girls certain skills. The first and most basic is centering. I recommend that they find a quiet place where they can sit alone daily for ten to fifteen minutes. I encourage them to sit in this place, relax their muscles and breathe deeply. Then they are to focus on their own thoughts and feelings about the day. They are not to judge these thoughts or feelings or even direct them, only to observe them and respect them. They have much to learn from their own internal reactions to their lives.

Another basic skill is the ability to separate thinking from feeling. This is something that all healthy adults must be able to do. It's particularly difficult for teenagers because their feelings are so intense. They are given to emotional reasoning, which is the belief that if something feels so, it must be so. In the sessions, as we process events, I ask, "How do you feel about this? What do you think about this?" Over time, girls learn that these are two different processes and that both should be respected when making a decision.

Making conscious choices is also part of defining a self. I encourage girls to take responsibility for their own lives. Decisions need to be made slowly and carefully. Parents, boyfriends and peers may influence their decisions, but the final decisions are their own. The bottom-line question is: "Does this decision keep you on the course you want to be on?" At first the choices seem small. Who shall I go out with this weekend? Shall I forgive a friend who hurt my feelings? Later the choices include decisions about family, schools, careers, sexuality and intimate relationships.

Making and holding boundaries is closely related to making conscious choices. Girls learn to make and enforce boundaries. At the most basic level, this means they decide who touches their bodies. It also means they set limits about their time, their activities and their companions. They can say, "No, I will not do that." They can make position statements that are firm statements of what they will and will not do.

Closely related to boundary-making is the skill of defining relationships. Many girls are "empathy sick." That is, they know more about others' feelings than their own. Girls need to think about what kinds of relationships are in their best interest and to structure their relationships in accord with their ideas.

This is difficult for girls because they are socialized to let others do the defining. Girls are uncomfortable identifying and stating their needs, especially with boys and adults. They worry about not being nice or appearing selfish. However, success in this area is exhilarating. With this skill, they become the object of their own lives again. Once they have experienced the satisfaction of defining relationships, they are eager to continue to develop this skill.

Another vital skill is managing pain. All the craziness in the world comes from people trying to escape suffering. All mixed-up behavior comes from unprocessed pain. People drink, hit their mates and children, gamble, cut themselves with razors and even kill themselves in an attempt to escape pain. I teach girls to sit with their pain, to listen to it for messages about their lives, to acknowledge and describe it rather than to run from it. They learn to write about pain, to talk about it, to express it through exercise, art, dance or music. Life in the 1990s is so stressful that all girls need predictable ways to calm themselves. If they don't have positive ways, such as exercise, reading, hobbies or meditation, they will have negative ways, such as eating, drinking, drugs or self-mutilation.

Most girls need help modulating their emotional reactions. I encourage them to rate their stress on a one-to-ten scale. I challenge extreme statements. A girl who comes in saying "This is the worst day of my life" likely needs help reframing her day's experiences. One of my favorite questions for this reframing is: "What did you learn from your experience?"

Girls are socialized to look to the world for praise and rewards, and this keeps them other-oriented and reactive. They are also vulnerable to depression if they happen to be in an environment where they are not validated. I teach them to look within themselves for validation. I ask them to record victories and bring these in to share with me. Victories are actions that are in keeping with their long-term goals. Once a girl learns to validate herself, she is less vulnerable to the world's opinion. She can orient toward true North.

Time travel is another survival skill. All of us have bad days, lost days. Sometimes on those days it helps to go into the past and remember happy times or times when problems were much worse. Sometimes traveling to the future helps. It reminds a girl that she is on course toward her long-term goals and that certain experiences will not last forever. Traveling in time is just like traveling in space. Going somewhere different gives girls perspective on the experiences of the day.

Finally I teach the joys of altruism. Many adolescent girls are self-absorbed. It's not a character flaw, it's a developmental stage. Nonetheless, it makes them unhappy and limits their understanding of the world. I encourage girls to find some ways to help people on a regular basis. Volunteer work, good deeds for neighbors and political action help girls move into the larger world. They feel good about their contributions and they rapidly become less self-absorbed.

As a therapist and teacher, I have found adolescent girls quirky, fragile and changeable. I have also found them to be strong, good-hearted and insightful. I think of the girls I've seen this week: the girl with lemon-colored hair in a rock band, Veal, who is flunking out of school; the girl in forest-green Dr. Martens shoes who insists on nose and lip rings; the eighty-eight-pound twirler who feels too fat and the deaf girl who insists on being sexually active to demonstrate her normalcy.

But all these girls are at the same developmental stage and moving into the same culture. They must figure out ways to be independent from their parents and stay emotionally connected to them. They must discover ways to achieve and still be loved. They must discover moral and meaningful ways to express their sexuality in a culture that bombards them with plastic, pathetic models of sexuality. They must learn to respect themselves in a culture in which attractiveness is women's most defining characteristic. They must become adults in a culture in which the feminine is defined as docile, weak and other-oriented.

Girls' symptoms reflect the grief at the loss of their true selves. Their symptoms reflect the confusion about how to be human and be a woman. The basic issues appear and reappear in many guises. Girls must find, define and maintain their true selves. They must find a balance between being true to themselves and being kind and polite to others. Pathology often arises in girls because of the failure to realize their true possibilities of existence. The best treatment for this pathology is growth encouragement and resistance training.

Working with adolescent girls has changed me. I'm more humble and more patient, less sure of success than I am with adults. I am more respectful of families and aware of the difficulties that they encounter when girls are in adolescence. I'm more focused on our mass culture and the damage it does young women. I'm angrier. I'm more determined to help girls fight back and to work for cultural change.

After a lifetime of work, Freud claimed that he didn't know what women wanted. I think his ignorance came from his failure to analyze the cultural context in which women lived. Margaret Fuller was able to define what women need in a way that stands the test of time: "What a woman needs is not as a woman to act or rule, but as a nature to grow, as an intellect to discern, as a soul to live freely and unimpeded to unfold such powers as are given to her."

Chapter 14

LET A THOUSAND
FLOWERS BLOOM

■

MARGARET

Margaret grew up in the Northwest, where her father worked at a steel mill and her mother was a homemaker. She and her brother, Neal, attended school a block from their home and explored the nearby woods with the neighbor kids. With puberty, several things happened at once. Neal distanced himself from Margaret, her mother spent many evenings a week with her charismatic prayer group and her father grew disenchanted with the marriage.

Before, Margaret had never worried about who was popular or attractive, but with puberty everything changed. Her body developed rapidly and soon she was tall and full-breasted. As she put it, "I had the biggest boobs of any girl in junior high." All of a sudden her looks mattered. Boys who played games with her and Neal were suddenly looking at her breasts and making suggestive remarks.

Earlier, she had had two close friends and got on well with other girls. Now Kim and Marsha changed the situation. They picked scapegoats and encouraged the other girls to scorn their unlucky choices. The girls agreed because they were afraid that if they didn't they would be next.

At first Margaret went along with these girls. "I knew it was wrong," she said. "I was frightened of being their next victim." But soon

Margaret was picked as the scapegoat, ostensibly because she was flirty, but more likely because she was popular with boys and inspired jealousy. Also, she was a good student.

She was shunned by all the girls in her class, including her two close friends. No one would walk by her, sit by her or talk to her. If a girl accidentally touched Margaret she would rush to another girl and "rub off the germs." That girl would then rush to another girl with the germs and so on.

Margaret wanted to tell her family, but Neal no longer had time for her. He was off with his friends or on the phone to his girlfriend. Her parents were preoccupied—her mother with her prayer group, her father with his work. She doubted they would understand. She had never lied to her parents, but she faked illness so that she could miss school. She claimed her stomach hurt and that she had no appetite.

Margaret lost ten pounds in a month. Her mother would sit by her bed, read to her and beg her to drink tea. She loved the attention. Margaret promised herself that she would never go to school again. She decided to be as sick as she needed to be to keep that promise. When her mother suggested she return to school, she faked pain and writhed around on the floor.

Her mother carried her to the doctor's office and he admitted Margaret to the hospital. For three days she was tested and observed, then she was released undiagnosed. When her mother suggested she return to school, Margaret claimed she was having double vision and might be going blind.

Her mother took her to a neurologist to check for a brain tumor. The neurologist referred her to an ophthalmologist, who was the only one to call her bluff. After the eye tests he said, "Young lady, I don't know why you are doing this, but you are lying. I'm going to tell that to your parents and doctors." He did tell, but Margaret seemed so sick that no one believed him.

Margaret's mother took her to a charismatic prayer group, where an exorcism was performed. One woman told her, "There's an evil spirit in you, a spirit full of fear." The women surrounded her, prayed in tongues and chanted until Margaret burst into tears.

She sobbed that she hated what was evil in her. The group assured her that their prayers had removed the evil, just like a surgery would. Margaret didn't believe them.

By now it was Christmas and Margaret hadn't attended school since early October. She decided to buy the girls in her class Christmas presents. Hoping to bribe her way in, Margaret carefully selected expensive bath salts for Kim and Marsha.

She was tired of being sick, of lying to her parents and of doctors' offices. After vacation and her gift giving, Margaret tried school again. The boys with their sexual remarks and the girls with their shunning were still there. She endured two days of scorn and then told her parents, "I won't go back. I'll die if you make me go back."

Her parents tried everything—bullying, bribing, reasoning and pleading—to no avail. Finally they took her to a psychiatrist, whom Margaret hated. She described him as a middle-aged man in a suit and tie who sat behind a heavy desk and lectured her on responsibility. Later he told her parents she was spoiled and insisted she be in school.

Her mother had the horrible job of enforcing his orders. Every day she pulled Margaret out of bed and dressed her. Most days Margaret drooped passively as her mom put on her skirts and cashmere sweaters. Sometimes Margaret fought her and yelled obscenities. Her mother slapped her and cried. She carried her downstairs and out to the car. Margaret sobbed all the way to school. Then, when they pulled up at the school, she flashed her mother a look of hatred and went in.

Margaret threatened suicide. One day she jumped out of the car. Another day she swallowed a box of Ex-Lax. Finally, one Saturday, she ran away from home. It was a snowy day and she walked deep into the woods. She sat down under a tree far off the walking path and waited to die. Snow drifted around her. A rabbit approached and wrinkled his nose in her direction. At twilight people came searching for her and she bit her hand to keep herself from calling for help. She grew numb from the cold and could no longer move her legs or arms. Watching the starry winter sky, she fell asleep. At midnight a neighbor found her and carried her home. Monday, her parents and psychiatrist made her go back to school.

Finally the school intervened and recommended a new therapist. The math teacher knew about the cliques and figured out why Margaret was missing school. He called Kim and Marsha and told them to shape up or he would have them expelled. Kim and Marsha were shocked that their teasing had hurt Margaret so much. They claimed that they had had no intention of doing any real harm. That afternoon they came to her and said they were sorry, that they hadn't meant to hurt her so badly. A bewildered Margaret accepted their apologies. The rest of the year they left Margaret alone.

When Margaret came to see me, we talked about her school. She still had trouble with the boys. We talked about how she could avoid negative encounters and how, when she was cornered, she could fight her way out. I recommended a self-defense class for her so that she would be more in control. I called the school and her parents about the harassment.

Margaret wished she had talked to her parents about her problems at the time they occurred. But she was not sure that they would have appreciated her despair. "Adults don't take kids seriously," she said. She wished the school would have intervened with the girls sooner and that she had had a therapist who listened to her instead of enforcing the social order. But she was proud that she resisted doing something that was so hurtful to her. She was glad that she would not let herself be bullied by the girls in her class, by her parents or by doctors.

"I'm not going to let fear rule my life again," she told me. "I'll stay and fight rather than run. Next time I won't pretend that my stomach hurts when it's my life that is hurting."

I handed her a Kleenex and said, "As you told about your school, I had this image from Tiananmen Square. Remember that young Chinese man who stood all alone before the Red Army tanks? He looked so vulnerable and yet he was where he needed to be. He was courageous and so were you."

"I didn't feel brave at the time. I felt evil, dishonest and weak. Now, though, I can see that I was fighting for my life."

While dramatic, Margaret's experiences were in many ways typical. Until puberty, she was relatively free to be who she was. Then, as her body changed, her social environment became an emotional obstacle course that she couldn't maneuver. Margaret was exceptional in her resistance to an environment where she was devalued and objectified. She would not tolerate the shaming and the humiliation inflicted on her by anxious classmates. Even then, she realized that this was a "life and death" matter.

Ironically, what was strong about Margaret—her resistance to pressure—looked weak to the adults around her. They saw the surface symptoms and missed the deep-structure strength. This often happens with adolescent girls. The issues are so complicated that strength is labeled weakness and vice versa.

———

Many young women are less whole and androgynous than they were at age ten. They are more appearance-conscious and sex-conscious. They are quieter, more fearful of holding strong opinions, more careful what they say and less honest. They are more likely to second-guess themselves and to be self-critical. They are bigger worriers and more effective people pleasers. They are less likely to play sports, love math and science and plan on being president. They hide their intelligence. Many must fight for years to regain all the territory that they lost.

I entered adolescence confident, curious and loud. I knew I was smart and expected to make something of myself. I wasn't afraid of anyone. I changed. By the time I graduated from high school, I was shy and demure, more polite than it's healthy to be, worried about my weight and my facial features and desperately eager to be liked. Much of my adult experience has been the slow trip back to my preadolescent androgynous personality.

Early adolescence is when many of the battles for the self are won and lost. These are hard fights, and the losses and victories determine to a great extent the quality of women's future lives. While young women are in the midst of these battles, none of them look terribly strong. Surface behaviors reveal little of the deep struggles that are battles to hold on to true selves.

Alice Miller would say that strength in adolescence requires an acknowledgment of all parts of the self, not just the socially acceptable ones. Simone de Beauvoir would say that strength implies remaining the subject of one's life and resisting the cultural pressure to become the object of male experience. Betty Friedan would call it fighting against "the problem with no name." Toni McNaron calls it "radical subjectivism." Gloria Steinem calls it "healthy rebellion." Carol Gilligan refers to it as "speaking in one's own voice," and bell hooks calls it "talking back." Resistance means vigilance in protecting one's own spirit from the forces that would break it.

Margaret Mead defines strength as valuing all those parts of the self whether or not they are valued by the culture. She would encourage the survival of the ten-year-old androgynous self that is competent and connected, and she would emphasize the importance of developing innate potentialities and fighting efforts to limit value.

In America in the 1990s, the demands of the time are so overwhelming that even the strongest girls keel over in adolescence. The lessons are too difficult and the learning curve too steep for smooth early mastery. Strong girls manage to hold on to some sense of themselves in the high winds. Often they have a strong sense of place that gives them roots. They may identify with an ethnic group in a way that gives them pride and focus, or they may see themselves as being an integral part of a community. Their sense of belonging preserves their identity when it is battered by the winds of adolescence.

Strong girls know who they are and value themselves as multifaceted people. They may see themselves as dancers, musicians, athletes or political activists. These kinds of identities hold up well under pressure. Talent allows girls some continuity between past childhood and current adolescent lives. Being genuinely useful also gives girls something to hold on to. Girls who care for ill parents or who help the disadvantaged have a hedge against the pain of adolescence.

Strong girls generally manage to stay close to their families and maintain some family loyalty. Even if they come from problem families, they usually have someone in the family whom they love and trust. Through all the chaos of adolescence, they keep the faith with this person.

Almost all girls have difficulty with their families. Even the healthiest girls push their parents to validate them as adults before the parents are ready to accept the new situation. All girls do some distancing as part of their individuation process. But healthy girls know that their parents love them and stay connected in important ways. They keep talking and seeking contact. Even as they rage at their parents on the surface, a part of them remains loyal and connected to them.

While no girls look or feel strong at this time, often there are signs that they are fighting to save themselves. It's a good sign if they maintain some memory of their preteen selves and are able to keep the interests and relationships of elementary school years. It's good if they resist pressure to become ultrafeminine.

Often strong girls can articulate a sense that things are much tougher and not quite right in the outside world. They are aware that they're being pressured to act in ways that aren't good for them. The premature sexualization of their lives makes them nervous. They may be involved in cliques, but a part of them hates the snobbishness and actively resists hurting other girls.

Healthy girls, like all girls, are scared of many things. They lose perspective and are more likely to be conformists than at any other time in their lives. They are more likely to blame their parents for their troubles and to do things they really don't believe in. They want to be pretty and well liked, but it's a matter of degree. They won't sell their souls to be popular. When push comes to shove, they'll stand up for themselves. There are certain lines they will not cross.

Positive signs include beliefs in causes or interests in anything larger than their own lives. Girls who have some special passions can call on something that is greater than their experiences in the halls of junior highs. Often their passion can give them some perspective and sustain them through the toughest times. Strong girls manage to avoid heavy chemical use and deal with pain in more adaptive ways. Often they have healthy stress-relieving habits such as reading, running or playing the piano.

In *Smart Girls, Gifted Women,* Barbara Kerr explores the common experiences of girls who grew into strong women. She studied the adolescent years of Marie Curie, Gertrude Stein, Eleanor Roosevelt, Margaret Mead, Georgia O'Keeffe, Maya Angelou and Beverly Sills, and she found that they had in common time by themselves, the ability to fall in love with an idea, a refusal to acknowledge gender limitations and what she called "protective coating." None of them were popular as adolescents and most stayed separate from their peers, not by choice, but because they were rejected. Ironically, this very rejection gave them a protected space in which they could develop their uniqueness.

Many strong girls have similar stories: They were socially isolated and lonely in adolescence. Smart girls are often the girls most rejected by peers. Their strength is a threat and they are punished for being different. Girls who are unattractive or who don't worry about their appearance are scorned. This isolation is often a blessing because it allows girls to develop a strong sense of self. Girls who are isolated emerge from adolescence more independent and self-sufficient than girls who have been accepted by others.

Strong girls may protect themselves by being quiet and guarded so that their rebellion is known by only a few trusted others. They may be cranky and irascible and keep critics at a distance so that only people who love them know what they are up to. They may have the knack of shrugging off the opinions of others or they may use humor to deflect the hostility that comes their way.

Many strong girls have found protected space in which they could grow. There are various ways to find that space. For example, athletics can be protective. Girls in sports are often emotionally healthy. They see their bodies as functional, not decorative. They have developed discipline in the pursuit of excellence. They have learned to win and lose, to cooperate, to handle stress and pressure. They are in a peer group that defines itself by athletic ability rather than popularity, drug or alcohol use, wealth or appearance.

Protective space can be created by books, interests, families, churches and physical or social isolation. It's a blessing. Girls who grow up unprotected, adrift in mass culture with little protective coating and no private territory are vulnerable to many kinds of problems.

This business of protected space is very complicated, however. Too much protection leads to the "princess and the pea syndrome," girls who are hothouse flowers unable to withstand stress. Too little protection often leads to addictions and self-destructive behaviors. The same stresses that help some girls grow, cripple others.

All lives have ups and downs. For most women, early adolescence is a big dip down. Strong girls, like all girls, do crazy things in junior high. They feel unstable and out of control. It's important to look beyond surface behavior to understand what's happening. For example, a girl can be depressed in junior high because she's bright enough to recognize our girl-poisoning culture and to feel defeated by it. A girl who withdraws may be acting adaptively. She may know that she's not ready to drink or be sexual and she may drop out of social life for a time while her friends grow up. Things are often different from the way they look on the surface.

Strong girls strive to define themselves as women and adults. They are trying to break away from family and remain close at the same time. They are trying to have friends without sacrificing themselves to do it. They attempt to define themselves as moral people and to take responsibility for their choices. They are trying to make good choices, often without much help. All of this is so difficult that weak often looks strong and strong looks weak. The girls who seem the happiest in junior high are often not the healthiest adults. They may be the girls who have less radar with which to pick up signals about reality. While this may be protective when the signals come fast and furious, later they may miss information. Or they may be the girls who don't even try to resolve contradictions or make sense of reality. They may be relatively comfortable, but they will not grow.

JUNE

The morning we met, June had worked a double shift at the Kawasaki plant, gone out for breakfast and driven across town to my office. June was big-boned with a round, pockmarked face. She wore her hair short and was dressed in a gray sweat suit. She lumbered into my office and sank onto the couch. She was so physically imposing that I was surprised by her delicate sensibilities.

Her language was personal, precise and earthy. She talked about herself softly and carefully as if psychotherapy, like dentistry, might hurt. She did not, thank goodness, talk like someone who had read too many self-help books.

June said, "I'm here because I am dating someone for the first time in my life. I'm twenty-seven and I've never been kissed. I thought I might need some coaching."

She'd been at Kawasaki for ten years. Her closest friend worked next to her on the assembly line. Dixie was a single parent and June helped her with her kids. She pulled out their school pictures to show me and said they called her Aunt June. "They're real good kids," she said, "once you get to know them."

June had met her boyfriend, Marty, at work too. He was the union representative for her group of workers. The last three Saturday nights he had dropped by with a pizza and a video. Last Saturday night he put his arm around June. That's when she decided to call me.

I asked her about her family and June sighed. "I was afraid you would bring them up."

"We can wait," I say gently.

"I might as well get it out," she said. "After you hear about my teenage years, you'll understand why I haven't dated much."

June's father was a farm laborer who "never had much to do with me." Her mother was a cook at a rest home. "She was hard-working and fun. She'd bring me treats from the rest home—cookies and crafts that the residents made for me. She showed them my pictures and kept them posted on my activities. Everyone at the home loved her."

June paused and looked at me. "Mom died at the start of my freshman year in high school. It was an awful time to lose her. I had just started my periods. I was clumsy and had bad acne. I had been slightly chubby and then I got fat. I was totally alone."

June blew her nose before continuing. "The year Mom died, I

watched the Miss America pageant all by myself. I stared at those thin, poised girls and knew I would never be like that. I had no looks and no talents. Only my mom had loved me as I was. I thought about giving up."

She rubbed her forehead as if to erase some memories too painful to consider. "I don't know how I made it through that year. Dad was never home. I had hardly any clothes. I did what housework and cooking got done and that was precious little. Dad almost never gave me money for groceries. I was fat and hungry at the same time."

I asked her about the kids at school. "They were terrible. Not so much mean, as totally indifferent. I didn't exist for them. I was too ugly and too sad to even be part of the class. I ate by myself and walked to and from school alone. No one would be my lab partner."

She rubbed her big face and continued. "One time a boy approached me in the cafeteria, in front of all the other kids, and asked me to go to a football game. I was such a goof that I thought he meant it. I thought maybe he could see past my appearance and like the real me. So I said sure, if I could get Dad's permission. Then he started laughing. His buddies all whooped it up too. They'd dared him to do it for a joke. He collected ten bucks for just asking me out."

June sighed. "After that I steered clear of boys."

Her father married Mercene a year after June's mother died. They took a honeymoon trip to Sun City and brought June salt and pepper shakers for her hope chest. "By then I had no hope," she said flatly.

"My stepmother was tight with money. She only let me wash my hair once a week. I needed to wash it daily it was so greasy, but she didn't want to pay for the water. My teeth were crooked and the school recommended braces. Mercene said, 'I've heard that can cost a thousand dollars. No way we'll spend that kind of money for straight teeth.' Once I cut my foot pretty badly when I was walking beans. She wouldn't pay for the doctor. I limped a little because of that."

I worked hard to remain neutral as June talked about this neglect. June herself had no anger. She continued matter-of-factly. "I was the black sheep. Once my stepbrother asked me why I lived with his family."

I asked how she survived those years when she was rejected at home and at school. "I thought about my mother and how she would have wanted me to behave. I decided that other people's bad behavior was no excuse for mine. I would do the best I could. I talked to Mom in bed at night. I told her about my days. I always tried to have something

I was proud of to report to her. I knew she had really loved me, and that got me through a lot. I knew I was lovable and that the people around me were too blind to see it."

She rubbed her broad face with a handkerchief. "At the time I desperately wanted friends. Now I think I learned a lot those years. I learned to take care of myself. I got so that other people's rejection didn't faze me. I had my ideas about right and wrong.

"After high school my life really improved. I started working at Kawasaki. Immediately I felt more accepted. I worked hard and people noticed. Women invited me to eat with them. The men joked around with me. My supervisor took an interest in me. He encouraged me to get my teeth worked on and have my foot evaluated. I wear a brace now that corrected the limp."

June smiled when she spoke of work. "I have a Halloween party every year for all the workers in my area. Fridays I bowl on the union team. I have earned merit raises every year I've worked there. I make good money.

"I've forgiven Dad and Mercene. I'm happy, so what is there to be angry about now? I am happier than they are. I try to do something for them every weekend. I take over a pie or mow their yard."

I asked how she gets along with her father. "Dad can't forgive me for being fat. He really wanted a beautiful daughter."

I thought of June's life. She has a spirit as delicate and strong as a spiderweb. She is gifted at forgiving and loving. Because she is unattractive by our cultural standards, she has been devalued by many, including her own father. But somehow she has managed to survive and even thrive through all this adversity. She reminds me of those succulent desert flowers that remain dormant for so many seasons and then bloom lavishly when there is a smattering of rain.

I said to her, "Your father has missed an opportunity to love someone who is marvelous."

We talked about Marty. He's a bulky man who is prematurely balding. June said, "His looks don't matter. I know how hard he works and that he doesn't put anyone down. He's not a complainer."

I suggested that daily she imagine herself successfully kissing him. "It's hard to do what you can't even imagine doing. Once you have the images down, the reality will be easier." I encouraged her to keep her expectations for that first kiss low. "Bells may not ring and the sky may not light up." I quoted Georgia O'Keeffe, totally out of context: "Nobody's good at the beginning."

I pointed out that the relationship was going well. Physical affection was only a small part of a relationship. She was already gifted at loving and forgiving, which were much more important qualities. I predicted that kissing would be easy once she was ready.

When I saw June again, she reported that kissing was great. She asked me if I thought she needed more therapy. "No," I said. "I think you could teach me some lessons about strength through adversity and the importance of forgiveness."

June is a good example of someone who, with almost no luck at all, fashioned a good life for herself. Almost all our psychological theories would predict that June would turn out badly. But as happens more frequently than we psychologists generally acknowledge, adversity built her character. What saved her was her deep awareness of her mother's love. Even though her mother was dead, June felt her mother's spirit was with her. That enabled her to feel valued at a time when she was rejected by everyone. June's belief in her mother's love gave her a sense of purpose. She was determined to live in a way that would make her mother proud.

June had the gift for appreciating what was good in her life. Once she told me, "I always get what I want." Then she winked and said, "But I know what to want." Her life, which might strike some people as difficult or dull, is rich and rewarding. She has friends, money, a boyfriend and the respect of her peers. She has that pride in her life that so many self-made people have. She has no bitterness or anger because she is basically happy. She's a desert flower opening to the rain.

CAROLINE (17)

Caroline asked to interview me for her high school psychology class. I agreed, provided we could trade interviews. Caroline had recently moved to town from Alabama, and I was interested in talking to girls from other states. We met at my house and Caroline interviewed me first. I was struck by her poise and sensitivity. Dressed in a dark blue skirt-and-sweater outfit, she looked older than her seventeen years. She could have been a college student in a journalism class.

After my interview, we jokingly traded chairs and switched roles. I asked her about her family. Her father was a military man with a drinking problem and a womanizing problem. He'd considered Caroline ugly and lazy. He whipped her for the smallest mistakes. Once when he was calling her names in front of his buddies, one of them told him to stop. Usually, though, his friends were too drunk or too insensitive to care when he belittled his daughter. Caroline said of her father, "He would have been a good horse trainer. He had lots of ways to break a person's spirit."

She continued, "Fortunately, he wasn't around all that much. When he was around, I'd grab a book and head for my room. Mom couldn't get away from him and he destroyed her."

I asked about the abuse. "It happened at night after he'd been out drinking. He'd stumble in, slamming doors and cursing. Mom yelled at him and he called her names. Then he hit her and she cried. Later she came to my bed for the night. I stopped it when I was twelve. I called the cops on him."

I must have betrayed my emotions because Caroline said, "It wasn't as bad as you think. I loved school. We moved a lot and I went to all kinds of schools—parochial, military and integrated public schools. But wherever I went, I was the best student.

"I was always the teacher's pet. The kids liked me too. I sang, danced, played sports, was good at art. I could joke my way into any crowd. Even though my home life was hell, I had high self-esteem from all the praise I got at school."

She said, "No one at school knew what my home life was like. I pretended my parents had rules for me, that I had birthday parties and dental appointments. When we had school plays, I explained that my parents were out of town on business. I was doing so well it was easy to fool the teachers."

She settled back into the couch. "My sixth-grade year was one of the best years of my life. That year Dad brought a girlfriend home and Mom tried to kill herself. I had to pull the gun away from her. But amazingly, I was a happy kid. I was in a good school in Boston and I loved my teacher. She arranged for special art lessons and she let me sing lead in the school musical. I maybe should have felt worse about my family, but I didn't. I was living my own life."

Caroline paused, and when she continued, the happiness had vanished from her voice. "The next year my parents divorced and Mom and I moved to Alabama to live with her parents. Everything good in my life stopped happening.

"The schools were horrible. Everyone with money went to private schools, and the public schools were broke. My social studies text was pre–Vietnam War, and our science labs didn't have microscopes. Once I had to go home and change clothes because I'd fallen in human excrement on the school yard. Another time I was cut by a broken beer bottle.

"That school sent us the message that we were nothing, we were dirt. Most of my classmates bought it. They gave up their dreams and planned to get factory jobs as soon as they could quit school.

"I was nobody in a school full of nobodies. I was an outsider, a Northerner. I actually got teased because my skin was too light and my manners were too good. After a few weeks I developed a speech impediment. I was trying to sound Southern and I slurred my speech. No one could understand me. I pretty much quit talking for a while.

"Meanwhile, my home life was miserable, Mom was a permanent invalid. My grandparents were well-meaning, but they didn't understand."

"What saved you?" I asked.

She pulled out her billfold and showed me a picture. "Sandra saved me, or rather we saved each other. I met her early in my eighth-grade year. She sat beside me in English. I noticed that she knew the answers to the teacher's questions. One day I asked her if she'd like to meet for an ice cream after school.

"Right from the first we understood each other. Sandra's dad was an alcoholic too. Her mother worked at the box factory and we had both raised ourselves.

"By the end of that first meeting we agreed to fight the system together. We promised each other we wouldn't do drugs or get pregnant. I'd traveled with my parents and I knew there were better places to be. Sandra loved to hear me talk about those places."

She laughed and continued. "We invented this game. I put my finger on a globe and spun it. Wherever it stopped, that's where we were for that day. If my finger landed in Bombay, we discussed the food, the music, the streets, the weather, the smells and sounds of Bombay. We vowed we would visit all those places when we grew up."

She put Sandra's picture away. "We pushed each other to achieve. We knew that the one way out was education. We memorized vocabulary words. We got a list of the classics from a librarian and read those books. We went to every free lecture we could. We were determined."

I asked her about high school. "By tenth grade, Sandra and I were straight-A students. We broke the curve in every class we took. We sang and were in the student government. We had transcripts full of activities that showed we were well rounded. Then last year we moved here."

"How did that happen?"

"Sandra's aunt and uncle said she could move in with them and have her senior year at a good school. She wouldn't come without me. We share a bedroom. We're closer than sisters. We've promised each other we won't marry until we get through college. We've divided up all the good schools so we won't be competing against each other for scholarships. But we'll stay close through college. We're family."

Since Caroline was a young girl, she had been determined to be the best at whatever she did. She had remarkable survival skills. In the language of popular psychology, Caroline was a "parental child." But as her life demonstrates, that's not always bad. Her experience left her responsible, achievement-oriented and able to take care of herself in any situation.

Often in stories of teenage girls, the relationships between girls are ugly and destructive. Margaret's story showed the harm girls do to each other. Caroline's story was different. She and Sandra helped each other survive and eventually escape their stormy environments. They helped each other stay focused on their dreams and optimistic about their futures.

Both June and Caroline lacked what we call today "emotionally available parents." June's mother was dead and her father insensitive. Caroline's father was absent and her mother was mentally and physically ill. This absence of parental support made it clear that, from the beginning, they had only themselves to depend on for happiness. That's a lesson all girls must learn. Ironically, it's harder to learn if parents take too much responsibility for their daughters' happiness.

Both girls had a focus that carried them beyond the painful days in junior high. June wanted to behave in a way that made her mother proud, and Caroline wanted to make something of herself academically. Even in their darkest times, they were preparing in their own ways for brighter futures.

Evonne's and Maria's stories are quite different. Both girls come from strong families with strong women. They learned from their parents the importance of fighting back and resisting others' efforts to define them. Evonne, like many black girls, saw strong women all around her. To Evonne, growing up female was compatible with growing up assertive and strong. Maria had grandparents who risked their lives for what they believed in. They taught her to be true to her own values no matter what the cost.

EVONNE (16)

Evonne was a black student who had toured with a women's gospel choir and starred in school and community musicals. She was an A student, she was on student council and popular with her classmates. I was curious about her social success and invited her to come to my house for an interview.

Evonne drove up in her new red sports car, a present for her sixteenth birthday. A week earlier, her parents had given her the keys at a dinner for twenty of her friends. Evonne was dressed in an olive silk blouse, black slacks and gold rings and earrings. She was beautiful, with butterscotch-colored skin, enormous black eyes and dimples. I asked her to tell me about her life.

Evonne was the only child of professional parents; her father was an attorney and her mother a physician. She'd been a loved and pampered child from day one. Every summer she spent with her maternal grandmother in Arkansas, and winter holidays she spent with her father's parents in Virginia.

She attended a private Montessori school in Chicago until she was in third grade, then she transferred to a racially diverse public school for gifted students. Her early school years were happy ones—she was immediately recognized as a gifted performer. She danced and sang her way through school and was in a children's choir that was on television regularly. Her parents had paid for private lessons with drama and singing coaches.

I asked about racism in Chicago. "As a kid, I only experienced one racist. This guy called me 'nigger' and said to stay out of his neighborhood when I rode my bike down his street. I avoided that street for a while, and finally Dad noticed. When I told him what happened, he insisted that I ride on that street. He told me I shouldn't give racists any power over my life, even the power to decide a bike route."

Evonne said that she liked school until fifth grade, when the girls at her school changed. She told me, "Everyone became materialistic. I could afford the right clothes but some of my friends couldn't and they were left out of everything. I never, ever teased anyone for wearing K Mart clothes, but other girls did."

She shook her head. "I wish I could tell you that I didn't fall for the snob scene, but I dumped my friends and hung out with the popular kids. I was a total bore in sixth grade."

She paused as our cat jumped on her lap. She petted Woody for a few moments before continuing. "Junior high was the pits. I went to a new school that was 95 percent whites. I felt alone. Even the nicest white students didn't invite me to their homes. But the blacks weren't like me either. They were poorer and from different backgrounds.

"I thought about where I fit in. I looked for black movies in the video stores and they were about drugs and gangs, which wasn't me. I felt like an invisible black person. I didn't want to be an Oreo, but I didn't want to hang out with crackheads. I couldn't find a place. Sometimes I was angry I wasn't white and sometimes I hated whites."

Evonne looked sober as she thought about race. She continued, "In junior high I prayed that I would wake up in a world where everyone was the same color. Simple decisions paralyzed me. Should I sit with black kids or white kids at lunch? Should I buy heavy metal or rap?"

I asked about her parents. "About then, Dad's company moved to New York City and he became a commuter father. I was mad at him and mixed up about myself. I got into trouble, which was easy to find. I smoked cigarettes and dope. I drank too. My parents were so trusting that I got away with murder."

I asked Evonne to elaborate. "I knew this girl Missy whose parents were divorcing, and we sneaked around and screwed up at school. Eventually my parents caught on, but until then we did whatever we felt like."

"What did your parents do when they found out?"

"They made up all kinds of rules and they took me to a therapist," Evonne said. "It was a tough year. We fought all the time. They were disappointed in me and I was mad at them. Then Mom got a job offer and moved me out of Chicago."

She paused. "That was good timing. I was almost raped at a party. I was sick of my racist school. Missy was turning into an alcoholic. I missed being in theater and music."

Woody purred as Evonne rubbed his back. "We moved here the summer before I started high school. I had plenty of time to think. Did I want to be a rebel or a high achiever? I realized that I was happier as an achiever. I decided to go back to my straight ways. I stopped smoking to protect my voice. I decided I wouldn't lie to my parents anymore. I'd study, make friends, try out for plays and choirs. I'd stay away from the druggies and boozers. I'd pick friends on the basis of interests, not skin color."

"Did your plans work?"

Evonne said, "I've been happy here. The school has lots of black and Hispanic kids, also Asian-Americans. Race is an issue, but not a big issue. I liked leaving my past behind, but I'm glad I experienced it. I got all my wildness out before high school. I'm not that tempted by evil."

I asked Evonne about dating.

She said, "I'm picky. I like guys, but nobody enough to date. I get mad at my friends who make a big deal of dating. I don't feel ready. I am in two musical groups at school plus the gospel choir. I try to be involved in a theater production at all times. I don't have time to date. I'd rather keep things casual."

I asked Evonne about her parents.

She said, "They have a commuter marriage right now, which is hard. Dad flies here once a month for a weekend and calls home every other night, but it's not the same. He likes his job, but I miss fishing with him and I miss him at all my performances."

Evonne was proud of her mother, who had overcome many obstacles. Her mother's father died when her mother was three. Evonne's grandmother had to work two jobs to raise the four kids. Evonne's mother studied so hard she needed special reading glasses in high school. She was one of the first black women to get a scholarship to Harvard.

I asked about her current life. "I'm happy now," she said. "I think for myself. I don't think any black person can say they have their racial issues worked out, but I like myself."

MARIA (16)

Maria was late to our meeting at the coffeehouse. She rushed breathless over to my table and plopped her book bag and sheaf of flyers on the spare seat. Maria was a tall young woman with straight dark hair and serious eyes. She explained that her VW, with its 200,000 miles and painted flowers, had died as she drove downtown.

I bought us both Italian sodas. As Maria drank hers, she told me about the previous day's march against the death penalty. Her talk reminded me of my friends from the sixties. I couldn't resist asking her if she was a Grateful Dead fan. She loved the Dead, with their wild abandonment and their community of fans. Maria wished she had been a teen in the sixties when people were idealistic and free. She hated corporate America and our town's emphasis on money.

Maria was the second child in a Hispanic family. Her dad was a social worker and her mother a schoolteacher. She had a brother, Alberto, two years older than she, and two younger sisters, Yolanda and Carla. Both her paternal and maternal grandparents lived in town, and Maria spent time with them almost daily. "The family is first" was the family motto.

Maria's family had a long tradition of social activism. In the late 1960s her maternal grandparents had fled for their lives from El Salvador. Her great uncle had been shot for his political activities. Her mother was an ardent feminist and active in the teachers' union. Maria said, "All of us were raised with the idea that we should work to make our society a better place. No one gets away with being indifferent. Even Alberto, who is a skateboarder, helps with Sanctuary work."

Maria felt especially close to Alberto. As children they rarely fought. In fact, Alberto was her main supporter and helper. "He could make anything out of cardboard. We played all kinds of games that he invented. We made movies together and sang duets. He let me play with his friends and him. I was never left behind."

Maria sipped her drink. "I loved elementary school. Every now and then I'd be called a racist name, but Alberto was there to protect me. His friends all liked me and made sure I was well treated. Until fourth grade my class was close."

"What happened then?"

"That's when cliques formed. My friends got together for cheerleading practice and I wasn't asked to join them."

She pushed her hair out of her eyes. "I wanted to fit in. I desperately tried to raise my coolness quotient. I even bought some Guess jeans, but they didn't help. The problem was my color."

She said, "Mom encouraged me to fight the pressure to be a certain way. She hates racism and elitism. Alberto was a nonconformist and he teased me about those jeans. Later I did fight, but in sixth grade I was a chicken."

I asked her about junior high.

"The first day was awful," Maria said. "It was a big school and I kept getting lost. I ripped my shorts in gym and I got called a wetback in typing class. I came home sobbing."

She frowned at the memories. "My family said I'd make friends quickly, but I didn't. I didn't like most of the kids. The girls tried to hurt each other and their talk drove me crazy. I spent time with my brother and his friends."

She ran her finger around the rim of her cup. "I was lonely and mixed up for a while. I took everything personally, and I thought there must be something wrong with me. But Alberto and my mom kept saying it wasn't me. They talked me into joining Amnesty International so I'd have an outside interest.

"I got interested, all right." She smiled. "The people were great. Their friendship saved me in junior high."

I asked about appearance. Maria sighed. "I wish I could say that I don't care about looks, but I do. I'm pleased when guys tell me I'm pretty, and I'm glad I'm not fat or homely. But being pretty isn't the most important thing about me, and I don't pick my friends on the basis of appearance.

"When I was in sixth grade we had a unit on self-esteem in Girl Scouts. I took it seriously. I tacked up a list of positives about myself on the mirror. I asked myself at the end of each day what I had done that I felt proud of. That work on self-esteem helped me in junior high. When I felt badly because my body wasn't perfect, I remembered my suggestions to think positively."

Maria continued, "In high school I found my own kind. I started a chapter of Amnesty International."

"Are the kids different?"

"Alberto is there and I like his friends. Some of the girls seem trustworthy. My school is the biggest school in town and I'm meeting more Hispanics and African-Americans."

"Have you dated?"

"This one guy really liked me. I liked him too, but I wanted friendship before we got involved romantically. He wanted too much of my time and he was jealous. Finally I had to break it off. Since then I've avoided close relationships with guys. I hate how quickly relationships get labeled. If I have lunch with the same guy three days in a row someone thinks we're going steady.

"Because of Alberto, I have high expectations," she continued. "I don't like macho guys. I like guys who can talk about their feelings and who respect women. In high school, not that many guys can."

Some friends of Maria's came in and she waved at them. "Another thing I don't like is competition. I love sports, but not competitive sports. Alberto's the same way. I think we learned that from our folks. They both try to set things up so that everyone wins in our family and no one is competing for anything."

I asked about sports. "Alberto and I like to play Ultimate Frisbee. We play on a volleyball team on Wednesday nights. We avoid school sports—too much pressure. We want sports to be fun."

I asked about the future. Maria said, "I'm dreading Alberto's graduation this year. We've been so close that I'll feel lost without him. He plans to go to Iowa and study writing. For myself, I want to be a political scientist. I am excited about graduation, but also scared.

"I will miss seeing my grandparents every day. They have helped me through things and now they are getting old. One of my sisters starts junior high the year I go to college. I wish I could help her through it."

I thanked Maria for our interview and told her I thought her "coolness quotient" was quite high. She rolled her eyes and laughed. When I said good-bye, Maria handed me a flyer for the protest against the situation in the Balkans. "Maybe you would be interested in this."

Both Maria and Evonne have extended families who have played an active role in their lives. Both girls felt close to their families and admired their parents. Their parents had experienced problems—Evonne's fought against racism and poverty in their youth, and Maria's grandparents had narrowly escaped death squads in El Salvador. These girls respected their parents' lives as separate from their own. They didn't have the belief that their parents were here to make them happy.

Both girls grew up as members of minority groups. This intensified their identity struggles in adolescence. In their cases, it sharpened the issues and helped them discover who they were. When they were young, both girls suffered from people who judged them because of their color. They learned to consider the source and discount such judgments. They were less overwhelmed by the idea that others might judge and reject them. This had happened to them before and they had survived and developed the inner resources to deal with it.

Because of race, Evonne and Maria were different from their peers. Instead of weakening them, this gave them strength. Evonne had a rich tradition of strong black women to draw upon as role models, and

Maria had a mother and a grandmother who fought back. Neither of the girls seemed slavishly obsessed with peer acceptance.

Neither of these girls had been a victim of violence or premature sexuality. Both were reluctant to date and had not been sexually active by the time of our interviews. They had resisted pressures to define themselves as sexual. It's interesting, given how mature they were compared to their peers, that they didn't feel ready for sex. Likewise, they both felt comfortable with their appearance. Evonne had lovely clothes and was beautiful. Almost in spite of herself, Maria was pretty. But neither defined herself on the basis of appearance.

This chapter tells the story of five strong young women: June, Margaret, Caroline, Evonne and Maria. It's not accidental that two of the young women are black, one is Hispanic and three are poor. Properly faced, adversity builds character. All of these women are fighters. June fought back by talking to her mother's memory. Margaret would not join a peer culture that was destroying her. Caroline fought her way out of an environment that could easily have trapped her forever. Evonne and Maria forged their own self-definitions independent of peer pressure. I'm reminded of that old chestnut "That which doesn't kill us makes us stronger."

Unlike Ophelia, most girls recover from early adolescence. It's not a fatal disease, but an acute condition that disappears with time. While it's happening, nobody looks strong. Even the girls in this chapter were miserable in junior high. From the vantage point of high school, they can tell their stories, but in junior high they had no perspective. It's impossible to have much perspective in a hurricane.

No girls escape the hurricane. The winds are simply too overpowering. Fortunately no storm lasts forever. By late high school the winds of the hurricane are dying down and trees begin to right themselves. Girls calm down. Their thinking is more mature and their feelings more stable. Their friends have become kinder and more dependable. They make peace with their parents. Their judgment has improved and they are less self-absorbed. The resisters and fighters survive. When it's storming, it feels like the storm will never end, but the hurricane does end and the sun comes out again.

A FENCE AT
THE TOP OF
THE HILL

■

On a misty Monday night Sara and I sit on the floor of the Georgian Room at the YWCA. It's a lovely room with high ceilings, peach carpeting and a grand piano. Baskets of dried flowers and an ancient grandfather clock adorn a marble fireplace. This room was designed for tea drinking by ladies wearing hats and gloves, but tonight twenty of us, dressed in sweat suits and tennis shoes, are here to learn self-defense.

There are several mother-daughter pairs, a trio of adolescent sisters, some college coeds and middle-aged women. Our teacher, Kit, alias Kitty Kung Fu, asks how many of us have hit another person, and two of the teenagers raise their hands.

Kit is aware of our anxiety and keeps the tone funny and relaxed. She hands out materials on prevention. She shows us whistles and Mace and warns us to read the instructions before we are attacked. She teaches us the vital points of the human body and how to punch, kick, break a stranglehold and escape when grabbed from behind.

We pair off and practice. Under crystal chandeliers, we attack each other and struggle to break free. At first we are wimps. We giggle and punch the air with gentle womanly moves; we apologize for our accidental aggression. We have to be reminded to scream, to go for the groin and the eyes.

Gradually we improve. We stop being ladylike and learn some power moves—the Iron Cross and the Windmill. We marvel aloud that these moves might really work. As we practice, Kit walks among us, correcting, coaxing, giving us something we have never had before— instructions on fighting back.

After our self-defense training we sprawl on the floor and watch a film on date rape. I'm gray-haired, I have been married for twenty years and I am unlikely ever to go on another date. This film doesn't hold my attention, so I look at the fresh faces reflecting light from the television screen. These young women are the granddaughters of the ladies who curled manicured fingers around china cups in this room. Their grandmothers never had lessons in how to bite, kick, scream and scratch. Perhaps some needed these lessons, but most led violence-free lives. These girls are growing up in a world where one in four women will be raped in her lifetime. I allow myself to hope this class will improve their odds.

There is something eerie about teaching our daughters how to fight off rapists and kidnappers. We need classes that teach men not to rape and hurt women. We need workshops that teach men what some of them don't learn: how to be gentle and loving.

I remember a poem about gender differences from my nursery school days. Little boys were made of "snips and snails, and puppy dogs' tails." Girls were made of "sugar and spice, and everything nice." I didn't ever dream that poems like this could become self-fulfilling prophecies.

Last week my friend Randy listened to a group of sixth-graders identify what living creature they would like to be. The boys all wanted to be predators: wolves, lions, grizzly bears and pumas. The girls chose soft and cuddly animals: pandas, koala bears, bunnies and squirrels. One girl said softly that she'd like to be a rose. When I heard that choice, I thought that the damage has already been done. Roses can't even move, and, while beautiful, they don't experience anything.

In order to keep their true selves and grow into healthy adults, girls need love from family and friends, meaningful work, respect, challenges and physical and psychological safety. They need identities based on talents or interests rather than appearance, popularity or sexuality. They need good habits for coping with stress, self-nurturing skills and a sense of purpose and perspective. They need quiet places and times. They need to feel that they are part of something larger than their own lives and that they are emotionally connected to a whole.

Many women tell stories about what saved them from the precipice. One girl was saved by her love of books, by long summer afternoons when she read for hours. Another was saved by thinking of faraway places and people. One was saved by her love of music, another by her love of horses. Girls can be saved by a good school, a good teacher or a meaningful activity.

In the past, many young women were saved by conversations and support from a beloved neighbor, a kindhearted aunt or a nearby grandmother. Many women report that when they were in adolescence, they had someone they could really talk to, who encouraged them to stay true to who they really were. Now, in our more chaotic, fragmented world, fewer girls have that option available. In the 1990s therapists often play this role. They are calm outsiders who can be trusted with the truth of each girl's experience.

Certain kinds of homes help girls hold on to their true selves. These homes offer girls both protection and challenges. These are the homes that offer girls affection and structure. Girls hear the message "I love you, but I have expectations." In these homes, parents set firm guidelines and communicate high hopes. With younger children, rules are fine, but with teenagers, guidelines make more sense. With older girls, there will be more negotiating. It's important to remember that rules, in the absence of loving relationships, are not worth much. Almost anyone can figure out how to break rules. What holds girls' lives in place is love and respect for their parents.

Parents can help by listening to their daughters, who need as much parent time as toddlers. Teenagers need parents available when they are ready to talk. Usually girls want to talk when it's most inconvenient for their parents. This is no accident. I found that both my teenagers were more likely to talk if I had my nose in a book. If I seemed interested in their lives and eager to talk, they pulled back.

It's good to ask questions that encourage daughters to think clearly for themselves. When listening, parents should listen to what they can respect and praise in their daughters' talk. Whenever possible, they can congratulate their daughters on their maturity, insight or good judgment. It's important to validate their autonomous, adult behavior and support their barely emerging maturity. It is almost never helpful to label girls as young and immature. To girls, that feels contemptuous.

It creates anger and resistance and negates their own sense of themselves as growing.

When teenagers temporarily lose their heads, which most do, they need an adult there to help them recover. When daughters have problems, it's important not to panic. It's a tough world for daughters. At times, girls from strong, healthy families can experience serious problems. Panicky parents make things worse.

It's important for parents to watch for trouble and convey to their daughters that, if it comes, they are strong enough to deal with it. Parents who send their daughters the message that they'll be overwhelmed by problems aren't likely to hear what's really happening.

Good parents manage to stay reasonably calm through the storms. They have a direction and order to their own universe. They can be reassuring. I encourage parents to model themselves after Mr. Rogers of television fame. He's reassuring when he says things like "Tomorrow is another day." "Nobody is perfect." "Everyone makes mistakes." "Most people feel awkward at parties." "Nobody is liked by everybody." This soothing voice helps girls to calm down in the short term. And in the long term, girls internalize these soothing words and say them to themselves when they are upset.

It's important for parents not to take things too personally or to be too hurt by rejection from adolescent girls. Girls' moodiness and irritability are usually related to problems outside the home, problems with school or friends. It's okay to have consequences for disrespectful behavior, but it's good to have a sense of humor and not "make a federal case" out of cranky remarks. Good parents ask their daughters what is wrong when they are particularly temperamental. They may need help.

Janet Reno said recently, "Growing up as a child today in America is even more difficult than raising children." That thought may help parents stay patient. Another thing that may help is recognizing "hot cognitions." Parents can learn to catch themselves before they react. For example, the thought that a daughter is selfish can be rethought: All adolescents are self-absorbed. It helps to remember the difference between the deep and surface structure of a daughter's behavior. When a girl says, "I hate Mom," it doesn't necessarily mean that. It can mean: "I'm trying to find out who I am."

One important reason to stay calm is that calm parents hear more. Low-key, accepting parents are the ones whose children keep talking to them. Later these parents may react by saying, "Here's what I liked about how you handled that. . . ." I recommend the sandwich technique for giving feedback: Start positive, slip in the criticism or concern and then end positive. For example: "I appreciate your honesty about drinking with your friends. I'm concerned that could be dangerous for you in a variety of ways. I'm glad you trusted me enough to tell me. I love you."

Good communication with teenage daughters encourages rational thought, centered decisions and conscious choices. It includes discussions of options, risks, implications and consequences. Parents can teach their daughters to make choices. They can help them sort out when to negotiate, stand firm and withdraw. They can help them learn what they can and can't control, how to pick their battles and to fight back. They can teach intelligent resistance.

Good parents model the respect and equality that they want their daughters to experience in the outside world. This takes work. All of us have been socialized to behave in gender-stereotyped ways. Parents must think about what their behavior teaches their daughters. Having a home with true equality between the sexes is an impossible ideal, but it helps girls to see that their parents are working toward this. They will respect the effort.

Many parents worry about rigid sex-typing when their daughters are small. They carefully dress their girls in blue and buy them tractors. That's okay, but the time to really worry is early adolescence. That's when the gender roles get set in cement, and that's when girls need tremendous support in resisting the cultural definitions of femininity.

Parents can help daughters be whole by modeling wholeness. Androgynous parents are the best. Good fathers are nurturing, physically affectionate and involved in the lives of their daughters. Good mothers model self-sufficiency and self-love and are responsive, but not responsible for their family members.

Mothers are likely to have the most difficult time with adolescent girls. Daughters provoke arguments as a way of connecting and distancing at the same time. They want their mothers to recognize their smallest changes and are angry when their mothers don't validate their every move. They struggle with their love for their mothers and their desire to be different from their mothers. They trust their mothers to put up with their anger and to stand by them when they are unreasonable. This is an enormous compliment, but one that's hard for most mothers to accept because it's couched in such hostile terms.

Many feminist mothers are upset by their daughters' willingness to be sexualized and feminized by the culture. These mothers support the development of whole, authentic daughters, and they encourage their daughters to fight back. Instead their daughters fight their mothers for the right to adopt the junk ideas of mass culture. I encourage the mothers to keep sharing their thoughts and values. They are planting seeds and there will be a later harvest.

Parents can educate themselves about the complicated world of junior high. It's good to know the teachers and to visit the classes, especially math and science classes. I recommend reading teen magazines and books, listening to the music, going to the movies, supervising activities and talking to other parents. It's important to discuss alcohol, drugs, violence, social pressure and appearance. If these topics aren't coming up, parents are missing out on what's important to their children.

When girls talk about their drug and alcohol use, it's important to listen for how often, how much and when and where chemical use is occurring. Is it experimental, the result of peer pressure or boredom, curiosity or a need to escape reality? Parents can discuss what need chemicals are meeting in their daughter's life. How else could she meet that deep-structure need?

There are many issues to discuss involving sexuality: romance, birth control, values, feelings, sexual decision-making, other teens' behavior, the media treatment of sexuality, gender differences, the double standard, abortion, teen mothers and STDs. Parents can communicate their values about sexuality to their daughters. Often parents are shy about this, but I tell them, "You must speak. Guess jeans, Madonna and 2 Live Crew are not shy about communicating their sexual values. You must present her with your message."

Parents can encourage their daughters to have friends of both sexes and to resist sexualizing relationships in junior high. I encourage parents to view boy-girl relationships in junior high as friendships. It's generally not a good idea to tease girls about boyfriends. Treating male-female relationships in a matter-of-fact way promotes relaxed, open behavior between the sexes. When parents ask if they should allow their junior-high daughters to date, I recommend they say, "We want you to have friends of both sexes. Invite your friends over anytime for games or movies with our family." This desexualizes things and brings boys into the realm of the everyday.

Ralph Nader said, "The main things that kids learn from television are addictions, violence and low-grade sexuality." They also learn to be lookist and sexist. The average teen watches four and a half hours of television a day. Parents can help their daughters interpret the media. It's a good idea to share viewing experiences and to read aloud from newspapers and magazines. The media offers parents many opportunities for consciousness raising.

As a critical human dimension, appearance should be downplayed. It's healthy for daughters to have other things to feel proud of besides their looks. Parents can fight their daughters' focus on appearance and weight. It's not a good idea to have a scale in the home or to allow girls to diet—better to have healthful meals and family exercise. While it's fine to empathize with how important looks are to students, it's also important to stand firm that in any decent value system they are not all that important.

It's good to encourage positive peer relations. This cannot be over-emphasized. One of the best things that can happen to a girl is that she have well-adjusted friends. Parents have some power to influence this by who they invite on trips, where they live and what activities they encourage. Girls are more likely to make healthy friends on a swim team than at a pinball arcade parlor. Money spent on pizzas and lemonade for a daughter's friends is money well spent.

Often girls do well if they are allowed to travel during their adolescent years. Camps, foreign exchange student programs and long summers with faraway relatives are great opportunities for growth. It gives girls a break from family. It helps them have some perspective on their lives, something almost all adolescents need. Jobs are useful too. Of course, hours need to be reasonable and job sites safe, but jobs allow girls to learn lessons from the real world and to see something outside peer culture.

It's good to remind girls that junior high is not all of life. There are other places—the mountains and beaches, the family cabin on the lake or the neighborhood clubhouse. There are other people—neighbors, relatives, family friends, old people and babies. And there are other times. They will not always be trapped in teenagehood; people do grow up. Along with this reminder, it's good to encourage non-peer activities: work at a soup kitchen or for Meals on Wheels, go rock climbing or join computer clubs. These activities help girls to stay in contact with the nonadolescent portion of the human race.

Plato said that education is teaching our children to find pleasure in the right things. Parents can share their own pleasures with their daughters by introducing them to the natural world and the world of books, art or music. They can take them backpacking and teach them to fly fish, tune up engines, collect political buttons, play cello, knit afghans or go hang gliding. Especially during this turbulent time, it's important to have regular ways that the family can have fun together.

But even as I encourage parents to help, I admonish them to be gentle with themselves. Their influence is limited. Parents can do only so much, and they are not responsible for everything. They are neither all-knowing nor all-powerful. Parents can make a difference in the lives of their daughters only if their daughters are willing to allow this. Not all daughters are. Daughters have choices and responsibilities. Friends will have an impact. The culture will have an impact.

While parents can do some fence building, we need to change our institutions. For example, junior highs are not user-friendly for adolescent girls. Most of what girls read in schools is written by men and about men. We need more stories of women who are strong, more examples of women in a variety of roles. History needs to include the history of women; psychology, the psychology of women; and literature, the writing of women.

Adolescent girls need a more public place in our culture, not as sex objects but as interesting and complicated human beings. Chelsea Clinton has become a hero for many young teens. Sixth-grade girls light up at the mention of her name. She's not a sex object or a victim of violence but a person, and she is much respected by other girls. With the exception of some Olympic athletes, who girls also love to see, I can think of no other adolescent girls who are positive public figures.

Girls benefit from the limelight. Girls' schools, clubs and groups allow girls to be leaders. Girls' art shows, literature festivals and athletic events give girls' lives dignity and public importance. Girls need to see reflections of themselves in all their diversity—as workers, artists and explorers.

Inclusive language helps girls feel included. One client said, "My aunt is a mail carrier. It's been hard to know what to call her—'mail person' didn't sound right and 'mail woman' sounded like something from the circus. I'm glad we have a word now for lady mailmen." Another noticed that artists are generally referred to as "he." She said, "That makes us say 'women artists,' which doesn't sound like they are real artists."

Teachers need equity training. Most teachers are well intentioned and think they are gender-fair, but they aren't. They discriminate inadvertently. The teacher who found girls' science projects trite probably didn't see himself as discriminating. Until I read the research on teachers' differential treatment of the sexes, I was unaware of the subtle ways I discriminated in the classroom. Schools need to be structured in ways that validate and nurture strengths in female students. Girls do better in cooperative environments and in all-girl math and science classes.

Junior highs often ignore what is happening to students as they are herded from one class to another. Between the ages of eleven and fourteen, students' issues are relationship issues, and their problems are personal and social. Academics take a backseat to urgent developmental concerns. Schools could foster groupings organized around talents, interests and needs, rather than cliques. They could offer students the clarity they desperately need—supervised activities in which adolescents work and relax together, conflict-resolution training and classes in which guidelines for chemical use and sexual decisions are discussed. They could offer awareness training in areas such as lookism, racism and sexism. They could take responsibility for helping adolescents structure all the social and emotional turmoil they are experiencing.

Schools could offer clear sexual and physical harassment policies that protect students and establish norms for conduct toward the opposite sex. They could offer guidelines for appropriate sexual behavior and teach how to say no. This work with young teens might help prevent the "gang bangs" and the date rapes of the high school years.

"Manhood" needs to be redefined in a way that allows women equality and men pride. Our culture desperately needs new ways to teach boys to be men. Via the media and advertising, we are teaching our sons all the wrong lessons. Boys need a model of manhood that is caring and bold, adventurous and gentle. They need ways to be men that don't involve violence, misogyny and the objectification of women. Instead of promoting violence as a means of solving human problems, we must strengthen our taboos against violence. Some Native American cultures have no words in their language for hurting other humans. What do those cultures think of us?

We need places for kids to go. We need ball fields and gyms, community centers, halls where bands can play music and young thespians can put on plays. Except for movie houses and video arcades, teens have few places they are welcome. They need no-cost supervised places where they can be together to talk, dance and play.

Much of the horrible behavior that now happens between the sexes comes from ignorance of proper behavior and lack of positive experiences with the opposite sex. We adults can provide that. For example, in my town the Red and Black Cafe was opened by adults who wanted their teenagers to have a safe, cheap place to congregate. It stays open late and hosts local bands. Teens love it. Or teens can work together in volunteer activities. By working side by side they can learn to see each other as people worthy of respect.

As a culture, we could use more wholesome rituals for coming of age. Too many of our current rituals involve sex, drugs, alcohol and rebellion. We need more positive ways to acknowledge growth, more ceremonies and graduations. It's good to have toasts, celebrations and markers for teens that tell them, You are growing up and we're proud of you.

Adolescent girls come of age in a culture preoccupied with money, sex and violence, a culture with enormous problems—poverty, pollution, addictions and lethal sexually transmitted diseases. And it's a culture in which more than half of all children will be raised by only one parent for at least part of their childhood.

The ways the media have dehumanized sex and fostered violence should be the topic of a national debate. After a five-year study, the American Psychological Association found that watching television can lead to antisocial behavior, gender stereotyping and bad grades in school. The APA warned that television has become a dominant and disturbing influence on the national psyche. They recommended that the government develop a national policy to promote quality and diverse programming and to protect society and individual citizens from its harmful effects.

Although I believe that the First Amendment has become the last refuge of scoundrels, I don't advocate censorship. I believe that the best defense against bad ideas is better ideas. But now in our culture the problem is that many people make their living by telling lies and spreading bad ideas. The truth is not getting equal time. We need more public media that exists to enliven and enlighten, not to sell.

Our society teaches that sex, alcohol and purchasing power lead to the good life. We really do know better. We need to rebuild the media so that its values are not antagonistic to the values we must adopt in order to survive and move into the twenty-first century. These changes will not happen overnight. But we can work together toward a new century in which men and women truly have equal power in our culture.

In the last few years violence has become part of ordinary life. A study by the American Psychological Association released in August 1993 found that teens are 250 percent more likely than adults to be crime victims. In some of our cities, seven out of ten kids have seen someone shot or killed. In America today the number-one cause of injury to women is battering. Women are kidnapped and murdered in numbers that were unthinkable in the fifties. It's hard for girls to grow into independent, autonomous people when they are fearful for their physical safety.

This vulnerability curtails the freedom of every young woman. For instance, Tammy Zywicki, a Grinnell student, was kidnapped and murdered when her car broke down on Interstate 80. One of her friends, Natasha Spears, pointed out that our society's current response to safety issues is to restrict the freedom of women. She noted that first women were urged not to walk by themselves, then not to live by themselves and now not even to drive by themselves. She said, "When I was in junior high I had more freedom than I have now."

My grandfather liked a poem about a town that had people falling off its cliffs. The city elders met to debate whether to build a fence at the top of the cliffs or put an ambulance down in the valley. The poem summarizes the essential differences between treatment and prevention of social problems. My work as a therapist is ambulance work, and after years of ambulance driving, I'm aware of the limits of the treatment approach to major social problems. In addition to treating the casualties of our cultural messages, we need to work for cultural change.

I believe, as Miller, Mead and de Beauvoir believed, that pathology comes from failure to realize all one's possibilities. Ophelia died because she could not grow. She became the object of others' lives and lost her true subjective self. Many of the girls I describe in this book suffer from a thwarting of their development, a truncating of their potential. As my client said—they are perfectly good carrots being cut into roses.

Adolescence is a border between childhood and adulthood. Like life on all borders, it's teeming with energy and fraught with danger. Growth requires courage and hard work on the part of the individual, and it requires the protection and nurturing of the environment. Some girls develop under the most adverse conditions, but the interesting question to me is, Under what conditions do most girls develop to their fullest?

Carol Bly coined the term "cultural abuse" for those elements in the culture that block growth and development, and she wrote: "A century from now, it will be thought ridiculous that we have not laid out lists of what influences people to be full-hearted, free-spirited and daring-minded."

Long-term plans for helping adolescent girls involve deep-seated and complicated cultural changes—rebuilding a sense of community in our neighborhoods, fighting addictions, changing our schools, promoting gender equality and curtailing violence. The best "fence at the top of the hill" is a culture in which there is the structure and security of the fifties and the tolerance for diversity and autonomy of the 1990s. Then our daughters could grow and develop slowly and peacefully into whole, authentic people.

I quoted Stendhal in Chapter One: "All geniuses born women are lost to the public good." Some ground has been gained since he said that, and some lost. Let's work toward a culture in which there is a place for every human gift, in which children are safe and protected, women are respected and men and women can love each other as whole human beings. Let's work for a culture in which the incisive intellect, the willing hands and the happy heart are beloved. Then our daughters will have a place where all their talents will be appreciated, and they can flourish like green trees under the sun and the stars.

Recommended Reading

Apter, Terri (1990). *Altered Loves.* New York: Fawcett-Columbine

Bepko, Claudia, and Jo-Ann Krestan (1990). *Too Good for Her Own Good.* New York: HarperCollins

Bliers, Ruth (1984). *Science and Gender.* New York: Pergamon

Brown, Lyn Mikel, and Carol Gilligan (1992). *Meeting at the Crossroads.* Cambridge, MA: Harvard University Press

Chodorrow, Nancy (1978). *The Reproduction of Mothering.* Berkeley: University of California Press

Cline, Sally, and Dale Spender (1978). *Reflecting Men at Twice Their Natural Size.* New York: Seaver Books

de Beauvoir, Simone (1952). *The Second Sex.* New York: Knopf

Faludi, Susan (1991). *Backlash.* New York: Crown Publishers

Friedan, Betty (1963). *The Feminine Mystique.* New York: Norton

Gilligan, Carol (1982). *In a Different Voice.* Cambridge, MA: Harvard University Press

Gilligan, Carol, A. G. Rogers and Deborah Tolman (1991). *Women, Girls and Psychotherapy.* Binghamton, NY: Haworth Press

Griffin, Susan (1981). *Pornography and Silence.* New York: Harper & Row

Hancock, Emily (1989). *The Girl Within.* New York: Fawcett Books

Hare-Mustin, R. T., and J. Maracek (1990). *Making a Difference: Psychology and the Construction of Gender.* New Haven, CT: Yale University Press

Kerr, Barbara (1985). *Smart Girls, Gifted Women.* Columbus, OH: Ohio Psychology Publishing

Lerner, Harriet (1985). *The Dance of Anger.* New York: Harper & Row

Marone, Nicky (1988). *How to Father a Successful Daughter.* New York: McGraw-Hill

Mead, Margaret (1971). *Coming of Age in Samoa.* New York: Morrow

Mead, Margaret (1949). *Men and Women.* New York: Morrow

Miller, Alice (1981). *The Drama of the Gifted Child.* New York: Basic Books

Orbach, Susie (1986). *Fat Is a Feminist Issue II.* New York: Berkley Books

Pipher, Mary (1985). *Hunger Pains: The American Women's Tragic Quest for Thinness.* Lincoln, NE: Barking Gator Press

Rich, Adrienne (1976). *Of Woman Born.* New York: Norton

Schurr, Edwin (1984). *The Americanization of Sex.* Philadelphia: Temple University Press

Skolnick, Joan, Carol Langbort and Lucille Day (1982). *How to Encourage Girls in Math and Science.* Englewood Cliffs, NJ: Prentice-Hall

Tavris, Carol (1992). *The Mismeasure of Women.* New York: Simon & Schuster

White, Michael, and David Epston (1990). *Narrative Means to Therapeutic Ends.* New York: Norton

I n d e x

Puberty, definition, 53
Purging. *See* Bulimia

Racism, 241, 275, 276, 280
Rape. *See* Sexual assault
Reading, 243
Reality distortion, 61
Reasoning, emotions affecting, 60, 256
Recreation facilities, 290–91
Religion, 71–73
Reno, Janet, 13, 285
Repression, 36–37
Role models, 62, 252, 280, 286, 289
Roosevelt, Eleanor, 266

Scapegoating, 68–69, 260–62
Schools, 62–64. *See also* Junior high
    school; Peers
  drug/alcohol programs, 201
  gender discrimination in, 42, 62–63,
    237–38, 290
  as negative environment (case
    story), 260–63, 272–73
  as positive environment (case
    story), 272
  reasons for girls' academic fading,
    64
  sexual harassment in, 34, 69–70,
    104, 263, 290
Schopenhauer, Arthur, 42
Schreiner, Olive, 19, 22
Science, girls' problems with, 19, 290
Self. *See* Personality; True self/false
    self conflict
Self-absorption, 258, 285
Self-defense classes, 218, 224, 225,
    282–83
Self-denial, anorexic, 174, 177
Self-esteem, 63, 95, 118, 272, 279
Self-mutilation, 157–65. *See also*
    Suicide attempts
  case stories, 159–65
Sex. *See* Sexuality
Sex education, 206–7, 208–9
Sex objects, 55–56, 66
Sexism. *See* Misogynistic culture

Sexual assault, 70, 218–31, 248
  by acquaintance, 225–28, 233, 290
  by family member, 227–28
  case stories, 220–24, 226–29, 232–33
  compulsive eating linked to fear of,
    182–83
  incidence statistics, 219, 224, 230
  initial reaction to, 230
  as major issue for adolescent girls,
    205–6, 245–46
  trauma of, 219–20, 224, 228–29
Sexual harassment, 34, 41, 69–70,
    104, 245, 263, 290
Sexuality, 203–18
  alcohol use and, 194–96
  case stories, 34–36, 203–4, 210–18
  confusion over, 204–7, 208, 238–40,
    245
  decision-making on limits, 209–10
  earlier age for, 207–8
  intercourse vs. other expressions of,
    208
  media depictions in 1950s, 235, 244
  media depictions in 1990s, 33–34,
    66–67, 71, 244
  multiple partners, 208
  1990s openness about, 245
  overeating and fears of, 182–83
  parental sensitivity to issues of, 287
  parental values, 66–67, 104
Shakespeare, William, 20
Shigellae, 69
Sills, Beverly, 266
Single-parent homes, 65, 80, 134, 291
  father-daughter case stories, 119–30
Small-town life (1950s), 234–41, 246
  contrasted with 1990s' anonymity,
    242–47
Smart Girls, Gifted Women (Kerr),
    266
Smoking, 46, 202, 242
Social learning theory, 249
Social pressures. *See* Cultural
    pressures
Social selves. *See* Family; Peers
Spears, Natasha, 292
Spender, Dale, 40–41